BLOCKCHAIN
Empowering Digital Economy

BLOCKCHAIN
Empowering Digital Economy

Yang Yan
Bin Wang
Jun Zou

Zhongguancun Big Data Industry Alliance, China
Zhongguancun Digital Media Industry Alliance, China
Terminus Technologies Group, China

机械工业出版社
CHINA MACHINE PRESS

World Scientific

Published by

World Scientific Publishing Co. Pte. Ltd.

5 Toh Tuck Link, Singapore 596224

USA office: 27 Warren Street, Suite 401-402, Hackensack, NJ 07601

UK office: 57 Shelton Street, Covent Garden, London WC2H 9HE

Library of Congress Cataloging-in-Publication Data

Names: Yang, Yan (Writer on blockchains) author.

Title: Blockchain : empowering digital economy / Yang Yan, Bin Wang,
    Jun Zou, Zhongguancun Big Data Industry Alliance, China.

Description: Hackensack, NJ : World Scientific/China Machine Press, [2022] | Includes index.

Identifiers: LCCN 2021009775 | ISBN 9789811236501 (hardcover) |
    ISBN 9789811236518 (ebook for institutions) | ISBN 9789811236525 (ebook for institutions)

Subjects: LCSH: Blockchains (Databases)--China. | Big data--China.

Classification: LCC QA76.9.B56 Y36 2022 | DDC 005.74--dc23

LC record available at https://lccn.loc.gov/2021009775

British Library Cataloguing-in-Publication Data

A catalogue record for this book is available from the British Library.

区块链+赋能数字经济

Originally published in Chinese by China Machine Press

Copyright © China Machine Press 2018

For any available supplementary material, please visit
https://www.worldscientific.com/worldscibooks/10.1142/12264#t=suppl

Desk Editors: Balasubramanian Shanmugam/Steven Patt

Typeset by Stallion Press
Email: enquiries@stallionpress.com

Printed in Singapore

This is an introduction for the book on the title page of the Chinese version of China Machine Press.

This book systematically describes the relationship between blockchain and the digital economy, introduces the development of blockchain technology at home and abroad and the application and development of blockchain in various key areas. The book also focuses on the role of local governments in promoting the application of blockchain in the innovation process. It also details the legal and regulatory aspects of blockchain technology.

This book can be used by personnel from national ministries and commissions, relevant personnel from state-owned enterprises, local government and industrial park personnel, those who work with the Internet and big data, artificial intelligence, blockchain, and in other industries, as well as teachers and students from institutions of higher learning and those who work in research institutions.

Expert Advisory Committee

Wang Lianzhou: Former Deputy Director of the Office of the Financial and Economic Committee of the National People's Congress and Chief Consultant of CIFC

He Jiazheng: Chairman of the Zhongguancun Digital Media Industry Alliance and Former President of the People's Network

Wang Lu: Executive Deputy Secretary General, China Society of Administrative Reform

Zhao Jianjun: Professor of the Central Party School, Chairman of the Science and Technology Innovation Committee of the China Dialectics Research Association, CIFC Think Tank Expert

Ni Guangnan: Academician of the Chinese Academy of Engineering, Vice Chairman of the Zhongguancun Digital Media Industry Alliance Expert Committee

Li Baomin: Director of the Supervisory Committee of the State-owned Assets Supervision and Administration Commission, CIFC Think Tank Expert

Wang Ning: President of the China Electronics Chamber of Commerce

Yang Dong: Deputy Dean of the School of Law, Renmin University of China, Director of the Center for Financial Technology and Internet Security, Renmin University of China, CIFC think tank Expert

Series Editorial Board

Members

Zhao Guodong: Secretary General of the Zhongguancun Big Data Industry Alliance

Han Han: Chief Engineer of the China Information and Communication Research Institute and Director of the Office of Big Data Development Promotion Committee

Zheng Zhibin: Vice President, Strategy Department, Huawei Technologies Co. Ltd., General Manager, Global Smart City Business Unit

Zhang Yande: Huawei Technologies Co., Ltd. EBG President, Smart City Business Unit, China

Zhang Jun: Planning Research Department General Manager, Huihua Fund Management Co. Ltd.

Li Wenkang: Assistant to the Secretary of China Society of Administrative Reform

Shen Jie: Chief Scientist of the Six Domain Chain

Wang Yunjia: Founder & CEO of Fengyu Technology, CIFC Think Tank Expert

Kang Chunpeng: Associate Researcher, Information Center, Ministry of Agriculture and Rural Affairs

Ge Zhenbin: Director of Internet of Things, Xinhuanet Co. Ltd.

Recommendations
(Translated according to the Chinese version)

Recommendation 1

Society will soon enter the era of digital economy, and the new era calls for a new system of network applications. The blockchain has emerged. A lot of information and unique analysis in the book *BlockChain + Empowering Digital Economy* is of great significance for understanding the blockchain and its application. Blockchain technology, application and management are still in the process of development, and there is still a lot of room for innovation. I hope this book can provide important reference value for the development and application of blockchain technology.

Wu Hequan
Chairman of China Internet Association,
Academician of Chinese Academy of Engineering

Recommendation 2

New generation information technologies such as blockchain and artificial intelligence are developing rapidly. This will bring about a new period of economic development led by the digital economy. It will be necessary to find out how to guide the healthy development of the blockchain industry, establish an ecosystem of production, education and research, break through the frontier technology and key technologies of the blockchain, promote the innovation and application of blockchain + industry, and empower the digital economy. These are important issues and they are also the key to the development of the blockchain industry.

The book *Blockchain + Empowering Digital Economy* by CIFC think tank experts contains research on its "blockchain +" innovation system and its results. This book systematically explains the principles and development trends of blockchain technology application, and reveals the close relationship and development of blockchain, big data and digital economy, especially the detailed introduction of "blockchain +" finance, agriculture, medical industry, real estate and other application scenarios, existing problems and development models. It will play an important role in the healthy development of the blockchain industry.

Ni Guangnan
Academician of Chinese Academy of Engineering,
Vice Chairman of the Expert Committee
of Zhongguancun Digital Media Industry Alliance

Foreword

Networks characterized by big data, big connections, large broadband, big computing, and big intelligence have unprecedented capabilities, and have increased the extent of Internet penetration. Government Internet and consumer Internet now have more applications, and the integration of the Internet and the real economy has led to the growth of the real economy. Society will enter the era of the digital economy, and the new era calls for a new system of network applications. The blockchain has emerged. The blockchain subtly combines multiple technologies such as peer-to-peer networking, distributed accounting, digital signatures and smart contracts. It has led to the development of new methods in access authentication, transaction tracing, data encryption, privacy protection and notarization. The innovations can be said to be occurring in areas such as trade, production, government affairs and the entire chain, providing a more secure guarantee for data circulation and protection.

The book *Blockchain + Empowering Digital Economy* first introduces the technical architecture of the blockchain and the ins and outs of its evolution. It will also discuss the blockchain's role in supporting the compliance management of big data sharing transactions. The focus is on the applications of blockchain, including applications in finance, insurance, health care, agriculture, commerce, supply chain, real estate, cultural innovation, government affairs, notarization, etc. Finally, the legal issues and challenges related to blockchain are discussed. The authors of this book are experts who have worked in the Zhongguancun Big Data Alliance as well as researchers who have worked in national research institutions for many years. They have long been concerned about the blockchain, and much of their time is spent researching a large number of enterprises and understanding the blockchain in various fields. They have used their expert knowledge to write this book.

Data and unique analysis are important for understanding blockchains and their applications. Blockchain technology, applications and management are still in the process of development, and there is still a lot of room for innovation. I hope this book can provide important reference value for the development and application of blockchains.

Wu Hequan
Chairman of the China Internet Association,
Academician of the Chinese Academy of Engineering

In the report of the 19th National Congress of the Communist Party of China and the "two sessions" of 2018, it was proposed that a network power, a digital China and a smart society should be built, further construction of information infrastructure should be undertaken, the integration of the Internet, big data, artificial intelligence and the real economy should be promoted, the digital economy and the sharing economy should be developed, new growth points should be cultivated and new kinetic energy should be produced.

With the rapid development of new technologies and new models such as artificial intelligence, blockchain and big data, the digital economy has become a new engine with new kinetic energy for the development of the new era.

The blockchain has been an important concept of 2018. Some people call it a new wind. I think, however, that the blockchain technology is still in the early stages and needs to be developed correctly. It is necessary to seize the opportunity to stimulate development, but to avoid creating "virtual heat". It is hoped that the relevant departments, the blockchain industry and the media will actively and correctly guide the development of blockchain technology applications, vigorously resist the pseudo-blockchain projects, air project speculation, illegal fund-raising and ICO, and provide the necessary scientific supervision to jointly safeguard the healthy development of the industry.

An active exploration of the blockchain + industry innovation model has unearthed a new round of technological and industrial revolution. This has injected a strong impetus into economic and social development, which has not only promoted the digital economy, but also helped the traditional industry to carry out comprehensive digitization, and transform and achieve better innovation and development. Blockchain, big data and artificial intelligence are the new engines for upgrading traditional industries. It is expected that more blockchain + industry applications and innovations will emerge.

Let the blockchain empower the development of the digital economy. In the field of digital economy, China is gradually becoming a leader. To further promote the development of the digital economy, we must strengthen the advancement of digital technology and deepen the application of advanced technology. New technologies such as blockchain, artificial intelligence and quantum computing are the driving forces for the development of the digital economy.

Experts from the CIFC think tank and the Zhongguancun Digital Media Industry Alliance have written this blockchain + industry and digital economy monograph *Blockchain + Empowerment Digital Economy*. It will be very important for the development of blockchain technology applications. It will promote the role of the blockchain and industry, provide a model of exploration and innovation, and actively promote the healthy and rapid development of blockchain and industry as well as the digital economy.

He Jiazheng
Chairman of Zhongguancun Digital Media Industry Alliance,
Former President of People's Network

Preface

In March 2014, I went to Silicon Valley to research Internet finance and big data applications with representatives from the financial industry. I visited PayPal, which is more concerned about the industry. PayPal launched the IMF in 1999, but it didn't last long. With the US dollar interest rate falling sharply in 2000, PayPal not only could not obtain management fees, but even used its own funds to subsidize the users' income. After the subprime mortgage crisis, the entire money fund market was also hit hard, so in 2011 PayPal gave up the money fund market. Since then, they have paid more attention to the integration and service of traditional industries. Compared with the domestic market at that time, the Internet financial market was in full swing. After investigating a number of companies in Silicon Valley, we raised the issue of the application of Internet finance and big data.

In the second half of 2014, on behalf of the Zhongguancun Big Data Industry Alliance, I undertook a key research topic for the National Development and Reform Commission. I worked on "Informatization (Big Data) Enhancing the Government's Governance Capability Research", focusing on "Big Data Technology" and "Application Development Strategy Needs Research". In the project report, we proposed a big data investment and financing strategy with top-level design as the traction. Investment and financing strategy would be used to promote it, and community organization would be an important factor. With regard to using big data to improve the governance capabilities of the government, we proposed that there were five important aspects: strategic level, organizational system, laws and regulations, government development and the data trading market. The data trading market, we felt, was an especially important aspect. We proposed to establish and improve China's big data trading market system, establish a system of big data trading centers, encourage qualified centers to conduct big data trading center pilots, and promote the establishment of the big data trading market. The multi-level big data trading market model of off-site and on-market, public and private equity, standard and non-standard big data products has opened up more space for the big data investment and financing market. At the same time, it fundamentally solves the problems of big data openness, big data intellectual property and governance. Particular emphasis is placed on the importance and role of scenario applications in data exchange and transactions.

With the deepening of big data application, I continued to host the research project of the National Development and Reform Commission in October 2016. At this point, I was conducting research on big data transaction standards. The domestic big data trading market was in the process of development, and the bottleneck problem in the market was solved through data sandbox, data lockbox and data hosting. However, the trading market of the Bitcoin World is very different from the trading market of our atomic world. The encryption mechanism of blockchain, the consensus mechanism, the smart contracts, the incentive mechanism, etc. have had a great impact on the development of big data applications and the integration of data.

Last year, Chairman Wang Bin of the Zhongguancun Digital Media Industry Alliance and I began planning to write a book on the application and development of blockchain technology. We had previously published the book *Internet Finance +: The New Engine of China's Economy* through "crowdfunding", and also, miraculously, published *VR+: Integration and Innovation* within three months. Jingdong Online also achieved good sales results.

In preparation for the publication of this book, we organized two closed-door seminars on January 27 and March 11, 2018. The number of participants in the two closed-door seminars exceeded expectations, and some local governments and regulatory authorities also sent people to participate. The in-depth discussion we had during the two closed-door seminars became a face-to-face debate. We all thought that it was imperative to write and publish the book as soon as possible.

The application of big data in China has become more sophisticated. Various industries and local economies are all looking for business models of big data applications to promote the development of China's digital economy. The establishment of an innovative production relationship has helped solve some bottlenecks in the development of the digital economy in recent years.

Last year, the popularity of the currency circle, a further development in the field of blockchain, had also raised many legal and regulatory issues. One view was that the blockchain will make all previous technical accumulations, resource reserves and management concepts clear, and that everyone is at the same starting line. In 2018, we also saw that the investment circle favored the blockchain technology almost one-sidedly.

The more the developments that arise in blockchain, the more we have to look at the blockchain hype rationally. Chairman Wang Bin and I agreed that "blockchain +" is the road to the development of China's blockchain industry for the following reasons:

First, the application of blockchain in China is still in a fragmented stage. It is still in the process of being integrated with industry. There are legal and regulatory issues, as well as industrial foundation issues, and more social and economic issues. The problem is one of theoretical change.

Second, the development of emerging technologies such as the Internet, cloud computing, big data, Internet of Things and artificial intelligence has enabled us to see the prominent role of the mutual promotion of advanced productivity and means of production for local economic development.

Therefore, just like the Internet and other industries, the technology first follows the development path of "Internet +". When the consensus in the industry reaches a certain level, it enters a relatively mature stage, that is, the stage in which industry expands due to developments made possible by the Internet.

At this stage, the digital economy has reached consensus as we are currently in a relatively mature period of big data development. However, the applications of blockchain are basically the same as those of the above-mentioned developments made possible by the Internet: technology streaking, industry wait-and-see, local desire, market chaos, laws and regulations and many blank or fuzzy boundaries. "Blockchain +" means that technology still leads, and business follows. When the separate applications reach a certain scale, they will usher in the stage of "+ blockchain" and a new leapfrogging stage of the digital economy will have been reached.

According to Moore's Law, the application cycle of blockchain may accelerate in theory, but according to socio-economic theory, it must adapt to the development of production relations and productivity (see Chapter 3 for details), so its development speed also has a particular certainty. But there is no doubt that 2018 was the first year of the blockchain, which with the involvement of industry, also became the first year of "blockchain +".

During the "two sessions" in 2018, blockchain applications were addressed. Blockchain technology served the real economy, and there were high hopes that blockchain would become the norm.

Chapter 1 of the book describes what the blockchain is, where it comes from, how it is likely to develop further, the global development of blockchain and the domestic situation. Chapter 2 explains the technical architecture and development of the blockchain. Chapter 3 mainly describes the relationship between blockchain and digital economy from the perspective of business models and socio-economics, and explains the progressive path of the impact of blockchain on the real economy. Chapter 4 mainly introduces the relevant laws, regulations, supervision and application of blockchain. Chapter 5 mainly introduces how the local government promotes the development of the digital economy by the blockchain industry, and promotes the construction and operation of the industrial ecology through the model of the industrial park economy. Chapter 6 introduces the blockchain's impact on the big data industry, the Internet of Things and artificial intelligence. Finally, Chapter 7 focuses on the application mode and development status of the blockchain in several key industries.

I especially miss the fulfilling time spent in the process of planning this book with Chairman Wang Bin. I would like to thank Dr. Zou Jun for his technical support despite his busy schedule. I am grateful to Zhao Guodong for his ingenious and innovative thinking. Special thanks to Ms. Chen Junxi for her meticulous and thoughtful service and hard work, which has made an important contribution to the publication of this book at the Digital China Forum this year. I also thank Professor Zhang Jinang for his contribution to this book.

Finally, I want to dedicate this book to the families of the authors and the friends who gave us support.

Yan Yang

About the Authors

Yan Yang has a Ph.D. in Management from Tianjin University. He is a Senior Engineer with the Internet Finance Committee of China Internet Association, the Deputy Secretary General of Zhongguancun Big Data Industry Alliance, a Researcher with the CIO Research Center of Renmin University of China, the Co-founder of the Blockchain + Hundred People Summit, and a Global Member of the Expert Working Committee of the Data Research Center (World Wide Web). He has served as the Technical Director of Minsheng Securities Co. Ltd., the General Manager of the National Securities Information Technology Department and the Director of Business Technology for the information Technology Department of Everbright Securities Co. Ltd. He participated in the drafting of the "Technical Guidelines for Securities Companies' Online Securities Information System" for the China Securities Industry Association. With nearly 23 years of experience in securities IT development, construction and management, he is one of the early securities IT personnel in China. In 2009 and 2011, he won the Science and Technology Award for the Securities and Futures Industry two consecutive times. He has presided over large-scale projects or projects such as the cloud computing project and the localization demonstration project, both for the securities industry. In recent years, he has been awarded the CIO title by the media.

Wang Bin is the Chairman of Puzhong Capital, the Founder of CIFC Financial Alliance, and the Executive Deputy Director of Zhongguancun Digital Media Industry Alliance. He is a Founder and an Active Promoter

xxiv   *About the Authors*

of the new economy, new finance and new media, sharing his insights with economic platforms, Internet professionals, new economic experts and investors. In 1997, he began working on the Internet. In 2007, he founded the New Media Industry Alliance and the New Media Network. In 2011, he established the Zhongguancun Enterprise Alliance New Media Incubator. In 2013, CIFC Financial Alliance was established, and in 2014–2017, CIFC Think Tank, CIFC Lead Accelerator, CIFC Financial Coffee, CIFC WuzhenPuzhongChuangke Space, VR Factory, Puzhong Block Chain Research Institute and other leading innovation and entrepreneurial platforms were established. These have successfully incubated more than 50 entrepreneurial teams and growth companies, providing services such as equity investment, financing listing, new media brand marketing, marketing, innovation and entrepreneurship for hundreds of companies. He is the author of *Internet Finance +: New Engine of China's Economy*, *VR + Virtual Reality Detonating New Economy*, and the executive editor of "China Economic Development Report" (2001).

Zou Jun is the Author of the best-selling Blockchain Technology Guide in the Blockchain Field. He has a Ph.D. in Computer Science from Macquarie University, Australia, and an MBA from Macquarie Business School. He is currently the CEO of Guangdian Express Blockchain Technology Co. Ltd. and concurrently the Deputy Secretary General of the Zhongguancun Blockchain Alliance. He used to be a chief architect in the financial industry for the IBM Australia Software Department. In 2011, he returned to China and participated in the planning of the Beijing "Xiangyun Project", the Guangzhou "Tianyun Project" and the Chongqing "Cloud Project". He has served as a senior executive of several cloud computing companies. He was named a senior overseas talent in the Beijing Yizhuang Economic Development Zone, a high-end foreign expert in Beijing, and an expert in the Zhongguancun Blockchain Industry Alliance. Zou Jun's research interests are cloud computing service contracts, blockchain finance and regulatory technology, and blockchain consensus algorithms. He has published more than 20 papers in leading international conferences and journals, and participated in the editorial committee of Software-Defined Storage. In 2015, the Australia China Alumni Association (ACAA) was awarded the 2015 Outstanding Alumni Award for ICT and Media by the Australian Ambassador to China. In 2016, the IEEE International Web Services Conference

(ICWS) published a blockchain paper and won the Best Paper Award. In 2018, Zou Jun's consensus algorithm paper was accepted by the international service computing journal *Transaction on Service Computing* and was published in the first half of 2018. In view of Zou Jun's outstanding achievements during his doctoral research, the President of Macquarie University awarded him the "Principal Award".

Contents

Expert Advisory Committee   vii

Series Editorial Board   ix

Members   xi

Recommendations   xiii

Foreword   xv

Preface   xix

About the Authors   xxiii

Chapter 1 Blockchain: Past and Present   1

1. What is the Blockchain?   1

2. The Development of Blockchain   2

3. Transformation Brought about by the Blockchain   4

4. Supervision Related to the Blockchain   7

Chapter 2 Blockchain Technology Architecture and
Development Trends   9

1. We Examine the Relationship Between Technology
and Architecture   9

2. We Discuss the Development of Blockchain
Architecture — from 1.0 to 3.0   10

3. The Problems and Challenges of the Blockchain Architecture   12

    3.1. Typical problems of the current blockchain platform   13

    3.2. Typical requirements for blockchain applications   15

4. Blockchain 3.0 and Its Development Direction   18
   4.1. Blockchain operating system   18
   4.2. Blockchain middleware   18
   4.3. Blockchain network   18
   4.4. Blockchain side chain technology   18
   4.5. Block expansion   19
   4.6. Off-chain computation   19
   4.7. Sharding   19
   4.8. Blockchain storage   19
   4.9. Consensus mechanism   19
   4.10. Blockchain platform adapted to the application scenario 20
   4.11. Data authenticity guarantee   20
   4.12. Security and privacy   20
   4.13. Formal proof   20
5. Profiles of Blockchain Projects that Claim to Represent the
   Blockchain 3.0 Architecture   20
   5.1. The blockchain operating system known as
        blockchain 3.0 — EOS   21
   5.2. Competition candidate projects for blockchain middleware 22
   5.3. Blockchain network project   22
   5.4. Blockchain projects based on side chains   24
6. Ethereum's Blockchain 3.0 Tour   28
7. The Outlook for Blockchain 4.0   31
8. Blockchain and Storage   32
9. Alternative Platforms to Blockchain   33
   9.1. R3 Corda   33
   9.2. DAG directed acyclic graph system   33
   9.3. Hashgraph   34
10. Security and Privacy Protection   35

Chapter 3 Digital Economy and Blockchain   37
1. The Digitalization of Industry   38
2. Digital Industrialization   41
3. The Digital Economy Era   45

Chapter 4 Relevant Laws, Regulations, Supervision and
               Application of Blockchain   53
1. Legal Regulation of Blockchain Technology   53
   1.1. Technology and legal regulation   53
   1.2. The dimension of the legal regulation of blockchain   55

1.3. The status quo of blockchain legal regulation 55
1.4. The legal issues of the blockchain business model
reconstruction 63
1.5. Legal extension and improvement of blockchain application 65
1.6. Reflection on the legal regulation of blockchain 66
2. Application of Blockchain Technology in the Field of
Proof-of-Existence 67
2.1. The nature of the problem of proof-of-existence 67
2.2. The value of proof-of-existence 67
2.3. The macro dilemma of proof-of-existence 68
2.4. The status quo in the field of proof-of-existence 68
2.5. There is a real dilemma in the proof-of-existence 69
2.6. Feasibility of application of blockchain technology
in the field of depository certificates 71
2.7. The necessity of applying blockchain technology in
the field of depository certificates 72
2.8. The solution case of blockchain technology applied in
the field of proof-of-existence 73
2.9. The development trend of blockchain in the field
of notarization and proof-of-existence 76

Chapter 5 Blockchain + Local Government Innovation 79
1. The Central Role of the Government in the Development
of Blockchain Innovation 79
1.1. Government innovation based on blockchain is the key
to seize the commanding heights of competition 79
1.2. Government innovation based on blockchain is a powerful
guarantee for the development of digital economy 80
1.3. Government innovation based on blockchain is an
objective requirement for the government to adapt
to new developments 81
2. Government Innovation Application Scenarios and Practice 81
2.1. Blockchain + targeted poverty alleviation 81
2.2. Blockchain + food and drug supervision 87
2.3. Blockchain + digital identity 90
2.4. Blockchain + tax management 93
2.5. Blockchain + city management 96
2.6. Blockchain + education governance 99
2.7. Blockchain + customs border inspection 103

3. Governments have Issued Blockchain-Related
   Development Policies   107
4. Suggested Measures to Promote Healthy Development
   of Blockchain Applications   113
   4.1. Strengthen the top-level design of blockchain development   113
   4.2. Enhance support for core technology research   113
   4.3. Select key industries to demonstrate first   114
   4.4. Strengthen supervision of industrial development
        and application   115
5. Actively Promote the Construction of Standards and Norms   116
6. Promote Industrial Chain and Ecosystem Construction   117

Chapter 6 Promoting the Big Data Industry, the Internet
                 of Things and Artificial Intelligence   119
1. Application of Blockchain in Big Data Industry   119
   1.1. The problems encountered in the development of big data   119
   1.2. The application of blockchain in the big data industry   121
   1.3. The development of the integration of blockchain and
        big data   124
2. Blockchain + Internet of Things   126
   2.1. The blockchain escorts the Internet of Things   127
   2.2. The status quo of development and application   128
   2.3. The technical principle   130
   2.4. The application scenario   130
   2.5. Future prospects   132
3. Relationship between Big Data, Artificial Intelligence and
   Blockchain   132

Chapter 7 Application Cases of Blockchain Combined
                 with Real Industry   135
1. Blockchain + Finance   135
   1.1. The new power of financial technology — blockchain   135
   1.2. Blockchain + financial scenarios   137
   1.3. Blockchain + financial application in the banking sector 145
   1.4. Blockchain + application in asset custody   149
   1.5. Blockchain + insurance   152
   1.6. Blockchain + promote a new era of financial technology   155

2. Blockchain + Cultural and Creative Industry: Creating
   Infinite Space   161
   2.1. Blockchain + cultural entertainment   162
   2.2. Blockchain + media   165
   2.3. Blockchain + digital copyright protection   167
   2.4. Blockchain + development and recommendations
        of cultural and creative industries   170
3. Blockchain + Health and Medical Industry   173
   3.1. The background of digital medical   174
   3.2. The blockchain application scenario overview   175
   3.3. The global blockchain medical case   177
   3.4. Blockchain medical industry trends   182
4. Blockchain + Real Estate   183
   4.1. Blockchain + real estate application scenario   183
   4.2. New opportunities in blockchain + real estate   185
   4.3. Application case in blockchain + real estate   187
   4.4. Application value in blockchain + real estate   189
5. Blockchain + Agriculture   191
   5.1. Grasping the opportunities and challenges of the
        blockchain + agriculture   191
   5.2. The implementation of blockchain agricultural
        application scenarios   193
   5.3. Promote blockchain agricultural policy recommendations   196
   5.4. Blockchain + agricultural traceability   198

Appendix A: CIFC Blockchain + Hundred People Summit   203

Appendix B: Blockchain Events   209

Appendix C: Design of Digital Economy Industrial Park   217

Index   227

Chapter 1

Blockchain: Past and Present

Blockchains have increasingly become one of the hot issues in recent years. On December 15, 2016, the State Council issued the "13th Five-Year National Informatization Plan". In the Plan, it was decided that the development of quantum communication, future networks, brain-like computing, artificial intelligence, holographic display, virtual reality, big data cognitive analysis, new non-volatile storage, unmanned vehicles, blockchain, gene editing and other new technologies and frontier layouts should be strengthened to build the first-mover dominant advantage in the new fields. Since then, blockchain technology has become a hot topic of extensive discussion in various industries. It has had an impact on areas ranging from the financial industry to the national information strategy.

So what exactly is the blockchain? What is the history of the block-chain technology? What will the blockchain bring? What are the regulations related to it? This chapter will discuss the answers to those four questions in detail.

1. What is the Blockchain?

Although the concept of blockchain has become popular all over the world, a considerable number of people only have a preliminary under-standing of the blockchain. If you randomly ask a passerby which color blockchain they like, it is probable that you will get answers like red, orange, yellow, green, blue and purple. Closer to home, no matter what kind of technology is used as the means of implementing the blockchain, it provides a new means of accounting, helping the parties in business

1

networks to enhance mutual trust, thereby improving execution efficiency and reducing transaction costs.

Business is an industry with a long history. In the early days of human society, in the era of commodity trading thousands of years ago, the prototype of business was constructed. After thousands of years of technological development and social evolution, people today have successfully built a big network of interconnected businesses around the world, but this evolutionary millennium old business network still faces troubles that existed a thousand years ago in business dealings. Each participant maintains a set of their own proprietary books. When a transaction occurs, each participant records the transaction details into their own books. In order to keep the books of the participants consistent, there will be a lot of extra work required and accommodating the middle man increases the additional cost of the transaction and affects the efficiency of the overall business process.

Blockchain techniques have been proposed to solve the above problems. Blockchain, also known as Distributed Ledger Technology, allows multiple participants in a business to share the same encrypted ledger through a computer network (either public or private, depending on the needs of the business). Although each participant has obtained a complete copy of the distributed ledger, the account page is authorized for viewing only by decrypting it first. The distributed accounting work also needs to be done only after the parties reach consensus. Through the blockchain technology, the consistency and non-destructive modification of the distributed ledger can be realized, thereby further ensuring the authority of the ledger. A business network built on such a credible book has lower trust costs, so it will enjoy lower transaction costs and more efficient transactions. Blockchain technology is an important cornerstone to support the transformation of the Internet of Information into the Internet of Value. Based on cryptographic mechanisms, transactions of value transfer can be recorded completely without allowing anyone to tamper with them through the mathematics-based "consensus".The underlying technologies involved in blockchain are a mixture of innovations from various sciences including cryptography, consensus algorithms, peer-to-peer (P2P) communication, etc.

2. The Development of Blockchain

The blockchain, as an independent technology, has not been around for very long, and the earliest blockchain application that has been documented is the BitCoin, which remains controversial till today. The concept of bitcoin was originally proposed by Satoshi Nakamoto, a mysterious person who has never appeared in reality. In 2009, Satoshi Nakamoto, using point-to-point communication, built the bitcoin, a virtual currency system based on a shared ledger network and implemented a consensus algorithm based on proof of work. The workload proof mechanism is often called "mining". It searches for a number whose hash value is less than a specific value through a large number of dense hash calculations. This specific value becomes smaller as the computing power increases. Bitcoin program code dynamics control the difficulty of finding this number and make it possible to have a number that satisfies the above conditions. On average, such a number is found once every 10 minutes in the entire bitcoin network. Although the cost of finding this number is high, once this number is discovered, the method of verifying if the condition is met is simple. In an anonymous bitcoin network, the participant who finds the number needs to prove that he/she has the ability to account for all participants by doing a large number of intensive calculations, while the other participants simply verify the number and believe that it does have a record. At the same time, the book-entry party will receive a certain amount of bitcoins as a bookkeeping reward. This is the simple economic principle behind the workload proof consensus mechanism.

In 2014, the concept of blockchains with smart contracts was first introduced by Ethereum founder Vitalik Buterin, and the blockchain entered its 2.0 era. The so-called smart contract is a set of commitments defined in digital form, and an agreement on which contract participants can implement these commitments. The business rules in the smart contract can be embedded in the blockchain system and automatically executed in accordance with prior agreements during the transaction. Smart contracts are implemented using a programming language, and validated after they are electronically signed by the relevant parties.

Both bitcoin and Ethereum are blockchain networks based on anonymous identities. The anonymity of blockchain cannot hinder ordinary users of the Internet, but for enterprises, such an anonymous network cannot guarantee the authenticity of the transaction, nor can it protect the privacy of the transaction. Although there are many open-source-software enthusiasts or startups that have made a certain degree of security and privacy protection available based on bitcoins or Ethereum, there is a lack of architectural support. In 2015, the world-renowned open source software organization Linux Foundation, in conjunction with some world-renowned companies, launched an enterprise-level blockchain collaboration project called Hyperledger to create leading enterprise-level blockchain technology. The superbooks support a real-name authentication system based on Certificates of Authority (CA). At the same time, they provide targeted privacy protection and meet the regulatory and auditing requirements. In doing so, they provide strong support for business transactions based on blockchain smart contracts between enterprises. Unlike bitcoin technology and Ethereum, which are both associated with original virtual currencies, superbooks are not associated with any virtual currency at the architectural level. Instead, they focus on the design and implementation of enterprise-level smart contracts, and increasingly strengthen the regulation of virtual currency in various countries. At the moment, superbooks avoid these controversial factors that are not technical. Due to multi-party participation in the real-name system, the superbooks also circumvent the unavoidable billing rights competition in the anonymous network, thereby avoiding the consumption of a large amount of energy or other resource due to the workload of proof mechanism. Practical Byzantine Fault Tolerance (PBFT), which uses three rounds of voting to confirm distributed accounting, is the consensus algorithm used by the superbook. Since then, large enterprises and governments have begun to carry out extensive blockchain pilot projects.

3. Transformation Brought about by the Blockchain

As an emerging technology, blockchain is indispensable in creating real business value. Why use blockchain? What is the problem solved by using blockchains? In short, blockchain technology solves the problem of mutual trust by strengthening the trust mechanism so that it is as strong as the trust mechanism in a traditional contract. Specifically, there are two main features of blockchain applications:

The first of these features is cross-organizational collaboration. In the blockchain network, all participants record and verify the information on the chain. Almost all the data records on the chain, such as keys, hashes and key values, are copied and distributed by all participants to achieve full lifecycle protection. Participants can be widely distributed around the world, provided there is network interoperability.

The second of these features is the power of the collective. Blockchain participants have a dynamic synchronization mechanism. The participants are interconnected by technical means, hence, the information on the blockchain can be quickly distributed to all participants, and the blockchain network will not be subject to the control of a few participants. Even if some participants exit the blockchain network or maliciously attack it, the normal operations of the network will not be affected. The network will never stop, and the credit will be sustainable.

As far as the current research is concerned, blockchain technology has significant business value in at least five areas:

(1) It reduces the risk of trust
Blockchain is an open source and transparent technology. Many participants know the operating rules of the blockchain network. Blockchain technology ensures that each participant can verify the authenticity and integrity of the book's content and history through mathematical and cryptographic methods. This ensures that the transaction history is reliable and has not been tampered with, and is equivalent to increasing accountability and reducing trust risk systematically.

(2) The transaction process is flattened, reducing complexity and cost
In the blockchain, the process of confirming the transaction involves clearing, settlement and auditing, which can save a lot of manpower and material resources compared to the traditional business model. It is of great significance in optimizing business processes and improving the competitiveness of enterprises.

(3) Jointly implementing trusted processes is a powerful tool for achieving
    a shared economy
The purpose of a shared economy is to optimize resource allocation by reducing information asymmetry, ensure the implementation of the rights and interests of both parties in the transaction through strict third-party certification and supervision mechanisms, and conclude the transaction efficiently. By using blockchain technology, information and value can be more strictly protected, enabling information sharing with more efficient, lower-cost flows for value.

(4) The birth of a new business model
It's much easier to implement some business models with the advantages of blockchain technology. For example, in the Internet of Things (IoT)

industry, some organizations have proposed to manage the identity, payment and maintenance tasks of tens of billions of IoT devices with blockchain technology. With this technology, IoT device manufacturers can dramatically extend the lifecycle of their products and reduce the cost of IoT maintenance.

(5) The openness of blockchain technology encourages innovation and collaboration

Through the openness of source code, blockchain technology can facilitate collaboration among different developers, researchers and organizations, allowing them to learn from each other and solve problems more efficiently and safely. Now blockchain technology has been regarded as one of the basic technologies needed to support the next generation of global credit certification and value Internet. The importance of blockchain technology to China's industrial upgrading cannot be ignored.

Specifically, which kinds of businesses are best suited to blockchain technology? Plainly speaking, businesses that are best suited to blockchain technology have multi-party participation, and have lengthy processes, opaque information, friction or disputes, as well as capital-related business transactions that require strong credibility control due to the lack of a mechanism of mutual trust.

Of course, it must also be recognized that the blockchain is still in the early stages of development, and the following guidelines can be considered in applying blockchain technology:

(1) Selecting the right application field requires multi-party participation, but there cannot be too many participants. The multi-parties implement smart contracts jointly to resolve the substantial benefits brought by friction, which must be considered together with the main risks undertaken by all parties.

(2) Fully guaranteeing the feasibility of the technology and avoiding the introduction of new risks, such as the completeness, security and reliability of the mathematical and cryptographic algorithms.

(3) Taking into account the balance between open innovation and regulations.

(4) Taking into account the interests and timetable of each participant in the application and promotion of the blockchain.

4. Supervision Related to the Blockchain

As a technology, blockchain has received considerable attention at the global level. However, as an application of blockchain technology, virtual currency has been subject to intensive policy regulation in recent times. On September 4, 2017, the People's Bank of China, the Central Network Information Office, the Ministry of Industry and Information Technology, the State Administration for Industry and Commerce, the China Banking Regulatory Commission, the China Securities Regulatory Commission and the China Insurance Regulatory Commission jointly issued the "Announcement on Preventing the Risk of Subsidy Issuance Financing". The announcement pointed out that the financing of token issuance refers to the illegal sale and circulation of tokens, which is essentially an unauthorized public financing behavior. Other illegal public financing behaviors include selling tokens illegally, issuing securities illegally and engaging in criminal activities such as illegal fund-raising, financial fraud and pyramid schemes. The relevant departments will monitor developments closely, and strengthen their coordination with the judicial departments and local governments. Also, they will enforce the law strictly in accordance with the current working mechanism, and control market chaos resolutely. Once someone is discovered committing what is suspected to be a crime, they will be transferred to the judiciary. Tokens or "virtual currency", such as bitcoins and ethers, used in token financing are not issued by monetary authorities, and do not have legal and mandatory monetary attributes. Also, they do not have a legal status equivalent to physical currency, and should not be circulated as such for market use.

In early 2018, the US Congress held three hearings on blockchain-related content from technical, financial, and judicial perspectives. Overall, the United States has also carried out strict supervision of blockchain-related activities from the financial perspective. In fact, technology, finance and justice reflect the three potential attributes of blockchain applications. In summary, technical attributes are generally strongly supported and financial attributes are carefully explored under strict supervision. Relevant legislation work is also gradually progressing.

Chapter 2

Blockchain Technology Architecture and Development Trends

1. We Examine the Relationship Between Technology and Architecture

On May 24, 1844, in the conference hall of the Federal Supreme Court of the United States Capitol, Morse sent the first telegram in human history to Baltimore, 40 miles (about 64 km) away. The message that he transmitted read, "What hath God wrought!" Since then, human beings have entered the era of information and communication. More than 100 years later, the first universal computer "ENIAC" appeared at the Moore School of Electrical Engineering at the University of Pennsylvania, marking the start of the era of information processing. With the development of information technology, storage technology based on different media has also progressed from the early perforated tape machine to tapes, magnetic floppy disks, hard disks, optical disks and, now, electronic solid state hard disks.

Most people tend to attribute the progress of society and the changing of the times to the invention of a certain technology, and ignore the fact that a key role is often played by the innovation of the architecture. An obvious example is today's ubiquitous IT infrastructure. The Internet and cloud computing are based on a set of converged architectures which combine communications, computing and storage. It is not enough to do just one of those things any more.

Looking back to the history of IT development, every major change in human development is due to the emergence of new capabilities, or to

9

new applications that drive change. The relationship between architecture and technology is somewhat like that between a conductor and the musicians in his orchestra. Just like an outstanding conductor directing a variety of different musicians to play a magnificent piece of music, good architecture can provide different technical functions through the combination of technology modules, through the communication and coordination of information among those modules, to form a complete computing system with certain functions.

Blockchain is the same. If the technology involved in the blockchain is taken apart, in fact, whether it is cryptocurrency, cryptography, the consensus algorithm or P2P communication, most of the technologies have appeared before the invention of Bitcoin. The reason why the blockchain is important is that it organically combines these technologies to form a decentralized immutable ledger architecture that can establish trust among strange parties in the execution of autonomous transactions and autonomous management architecture. Therefore, rather than being a technological innovation, the blockchain is better described as an architectural innovation.

The term "architecture" comes from construction industry, that is the style of design and method of construction of buildings and other physical structures which are made of building materials to withstand various loads or forces to act as a skeleton. In IT, architecture has two aspects of meaning: one is the static aspect, mainly to outline system boundaries, structures, the components of components and the relationship between components; the other is the dynamic aspect mainly to regulate the behavior of components and the interaction protocol between components. The architecture of an IT system can be considered as the functional features and some non-functional characteristics of the system.

2. We Discuss the Development of Blockchain Architecture — from 1.0 to 3.0

There is currently no uniform definition of the blockchain. The National Institute of Standards and Technology (NIST) is working to provide us with one. Currently, the popular view is to divide the blockchain's architecture development into three phases. The first stage is Blockchain 1.0, represented by Bitcoin, which provides a programmable virtual currency through a scripting engine. At this stage, the blockchain platform has a relatively simple use scenario, which is mainly used for the issuance and circulation of virtual currency, provides decentralized anti-counterfeiting and anti-tampering mechanisms, and prevents the "double-spend" problem. Bitcoin's scripting engine is used for automated transaction verification and does not have Turing completeness. Bitcoin's blockchain platform can only provide storage capacity for other data not exceeding 83 bytes per transaction.

Since the introduction of Bitcoin, its blockchain architecture has attracted widespread interest, especially its ability to build trust in a non-centralized environment. This ability has led to a new concept: that of the "Decentralized Application (DApp)". DApps are different from traditional apps. A traditional application belongs to an owner, and runs on a node or a cluster; also, it does not require consensus on the results. DApp generally does not belong to a specific owner. It runs on a decentralized network at the same time. The result of the operation needs to be agreed upon in the network before it can be finalized. DApp's decentralization makes it particularly suitable for weak trust environments that involve multiple parties because it provides anti-counterfeiting, tamper-proof, fair, transparent and algorithm-based transactions rather than transactions based on trusting people or an organization. There are a wide range of application scenarios in the financial industry and in all walks of life related to data authenticity. Huge demand drives the evolution of the architecture of blockchain from 1.0 to 2.0, with the most prominent upgrade being the Turing Complete Smart Contract Platform, which is the foundation for supporting DApp applications. Among the many blockchain platforms that are advertised as blockchain 2.0 architecture, Ethereum has a grand vision of "the never-ending world computer". The advantages of distribution, circulation and especially support for the account system and the "World State" state machine, and the high-level programming language support for smart contracts, make Ethereum stand out as the typical representative of blockchain 2.0 architecture. Following the launch of the ERC20 standard, Ethereum became the de facto virtual currency and digital asset issuance and distribution platform. The era of blockchain 2.0 is also known as the "programmable finance" era.

As the hype surrounding the blockchain increases, many people's expectations for blockchain rise rapidly. Blockchain 2.0 can no longer match those people's imagination, and the concept of blockchain 3.0 has arisen. Blockchain 3.0 refers to the use of blockchain technology to transform organizational structures into "programmable organizations, programmable society". This means that future organizations, like companies or other social groups, can be made up of smart contracts on the blockchain. Smart contracts can automatically manage organizational activities, conduct business, assign responsibilities, rights, and benefits, and automatically account for disputes and arbitration. The practical execution of this concept seems to be as distant as Utopia at the moment, because neither the current technology nor the legal system supports it. Therefore, most people currently regard "blockchain 3.0" as an extension of "blockchain 2.0", specifically conceptualized to build a blockchain platform that truly supports DApp, and to solve the problems of "blockchain 2.0", of which a typical representative is Ethereum. The problems that have arisen range from insufficient performance to scalability and even security.

3. The Problems and Challenges of the Blockchain Architecture

A completely decentralized blockchain architecture can present performance and security issues. Traditional distributed architectures, such as cloud computing, perform their functions by slicing a task and distributing it to multiple nodes for parallel computing. The final result is aggregated back to a single node, so the efficiency is high, but the degree of centralization is also high. In a completely decentralized blockchain architecture, the same task is put on multiple nodes at the same time, and the execution results of all the nodes need to achieve consensus through a consensus algorithm, and the result of that consensus becomes the final state that needs to be synchronized across all the nodes. It is conceivable that its efficiency is far lower than that of more traditional methods. But, the degree of security and trust achieved by using a completely decentralized blockchain is much higher than that achieved through traditional methods.

The real world in which people live is not perfect, and it contains many impossible trinities. For example, there is a Mundell impossible trinity in economics. It is said that a country cannot take into account the autonomy of monetary policy, the fixed exchange rate and the free flow of capital. Only two out of three can be used.

In the field of distributed computing, the well-known CAP theory states that Consistency, Availability and Partition Tolerance cannot be achieved at the same time. In the blockchain, the currently recognized impossible trinity, the so called "trilemma" has decentralization, security and scalability as three competing characteristics.

According to the impossible trinity theory of the blockchain, it is obvious that the current Ethereum architecture favors decentralization and security at the expense of scalability. At present, Ethereum can do about 15 transactions per second on average, so for Ethereum, it is difficult to scale applications except for those such as digital asset issuance. In 2017, a blockchain cat game "CryptoKitties" caused congestion in the Ethereum network.

Therefore, many new blockchain platform projects flaunting blockchain 3.0 have proposed their own solutions to improve the performance of Ethereum. However, the current deployments of blockchain projects are mostly unsatisfactory. Let's first look at the pain points of the blockchain platform and the typical needs of industry customers.

3.1. *Typical problems of the current blockchain platform*

3.1.1. *Transaction performance limit*

Bitcoin's theoretical limit of transaction per second (TPS) is 7, but in practice, there are usually only 1–2 transactions made per second. Ethereum allows about 10–20 transactions to be made per second. Since a Bitcoin blockchain transaction requires more than six confirmations for its final certainty to be guaranteed with a high probability, the transaction confirmation time is also slow.

3.1.2. *Extensibility restrictions*

In scenarios where timely deterministic transactions, such as consortium chains or private chains, are required, the number of consensus nodes will be limited. For example, when using a blockchain platform, which runs on a state machine replication (SMR) consensus algorithm based on Paxos (distributed conformance) or BFT (byzantine fault tolerance), the number of nodes participating in the consensus cannot generally exceed two digits.

3.1.3. *Ease of use and support for applications*

At present, the development, deployment and invocation of smart contracts need to be carried out by professional blockchain programmers. Blockchain has obstacles in terms of ease of use and support for applications.

3.1.4. *Compatibility and interoperability*

At present, most of the blockchain platforms are independent systems, and do not support the transfer of assets between different chains. There is no standard to implement cross-chain integration and the integration of applications on different chains.

3.1.5. *Storage restrictions*

Blockchain has limited storage capacity for data, especially as the amount of data that needs to be stored in each node is increasing. There is an urgent need for a lower cost and more efficient chain storage solution.

3.1.6. *Data synchronization performance limit*

As the data on the chain grow all the time, the burden of data synchronization on the network is getting larger and larger, and the synchronization speed is getting slower and slower.

3.1.7. *Smart contract formal verification*

Once a smart contract is deployed, it cannot be modified, so if it contains bugs and vulnerabilities, it may give hackers the opportunity to take advantage of the situation. A formal proof of the contract code is a logical proof completed before the contract is deployed, proving that the execution of the contract is correct. In order to complete this formal proof, a programming language with strict logical completeness and automatic reasoning is generally required. At present, Ethereum's Solidity programming language does not have this capability, and some traditional formal proof tools and programming languages have not been effectively applied to blockchain.

3.1.8. *Consensus mechanism mathematical proof*

The consensus algorithm used by many blockchain platforms does not give a rigorous mathematical proof that it can reach consensus within a limited time in the hypothetical network communication environment or ensure that the consensus results are correct even in the presence of a limited number of faulty nodes. Especially in the case of public chains, many consensus algorithms, particularly the POS (Proof of Stake) consensus algorithm based on stake of the coins, lack strict mathematical proof.

3.2. *Typical requirements for blockchain applications*

The applications on the blockchain have different dimensions of requirements depending on different scenarios.

3.2.1. *Privacy protection*

The details of the trading participants and the transaction cannot be disclosed to unrelated parties. At present, Bitcoin, Ethereum, etc. only provide a semi-anonymity mechanism, and there is no guarantee that private transaction information will not be leaked under big data analysis.

3.2.2. *Chain security*

In the blockchain network, especially in the public chain scenario, it is important to know how to tolerate faulty nodes, especially the Byzantine fault, and prevent security attacks such as sybils, replay and DDoS (distributed denial of service). When a large-scale P2P system faces the threat of an adversary node, a malicious entity can control a large part of the system and undermine the system's redundancy strategy if it imitates multiple identities. This attack that mimics multiple identities is defined as a Sybil Attack. In a Sybil attack, an attacker destroys the reputation system of a peer-to-peer network by creating a large number of pseudonym identifiers, which are used to cause a serious security impact.

A replay attack occurs when an attacker sends a packet that the destination host has received to achieve the purpose of spoofing the system. It is mainly used for the identity authentication process and destroys the correctness of the authentication. Replay attacks can be performed by the initiator or by an enemy that intercepts and resends the data. The attacker uses network snooping or other means to steal authentication credentials and then resends them to the authentication server. Replay attacks can occur in any network process and are one of the common attacks used by computer hackers.

3.2.3. *Data authenticity*

Although the data on the blockchain cannot be tampered with, there is no way to prevent artificial fraud. Ensuring that the chain of data is real, and that there is no return to the centralized Oracle (source of truth) mechanism, is also a very critical requirement. Oracle is a guarantee mechanism for authenticity of data on the blockchain. An authoritative organization is usually required to act as Oracle, but how to prevent the Oracle's centralization?

3.2.4. *Proof of useful work*

Bitcoin mining has caused a huge waste of energy. It is estimated that the current amount of electricity used for bitcoin mining in one year is equivalent to the electricity consumption in Ireland for one year. If we examine Bitcoin's workload, we find that it is just doing hashing, and that the results are useless. If it can provide a useful workload and provide a more stable consensus mechanism, it will be very attractive, but this is also a difficult research direction.

3.2.5. *Public Key signature security*

Although quantum computing is still in its infancy, it may take another 20 years for it to be developed commercially. However, the Shor algorithm of quantum computing has theoretically cracked the public key encryption system. The public key signature system used in the blockchain is faced with the threat of being cracked by quantum computing. While the Grover algorithm of quantum computing cannot reduce the difficulty of cracking the hash algorithm from the exponential level to the polynomial time level, it can reduce the amplitude equivalent to a square root of the original calculation amount. Therefore, the anti-quantum cryptography algorithm has also become a research direction of interest to cryptography researchers.

3.2.6. *Governance and supervision*

Many blockchain projects are currently maintained by several core developers. The revision of some key parameters and the decision-making direction of the platform are still determined by a small number of people. Due to this, blockchain projects generally lack a transparent and strict governance structure and regulatory system. How to design a governance and supervision system suitable for the blockchain so that the blockchain platform can develop healthily is a problem faced by many blockchain projects.

3.2.7. *Smart contract upgrade and monitoring*

Once a smart contract is deployed, it cannot be changed, but traditional software needs to be constantly improved and upgraded. In addition, in many scenarios, the logic of smart contracts also needs to adapt to changes in demand. So, how to upgrade smart contracts and how to monitor the operation of smart contracts are also common requirements, especially for enterprise customers.

3.2.8. *Prevent the centralization of computing power*

As the price of bitcoin climbs, the interest drives bitcoin mining to become an area in which there is a computing "arms race". The computation power of Bitcoin mining is constantly being centralized. At present, the computation power of the five major mining pools has exceeded 70% of the total network computation power. In order to prevent the concentration of computation power, a proof of work mechanism that requires a large amount of storage is designed so that the cost of making an application-specific integrated circuit (ASIC) becomes higher, and ordinary people can still participate in mining with a general-purpose processor like a GPU.

3.2.9. *Identity authentication and access control*

Many blockchain applications, especially enterprise-level consortium chain applications, need to identify the user and grant different permissions based on their identity. Secure and efficient identity (ID) management, identity authentication and access control are important requirements.

4. Blockchain 3.0 and Its Development Direction

The problems of the blockchain that have been described above and the needs of users have driven the evolution of blockchain architecture from 2.0 to 3.0. The specific technology is developed in the following directions.

4.1. *Blockchain operating system*

The operating system of the blockchain is similar to the traditional computer operating system, in that it provides the underlying services for computer users and application development. The blockchain operating system also provides functions and environments to support the development and operation of the upper decentralized applications. These functions include supportive functions such as authentication, access control, data access, contract compilation and test-level deployment. The operating system provides ease of use, lowering the barriers to using blockchains, and developing and deploying DApps.

4.2. *Blockchain middleware*

Like traditional middleware, blockchain middleware shields interface differences between different blockchain platforms, enabling applications to easily develop DApps that support different chains, as well as cross-chain integration capabilities that enable applications to integrate multiple blockchain platforms.

4.3. *Blockchain network*

Unlike Bitcoin or Ethereum's single-chain technology, the blockchain network provides a network platform under which there are multiple chains, each of which can issue its own virtual assets. Cross-chain interconnection is achieved through a backbone or relay in a blockchain network platform.

4.4. *Blockchain side chain technology*

The side chain originally came from the concept that there is no need to change the main chain (this originally refers to bitcoin). Instead, it is possible to expand the main chain by establishing a side chain. The assets of the main chain can be safely transferred to the side chain for circulation, and finally safely returned to the main chain.

4.5. *Block expansion*

The block capacity is related to the number of transactions that can be packaged. Since the blockchain's block broadcast frequency is relatively fixed, the transaction volume per second (t/s) will increase accordingly after the block is expanded.

4.6. *Off-chain computation*

Although the transaction workload on the main chain can be safe and reliable, the consensus overhead is very high, so offloading some of the workload outside of the main chain is a natural choice to make in order to increase transaction throughput.

4.7. *Sharding*

The performance problems of Ethereum have made Ethereum's development community realize that when each transaction and each step of smart contract execution need to be completed at all consensus nodes, its scalability cannot support the application. Therefore, it is inevitable that local consensus is used instead of global consensus.

4.8. *Blockchain storage*

Storage space on the blockchain is limited. Generally speaking, it is only the transaction data and the hash value of the stored data, that is the "fingerprint" of the data, which can be stored. Therefore, how to store the ever-increasing blockchain data, especially code or state data, is a problem faced by today's blockchain platforms.

4.9. *Consensus mechanism*

The core part of the blockchain is its consensus mechanism. Different consensus mechanisms have different consensus attributes and their transaction volumes are determined per second. Therefore, the design of the consensus mechanism has become a key task in the underlying platform of the blockchain.

4.10. *Blockchain platform adapted to the application scenario*

Blockchain platforms need to support deployment of applications. In practice, applications have different requirements depending on which industry they are in. Therefore, in many areas of vertical subdivision in the future, there is a need for a corresponding blockchain platform.

4.11. *Data authenticity guarantee*

The data on the chain are not easy to tamper with, but before the data are put to the chain, it is not difficult to fake the data. Therefore, distributed Oracle systems are needed to guarantee data authenticity.

4.12. *Security and privacy*

Security is the lifeblood of the blockchain platform. It is necessary to ensure the security of the blockchain platform and to prevent disclosure of private transaction information through the use of cryptography.

4.13. *Formal proof*

When formal proofs are used to verify smart contracts, bugs and vulnerabilities can be found before contract deployment to enhance contract robustness and security.

5. Profiles of Blockchain Projects that Claim to Represent the Blockchain 3.0 Architecture

Currently, we are experiencing the transition from blockchain 2.0 to blockchain 3.0. New blockchain projects emerge in an endless stream and all claim that they represent the next generation of blockchains. However, most of them have not yet been formally on production. Whether the projects described in the white papers of various companies will be implemented remains to be seen. The following is a brief introduction of some of the typical representative projects that include the various aspects described above.

5.1. *The blockchain operating system known as blockchain 3.0 — EOS*

The EOS project was first proposed as a blockchain operating system. It provides similar operating system features and services required for DApp development and operation, including account systems, user authentication, authorization, database, asynchronous communication, scheduling and cloud storage. At the same time, EOS also supports both vertical and horizontal extensions. It specifically supports parallel processing in the operation of smart contracts, so transactions can be processed in parallel. The design goal is to achieve thousands of TPS per second. EOS is free of transaction fees for users, making it easy for users to deploy DApps. EOS was officially launched in June 2018.

EOS has revised its original white paper and released the 2.0 version of the EOS white paper. In the updated EOS white paper in the Github, EOS says that it has replaced the previous DPoS (delegated proof of stake) consensus algorithm with a BFT-DPoS consensus algorithm that can perform Byzantine fault tolerance. The block time has also been reduced from the past 3s to 0.5s. In the original 1.0 version of the white paper, 21 witnesses took out one block. The new algorithm changed to six blocks per witness, for a total of 126 blocks. Twenty-one witnesses will be selected by EOS stakeholders on the basis of who has the highest coin stake. The order of the blocks between the 21 witnesses is determined by a consensus scheduling algorithm that obtains no less than 15 consents in 21 cases. The new BFT-DPoS consensus algorithm prohibits witnesses from simultaneously appearing on the two chains of the fork. In addition to a system in which evil witnesses are identified by voting, it also implements a mechanism based on cryptographic evidence to automatically eliminate wrong doing witnesses.

The EOS blockchain can finally confirm the transactions on the blockchain within 1s, and the transactions can no longer be overturned after confirmation. EOS will use sharding for parallel execution and support for delayed transactions, which means that you can plan a future-initiated transaction to support long-running process transactions.

Another major change in EOS was dropping the original intention of Ethereum Virtual Machine (EVM) support. EOS's smart contract will be running on top of the WebAssembly (WASM) virtual machine.

In terms of governance, EOS can freeze accounts and change smart contract codes with the consent of at least 15 witnesses.

EOS was released on production in June 2018. It becomes a mainstream blockchain platform after Bitcoin and Ethereum.

5.2. *Competition candidate projects for blockchain middleware*

Two examples of the middleware-oriented project are an Ontology network and ArcBlock.

According to Ontology's white paper, it is a multi-chain, multi-system fusion chain group structure. In addition to the distributed network of the ontology network itself, the distributed ledger framework can support the blockchain system under different governance modes, and can also be from different business areas. Different chains in different regions cooperate through the various protocols of the ontology network to form the cross-chain and cross-system interaction mapping of various heterogeneous blockchains and traditional information systems, in order to create a blockchain middleware.

ArcBlock is an ecosystem for building decentralized applications. It provides the basic blockchain service component needed to integrate blockchain capabilities into existing systems. It contains Pub/Sub Gateway Adapters (publish/subscribe gateways) and an OpenChain Access Layer (a common layer that supports different blockchains) and provides different blockchains, and is also a typical blockchain middleware project.

5.3. *Blockchain network project*

Broadly speaking, the main design goal of the blockchain network is to provide scalability, and to achieve blockchain network interconnection, cross-chain assets movement and information exchange. In the specific implementation, there are different emphases. The following is a brief introduction to several blockchain network projects.

5.3.1. *Lightning network*

The bitcoin-based Lightning Network actually builds a peer-to-peer payment channel network outside the main chain, which can move peer-to-peer transactions from the main chain to the payment channel, and thus turns the main chain into a settlement system, thereby reducing the load on the main chain and improving the overall throughput. Combined with the main chain, it can support tens of thousands of transactions per second. The specific payment process is that the two parties first set up a payment channel on the lightning network, and then they can realize the micropayment of the instant confirmation through the payment channel. The final netting of transactions will be recorded on the main chain. If there is no direct point-to-point payment channel between the two parties, the two parties can be connected indirectly through multiple payment channels. The lightning network can also use this payment path to realize the reliable transfer of funds between the two parties.

The basic technology of the Lightning Network is to define a two-way micro-payment channel through RSMC (Recoverable Sequence Maturity Contract). The micro-payment channel has funds injected by each party in advance, and then each payment is mutually confirmed by a signature. A new balance is formed and the channel also records the balance of the funds of both parties. The Lightning Network also supports HTLC (Hash Timelock Contract) funding conditionally. For example, Alice and Bob can use HTLC to reach a protocol that will lock Alice's 0.5BTC before the time T arrives (T is expressed in a future blockchain height) if Bob can reach Alice. Presenting an appropriate S (called a secret) so that the hash value of S is equal to the previously agreed value $H(S)$, Bob can obtain the 0.5BTC; if Bob still fails to provide a correct S until time T, this 0.5BTC will be automatically thawed and returned to Alice.

Lightning networks can be extended into a network through point-to-point payment channels. For example, if there is a payment channel between Alice and Bob, and there is a payment channel between Bob and Eva, then Alice and Eva can use the first two payment channels to achieve point-to-point payment. At present, the Lightning Network has launched the Bitcoin main network on December 25, 2017. Currently, there are more than 14,000 nodes running on the Bitcoin main network.

5.3.2. *Raiden network*

The Raiden network is a chain payment channel network based on the idea of lightning networks in Ethereum. It uses smart contracts to achieve both parties' payments, including conditional payments. The Raiden network implements payment by submitting an "Update Transaction" message to the chain contract. The Smart Condition can be used to provide the HTLC richer conditional payment function of the Lightning Network. The Raiden Network released the preview version in 2017 and planned to release the original version in 2018. However, it experienced a near two-year delay; the Raiden network 1.0 version was only released on Ethereum in May 2020.

5.3.3. *Tendermint cosmos*

Unlike lightning networks, Raiden networks, etc., which are attached to bitcoin or Ethereum, Tendermint Cosmos builds a native blockchain network to fundamentally solve the problem of cross-chain interconnection. Tendermint Cosmos uses Tendermint Cosmos's BFT POS consensus algorithm. The Tendermint Cosmos Consensus is the first POS consensus mechanism that supports Byzantine fault tolerance. The traditional POS consensus mechanism can lower the cost of committing crime; in other words, the witness can make a block on multiple forks to earn the accounting fee without penalty. Tendermint Cosmos first proposed the concept of a deposit. If a witness is found to have a block on multiple forks, the deposit will be forfeited. On the contrary, by voting to confirm the block by more than 2/3 of the witness nodes, it is possible to effectively tolerate less than 1/3 of the Byzantine nodes. Tendermint Cosmos's BFT POS consensus mechanism will be inspired by the later Ethereum Casper and EOS, which both have similar mechanisms.

The Tendermint Cosmos architecture is a parallel multi-chain architecture. Different sovereign chains are placed in the Zone, and the Hub interconnects different chains. The first release of Tendermint Cosmos was Cosmos Hub, which was launched in 2018, and the main net was on production in March 2019.

5.4. *Blockchain projects based on side chains*

The concept of the side chain was first proposed by Blockstream, whose purpose is to extend the function of the main chain through the side chains without changing the structure and parameters of the main chain. There are a lot of side chain-based projects coming up, the most typical of which is Rootstock.

The special currency two-way hook supports Turing's complete smart contract and instant payment. Rootstock's virtual machine incorporates the EVM's instruction set, so it is compatible with smart contracts on the Ethereum EVM. Rootstock produces a block in every 20s, claiming to support 300 transactions per second at the time of release, and gradually expanding to 1,000t/s. Another big feature is that although Rootstock has its own blockchain, it is jointly mined with the Bitcoin block. So, it has the same security as Bitcoin.

Rootstock supports two-way hooking with Bitcoin. When an asset goes from the Bitcoin main chain to Rootstock, the corresponding Bitcoin is locked in the main chain, and the equivalent Rootstock Native Token RTC is unlocked on the Rootstock blockchain. When the RTC asset is to be transferred to the Bitcoin main chain, the corresponding RTC will be locked on the Rootstock, and the corresponding BTC that was previously locked on the Bitcoin main chain will be unlocked.

Rootstock's side chain technology extends the support of Turing's complete smart contracts without changing the bitcoin backbone architecture, and is forward-compatible with Ethereum smart contracts, as well as supporting assets between the main and side chains for instant payment.

Another very famous project is Polkadot. Polkadot is a heterogeneous multi-chain system developed by the Web3 Foundation, a Parity wallet team led by Ethereum Yellow Book author Gavin Woods. Its purpose is to enable companies or developers to build parallel chains (Parachain) using their platforms. There can be multiple Parachains, all sharing the Proof of Authority consensus mechanism on the platform. Each Parachain can have different characteristics. All parallel chains are seamlessly connected to a common blockchain called a relay chain, and cross-chain integration of parallel chains is achieved through the relay chain.

Each parallel chain has an equal number of complete nodes, which are specifically responsible for a parallel chain, known as the Collator. These checkers collect and validate transactions from users, and then transmit the verified transactions to the Validator responsible for the relay chain, which runs nodes equivalent to light nodes on the trunk chain. The certifier is responsible for verifying and broadcasting the block sent from the checker. To do this, each time a block is received, the certifier must mortgage their DOT (Relay Chain Token). In order to ensure that the verifier performs the correct behavior and does not broadcast invalid transactions, another type of participant, the Fisherman, monitors its behavior. They will get the DOT as long as they prove the wrongdoer's wrong behavior. In addition, the certifier needs to be approved by the Nominator, and the nominee also needs to mortgage their DOT to nominate the certifier. The verifier not only has the right to mortgage but also can vote for or reject a parallel chain. Through the above mechanism, Polkadot guarantees the security of the network.

How does Polkadot support trading from one parallel chain to another? Here's a simple workflow:

(1) The user creates a transaction on parallel chain A to send information to parallel chain B.
(2) The transaction is sent to a collator of parallel chain A.
(3) The checker ensures that the transaction is valid and is included in a block.
(4) The collating person presents this block and proof of state transition to a verifier of parallel chain A.
(5) The verifier verifies that the received block contains only valid transactions and mortgages their DOT.
(6) When there are enough nominees to mortgage their DOT and nominate the verifier, it is broadcast that their block to the trunk will be authorized.
(7) The transaction is executed and data from A are sent to B.

Polkadot is designed to guarantee Byzantine fault tolerance in an environment without trust. Once the checker transmits the error message, a proof of the action is generated and the checker may then be punished or cleared. At the same time, the verifier is under the surveillance of the phishers; in order to maintain the DOT, the nominee will tend to nominate a good certifier.

Polkadot can be used to bridge existing blockchains. Polkadot is able to connect the Ethereum main network to the Polkadot network through so-called Break-in Contracts and Break-out Contracts. In order to transfer data from Ethereum to the Polkadot parallel chain, some verifiers either need to run the full node of the Ethereum main network and listen to the logs of the specific contract, or they need to have a mechanism to receive the transaction certificate from the bound third-party full node. In the latter case, the certifier does not need to run the entire blockchain, but will rely on a Merkle proof to verify the transaction. In order to guarantee the canonicality of the transaction, the certifier needs to wait for a minimum number of block acknowledgments before trading on the broadcast relay chain.

In order to send information from Polkadot to Ethereum, one can give certain verifiers the right to mortgage their DOT to a transfer transaction. An inbound contract that knows the list of authorized verifiers can create a transaction after collecting the signatures of the specified number of verifiers.

In summary, most existing blockchains can be connected to the Polkadot network via a specific bridge. Building a bridge for a common blockchain may not be as straightforward as building one for Ethereum, but it is also possible. While exchanging information with Polkadot's parallel chain, these blockchains retain their existing consensus types and cybersecurity participants. Whether a bridge should be developed will depend on the use case and needs of the users. Parity Technologies has open sourced a bridge that can connect blockchains to any other Parity chain through authoritative proof.

Polkadot was rewritten using Substrate as the underlying framework. Substrate is a blockchain development framework provided by Parity. Parity Substrate makes it quick and easy to build the custom blockchain for your needs. Built on Rust and WebAssembly (WASM), you can choose Substrate to build a custom blockchain platform quickly.

In order to solve the problem of asset transfer in different ledgers, Ripple proposed the Interledger protocol in 2015. First, Interledger is not a blockchain, but a set of rules for transporting assets called ILP. In other words, ILP solves the problem that different books cannot be interconnected. ILP has four basic components: the first is the sender (Sender); the second is the receiver (Receiver); the third is the connector (Connector); and the fourth is the ledger (Ledger).

Both the sender and the receiver are easier to understand, and the connector connects the sender and receiver to complete the ILP. Connectors can also be connected to other connectors so that more senders and receivers can be connected. The ledger is used to record the balance of assets in each account. In the real world, the ledger can be a book with a traditional bank or a third-party payment, or it can be a block of the blockchain. If the sender and receiver are on the same ledger, then there is no need for a connector between them and they can carry out a transfer directly.

An Internet-like architecture has four layers (application layer, transport layer, cross-network layer, and network layer), and the Interledger architecture also has four layers (application layer, transport layer, cross-book layer, and ledger layer). Simply put, Interledger applies the concept of the Internet to the interconnection ledger to achieve interconnection between different blockchains, between blockchains and traditional ledgers, and even between traditional ledgers and other traditional ledgers. Interledger can solve the problem of information islands in the financial industry, providing a safe and efficient cross-book interconnection, which will have a wide range of usage scenarios.

6. Ethereum's Blockchain 3.0 Tour

Ethereum is currently one of the most widely deployed and mature blockchain platforms. Ethereum itself is constantly evolving and strives to upgrade itself to the blockchain 3.0 architecture. In addition to the Raiden network mentioned above, the following are five upgrades for Ethereum.

(1) Plasma
Plasma is a blockchain expansion solution proposed by Joseph Poon and Vitalik Buterin. The idea is largely analogous to the idea of lightning networks, which mainly freeze funds in the main network and use them for settlement under the chain, while transactions are carried out under the chain. The main chain is Plasma. The root chain is the Ethereum blockchain. And, the underlying chain trades on the sub-chains created by the main chain and is associated with the trading participants. If the party on the transaction finds that the other party has committed misconduct (such as violation of a pre-determined transaction agreement), evidence of the violations can be submitted to the main network, causing the evil party to be fined. The consensus protocol in the sub-chain and the execution of the participants' actions and functions are controlled by a smart contract in the main network. The sub-chain transaction data are organized using the Merkle tree, and its Merkel certificate is uploaded to the main chain, allowing external observers to monitor the status of the sub-chain.

Plasma uses sub-chains to reduce the burden on the root chain (Ethereum) to increase transaction traffic, while using the security of the root chain to ensure the security of the sub-chain. Plasma's scalability can even reach billions of transactions per second. The reason is that in a Map-Reduce-like way, sub-chains can be built on the sub-chains and expanded in a tree structure. Plasma consists of the following components:

(i) Client (Client) — Monitors the Ethereum and runs the sub-chain, leaving it immediately when it detects fraud.

(ii) Child Chain — Monitors the behavior of Deposit on Ethereum and performs all calculations related to the current state of the sub-chain.

(iii) Root Chain — Processes the business of depositing and leaving (withdrawal) on the sub-chain through the intelligent contract anchor chain in the Ethereum chain. Confirms and processes these deposits and withdrawals after receiving enough information, or rejects fraudulent withdrawals (departure).

(iv) Parent Chain — Protects the sub-chain. The parent chain is equivalent to the root chain in the minimum viable product (MVP). In the final version, however, there may be multiple parent chains on the sub-chain, but only one root chain.

(2) Blocking of blockchains (sharding)

In all current blockchain protocols, each full node holds all the states, including account balances, smart contract codes and "world state" storage for smart contracts. This provides a high level of security, but scalability is greatly limited. Because the blockchain transaction processing speed cannot exceed the processing speed of any one of the nodes, transactions in Bitcoin and Ethereum will be slow, and the number of transactions will not exceed 20 per second. What is the solution? According to the blockchain, it is impossible to increase the scalability by sacrificing a part of security or decentralization. The fragmentation of Ethereum is based on this idea.

The current fragmentation of Ethereum involves the division of the state and historical data into K shares, each of which is a piece (shard). For example, a sharding method can simply use the address segment to slice up the data. One shard has an address starting at 0x00, another has an address starting at 0x01, and so on. With a simple sharding mechanism, each piece has its own trading history, and the effect of the transaction is only limited to that piece. This mechanism is suitable for supporting multi-asset blockchains, with each asset placed in a single slice. More complex fragmentation mechanisms support slice-to-chip communication. Under this mechanism, an on-chip transaction triggers another on-chip event.

The designers of the Ethereum segment proposed a simple sharding scheme. On the blockchain, there are special nodes called certifiers that receive messages on shard K and establish a certification record.

Each certification record has a header, which includes the pre-certification header hash and the Merkle root that receives the message. The certification records in each slice are connected into a chain like a traditional blockchain. Under the fragmentation mechanism, the main chain still exists, but the function of the main chain is to save the certification headers of all the fragments. The longest certified record chain in each shard is the default consensus chain.

Fragmentation is still only an idea, and there are many challenges. The biggest challenge is the communication between slices and tablets.

(3) Truebit project

The Truebit project moves large computational tasks to the chain, which extends the computing power of smart contracts without being limited by Ethereum's "fuel limits". Similar to the idea of other expansion projects, Truebit uses layering above the blockchain to solve this problem. But, its specialty is to outsource the execution and verification of the calculations. Out-of-chain nodes can perform computational tasks, rather than computing every smart contract on every node in the chain. These participants are called "solvers", who propose a way to solve problems to get rewards, while "certifiers" check their work. The Truebit project development team includes Christian Reitwiessner, the creator of the network intelligence contract language Solidity, so many people also have high hopes.

(4) Status Channel

The State Channel is an "off-chain" technique for performing transactions and other status updates. Payment channels like lightning networks are also a type of status channel, except that the payment channel only focuses on the payment status, not the status of other smart contracts. The status channel can be used not only for payment but also for any status updates on the blockchain, including changes to smart contracts. The state channel submits the final state to the chain by deploying a rule contract on the blockchain. The Status Channel is best suited for applications with a clear set of participants, especially if long-term exchange or a large number of status updates are required. The Status Channel has strong privacy attributes because everything happens "inside" the channels between the participants, instead of there being public broadcasts that are recorded on the chain. Only open and close transactions must be made public. The authority of the Status Channel is immediate, which means that as long as both parties have signed a status update, it can be considered the final state. Both parties have a clear guarantee that they can "execute" the status into the chain if necessary.

(5) Casper consensus mechanism

The PoW consensus mechanism will always be a bottleneck in the performance of Ethereum. Therefore, from the earliest roadmap designed by Ethereum, plans were made to adopt the Casper PoS consensus mechanism in the future, but they were continuously delayed due to various reasons such as security. From the first draft of Casper's white paper, it was decided that in its first phase, Casper will be a hybrid mechanism of PoW and PoS. Specifically, the blocks are finalized after every 100 blocks. The first 99 blocks use the PoW mechanism, and the 100th uses the PoS mechanism. At the same time, the transaction data of the first 100 blocks are finally confirmed and cannot be overturned. Ethereum's PoS mechanism also draws on Tendermint's BFT design, using deposits and voting to ensure that witnesses cannot do evil things.

There are many blockchain platforms that use improved consensus mechanisms to increase transaction frequency, such as NXT (PoS Consensus), Ripple (with UNL local consensus instead of global consensus), Stellar (federal BFT consensus) and Bitshares/EOS (DPoS consensus).

7. The Outlook for Blockchain 4.0

More and more people are realizing that the blockchain 3.0 dream of "programmable organization, programmable society" is very far away, and they are gradually returning to the blockchain architecture that supports DApp applications in terms of performance and security as blockchain 3.0. Taking this as a starting point and looking forward, the industry has already positioned blockchain 4.0 as a blockchain platform that supports large-scale industrial applications, especially in combination with industry 4.0. If blockchain 3.0 focuses on performance, scalability and security, then blockchain 4.0 focuses instead on industry applications, such as application landing, addressing interoperability and adapting to different scenarios. A governance structure should be provided to ensure that the blockchain consensus mechanism changes to adapt to scenario requirements, and that parameter changes, software upgrades and smart contract modifications can be effectively implemented under a transparent, reasonable and fair governance mechanism. At the same time, the formal proof of smart contracts is also an important issue that needs to be solved in blockchain 4.0. Although the concept of blockchain 4.0 is still relatively advanced, it is expected that the blockchain 4.0 era will be the era of interconnected chains and the era of blockchain network interconnection. In this era, various digital assets can be interconnected securely and without barriers to create a true value Internet. At the same time, in terms of supervision, there are related laws and regulations that are compatible with technological development. Through the self-regulation and self-compliance of smart contracts linked to regulations, the value Internet moves toward the order Internet.

8. Blockchain and Storage

How to store a large amount of data on the blockchain is a problem. The following six distributed storage schemes are introduced:

(1) IPFS
IPFS (InterPlanetary File System) is designed to divide data into fragments and store them in a decentralized manner in participating nodes. It combines the ideas of distributed hashing (DHT), distributed version management (Git) and P2P protocol BitTorrent. Many people expect IPFS to be a P2P Hypermedia protocol based on domain name addressing instead of HTTP for content-based addressing. IPFS uses Merkle DAG to organize data. FileCoin supports smart contracts and supports token transactions using Proof-of-Storage and Proof-of-Replication consensus mechanisms.

(2) Swarm
Swarm provides a distributed storage and distributed CDN (Content Delivery Network) functionality under the P2P file sharing protocol on Ethereum. The code and data on the Ethereum are stored in Swarm nodes outside the main chain. Swarm nodes are connected to the chain, and data can be exchanged on the chain. Swarm can share storage and bandwidth, built-in peer-to-peer accounting mechanisms, incentive mechanisms and trading mechanisms.

(3) Sia
Sia supports smart contracts to define storage rules and requirements, and users can buy and sell storage space.

(4) MaidSafe

MaidSafe is positioned as a "crowdsourced internet" offering Marketplace and token transactions. User-stored data can be randomly obtained from the SafeCoin token in the form of a lottery ticket. The amount of SafeCoin tokens is related to the resources provided and the boot time.

(5) Storj

Storj files and data fragments are encrypted and stored on multiple nodes. Storj does not support smart contracts, and its token SCJx is paid to the storage nodes that contribute storage.

(6) BurstCoin

BurstCoin supports smart contracts based on the NXT blockchain, using the Proof-of-Capacity consensus algorithm, which is calculated by each miner to generate a large dataset with a miner's nodes for each new block. The miner will read a small portion of the dataset (0.024%) and return a time (the deadline), which is the time from the generation of the last block to the time a new block is generated, and the shortest time to get the block right.

9. Alternative Platforms to Blockchain

9.1. *R3 Corda*

R3 Corda is a financial industry distributed ledger and smart contract platform that provides decentralized workflow collaboration, manages legally binding contracts and links smart contracts to legal terms. The consensus mechanism uses the parties involved in the transaction to form a consensus rather than requesting for a global consensus. R3 Corda uses peer-to-peer communication, transactions are not broadcast, there are no tokens and compliance is emphasized, as is the adoption of industry technical standards.

9.2. *DAG directed acyclic graph system*

The DAG blockchain represents platforms with IOTA and Byteball. It is characterized by not packaging transactions into a block, rather each transaction can be confirmed individually on the network.

Each transaction is a unit, and no block structure is used. Later, the consensus node verifies the past transactions and forms a transaction-oriented acyclic graph. The Spectre Protocol project, which combines DAGs with blocks, can be used to package blocks, but with acyclic graphs instead of the traditional linked chain. The main feature of DAG is that it can greatly increase the transaction frequency. On the one hand, it does not have to wait for packaging; on the other hand, it does not have to connect transactions on the main chain. The difficulty of DAG lies in the consensus mechanism and the choice to use the main chain to prevent double-spending. The waiting verification problem when the transaction frequency is low also needs to be solved.

9.3. *Hashgraph*

Hashgraph is a fast, secure and fair data structure and consensus algorithm patented by Swirls. It is also a kind of DAG structure, but compared with IOTA and Byteball which also adopt DAG structures, the difference is the final confirmation of the transaction. Hashgraph's method implements asynchronous Byzantine fault tolerance and is more secure.

Projects using the Hashgraph technology Hedera (Ivy) were launched in the second half of 2018, using the Virtual Voting consensus algorithm to achieve honesty and transparency, while also saving the resources of the PoW algorithm. Using a protocol called "Gossip about Gossip", which records in which order and to whom Gossip is propagated, a network-interactive distributed ledger that enables the network to scale at an extremely high speed and efficiency is created. The current transaction speed with Hashgraph technology is up to 250,000+ t/s.

Gossip is a widely used protocol in distributed systems, and is mainly used to implement information exchange between distributed nodes or processes. When a computer trades, it randomly tells two other computers. Hashgraph has innovated the "Gossip about Gossip" protocol, which calls any random node and tells the node what it knows, and also attaches a small piece of information to this Gossip which contains information that has just been exchanged (Gossip). The two computers will tell four other computers, and the number will grow exponentially until all the computers on the network know about the transaction. "Gossip" plays an important role on the web. Each network participant will "Gossip" the information they learn, allowing data to be propagated through each member, as each member will randomly propagate information to other members. Unlike existing blockchain protocols, this protocol uses very little bandwidth overhead and prevents network bloat.

10. Security and Privacy Protection

Security and privacy have always been an important part of the core technology in the blockchain. Some of the innovative virtual currencies in this area are Monroe, which uses ring signatures to protect the privacy of the counterparty; Dash, which uses the X11 hash algorithm to guarantee password strength; and Zero Coin (ZCash), which uses non-interactive zero knowledge proof (zk-SNARKs), provides anonymity and hides transaction details. Other security privacy methods include Code Obfuscation and the use of ECDHM (Elliptic Curve Diffie–Hellman–Merkle) addresses to hide real addresses. In addition, it provides complete homomorphic encryption with full privacy protection. The development of an anti-quantum attack cryptography algorithm is also a research direction of the research community and the blockchain community.

Future blockchain development will be deeply integrated with the Internet infrastructure. The blockchain protocol based on the consensus algorithm and the Merkle tree proof will become the trust machine of the network protocol layer. The blockchain will also be combined with legal depth to build a legally meaningful smart contract, while using the traceable and transparent blockchain characteristics to create the core technology behind regulatory technology.

In the future, the broader development direction of the blockchain will involve deep integration with the Internet of Things and artificial intelligence. Future IoT smart devices will become distributed Oracle language machines, providing a trusted source of data for blockchains. At the same time, the combination of artificial intelligence and blockchain will play a huge role in the management and coordination of IoT smart devices. It can be foreseen that in the era of digital economy, the blockchain, as the basic platform of the value Internet, will improve the production relations that are incompatible with the development of the productive forces in the digital economy era and promote economic development and social progress.

Chapter 3

Digital Economy and Blockchain

Perhaps we are still reminiscing about the three-round battle between KeJie, who was called "the last hope of mankind", and AlphaGo. The final score was 0:3. KeJie was defeated by AlphaGo — the masterpiece of that unforgettable first year of artificial intelligence. At the end of 2017 and the beginning of 2018, the major media began to turn their attention to the hot news of the coming year.

The most striking thing is that on February 26, 2018, *People's Daily* reported on the blockchain in a full-page space, in which they explained the definition, function and prospects of blockchain technology. Also, they published the articles "Capturing the opportunity of blockchain" and "Being a leader in the digital economy". On January 23, 2018, the *People's Daily* (overseas version) published an article titled "The blockchain is so hot", and once again reported on blockchain technology. In these two coverages on blockchain, some NPC deputies and CPPCC members also expressed their views. The remarks by Ma Huateng, Zhou Hongyi and Ding Lei included in the two features also caused a lot of discussion, and their concerns about blockchain technology became the cause of much media competition. "Blockchain +" became a hot spot in 2018 or we can say that 2018 was the first year of "blockchain +".

The blockchain is closer to us, and we need to find out more about it.

Today, production, life, consumption and other fields are inseparable from the Internet. I am afraid that the Internet will become a "standard" in these fields. For example, the popularity of mobile terminals has made UGC (User Generated Content) commonplace. When we see a beautiful scenery, we always think of sharing it with friends, so we upload pictures, videos and sounds to the cloud.

(Cloud) — The Internet makes this easy. If an amateur team has a business opportunity, a professional team will also get involved and produce PGC (Professionally Generated Content, also known as PPC, Professionally Produced Content). Further, OGC (Occupationally Generated Content) is available. Numerous content production channels are transmitted through the Internet, recycling and generating a large amount of information, and in this way the related fields of big data came into being. The advent of the era of big data has also made information dissemination via the Internet more transparent.

1. The Digitalization of Industry

The impact of the Internet on the real world is self-evident, but our understanding of the Internet can be derived from the word "Internet" itself.

First of all, mutual connection, representing interoperability, refers to the connectable nature of the Internet, but it is not a "final state". If the atomic world did not have connectivity, there would not be Internet connections at all.

An overpass in a city makes the city accessible from all directions. If we go from *a* via the overpass to *b,* but if it is very difficult to return from *b* to *a,* then such a design is a failure. It can be said that the connectivity of the Internet world is very important. Even if connections do not exist (because of factors such as security requirements), they can be quickly established if these factors are eliminated. The ease of delivery enhances the competitive advantage and the likelihood of winning.

Secondly, the link refers to the state of the connection, which represents synergy and self-discipline. It is an ecological state, not just the narrow connection between people and machines. Broad associations include social organizations such as alliances and associations. The more valid the paths being connected, the more the resources that are available, and the greater the probability of winning in the process of competition.

Finally, the network refers to the physical and material resources available, and contains material and spiritual content (including laws and regulations, of course). The content and efficiency conveyed in the connection form its own business model, which is the key to the final value chain.

Therefore, the Internet mentioned in the material world should be a superposition of the three levels of "mutual connection", "union" and "net".

With the broad application of the Internet, more and more people are beginning to understand the term WiKi (wiki), but the word WiKIT may be unfamiliar. Use Baidu to find this word, there is only one search result, it is a small program; use Google to find the meaning of the word wiki (not WiKIT). Yes, the main meaning of the word WikIT refers to the development of Internet technology such that people can collaborate through an open environment, gain access to entertainment and communication channels, and perform transactions, which are new types of connections with new relationship potential. The huge social value of Internet technology is what we have neglected. WikIT is the "gold mine" that we have not yet explored. These are the changes brought about by the development of the Internet, and some changes are actually revolutionary. In the real world, we often espouse certain doctrines. In fact, the impact of the Internet is to allow us to participate in "sharedism". The sharing here is open, but it is orderly. Openness will produce value.

WikIT provides a better user experience (one actually inclusive of individual desires) while supporting adaptation (collaboration, sharing). Everything that is suitable for such traits will grow or fail. In this way, its marginal cost will be greatly reduced.

In the past few years, there have been some problems in the process of promoting smart cities. They can be described as "separation of expanding industries, lack of talent in academic circles, inconclusive research, unsuccessful investment, difficulties with local control and unsatisfactory application". How can this happen?

Here's the situation. Taking the construction of IT projects as a starting point to promote smart cities may lead to a separation of expanding industries, of course, but this may lead to faster performance when solving problems. With the development of the city of wisdom, its drawbacks have already emerged. The current innovation is too fast, such that the cultivation of talent naturally lags behind. Consequently, the talent that is available is not good. Many companies experience a large gap between the top-level designs they create and the actual implementation after obtaining the project rights, which is also a systemic problem.

Today's application results are such that it's more difficult for builders to profit, user experience is poor, and local governments are in a dilemma — so people often ask: "Tell me what smart cities do better?" In fact, this question is difficult to answer.

As early as in the "18th National Congress" report, it was clearly stated that we must adhere to the path of new industrialization, informatization, urbanization and agricultural modernization with Chinese characteristics. Now, urbanization is no longer just "urbanization", but also emphasizes consumption upgradation, informatized cities and intelligent cities. Therefore, building a smart city has become an important task in promoting new urbanization and building a new countryside. It can be seen here that the smart city is no longer a concept of the past. Urbanization is a complex systematic project that will bring about profound changes in the economy and society, and that requires various supporting reforms to advance.

To this end, let's take a look at the top-level design of the local government's smart city. The PSR (Pressure–State–Response) model was originally proposed by Canadian statisticians David J. Rapport and Tony Friend in 1979. Based on this model, according to China's actual situation, a big data-based feedback-economic model, WSS (Working–Sensing–Smart), has been proposed, which is the top-level model for smart cities.

As shown in Figure 3.1, human activities exert various pressures on the environment and resources. These pressures are perceived in certain ways by various organizations (tangible and intangible institutions), which produce a social response. The configuration, which affects various activities, forms a feedback economy in a shared form.

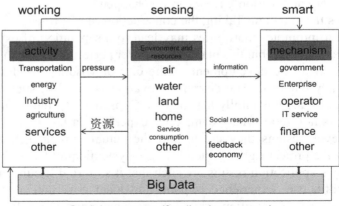

Figure 3.1.   Feedback economy in shared form

From the perspective of China's urban information advancement in these recent years, many cities have basically completed the informatization of industry (the initial stage of digitization). The previous problem was that big data from these three vertical blocks (operation, perception, wisdom) could not get through in smart cities.

So what are the solutions to the problems of the smart city? (See below for details.) One of them is to promote digital industrialization — the development of big data.

2. Digital Industrialization

As shown in Figure 3.2, innovation in the consumer field has already entered the "Competitive era", which is characterized by the "community economy", which can be passed down through niche power using a specific scene experience, relying on traffic to achieve realization. However, the business model of agriculture and industry on the left side of Figure 3.2 has become how to develop non-standard products through the data "refinement" process, sales and other links to achieve personalized customization, networked collaborative realization and social production. This shift from the life service industry to the productive service industry has

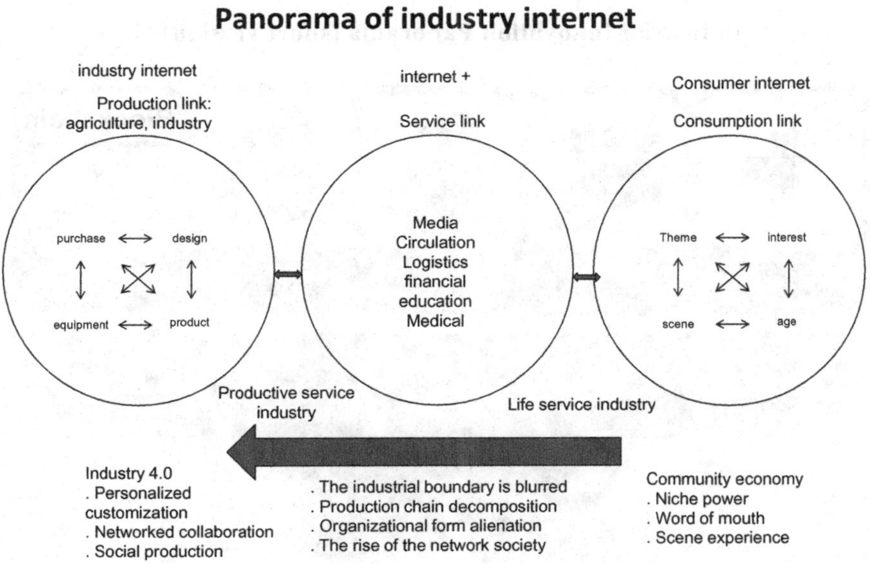

Panorama of industry internet

Figure 3.2. Panorama of industry Internet

gradually rewritten the traditional service industry. The characteristics of disintermediation are very obvious. The rise of the productive service industry is unlikely to develop from the original traditional enterprise. Because of the new format, its industrial boundary has been blurred, the production chain has been decomposed, and the organizational form has completely changed from that of the previous company form to form a networked, platformized production form. We call it EOP (Ecosystem Operating Platform or Ecological Operation Platform, which will be described in detail later). Currently, we call it the era of digital industrialization.

Figure 3.3 shows the interlaced relationship with each domain during the life cycle of big data. From a technical point of view, the digital industry includes: data collection (including the Internet of Things, etc.), data storage (including cloud computing, data cleaning, etc.), data processing (including data desensitization, data migration, pre-processing, etc.), data analysis (including data mining, data modeling, data prediction, etc.), data visualization (including VR, AR, MR, etc.) as well as data decision and data services. The various nodes of the data lifecycle form the various segments of the big data technology market. When these segments are superimposed with various industries (such as the industries in Figure 3.3), they contribute to the development of the digital industry.

Industrial Innovation Panorama (short version)

Figure 3.3. Industrial innovation panorama

In the past few years, the misunderstanding in the process of promoting digital industrialization has been to focus on the digital light industry. According to the results, from the Internet of Things to cloud computing to the evolution of big data, the companies that live well are actually those that rely on project contracting. On the surface, we seem to have returned to the era of industrial digitalization. The project is supreme, but what is the actual reason for this? There are seven main reasons: (1) the benefit the people derive from the service (competition model); (2) simplification of service; (3) the socialization of the (local) government functions; (4) the distribution of the ecological chain (zero marginal cost sharing economy); (5) data openness; (6) financial generalization and (7) trial and error, fault tolerance normalization (policy).

The specific interpretation is as follows:

(1) Humanization of service provision (competition model)
Learn the essence of taxi software. The services provided automatically in the design of the smart city platform should not be searched by users, but the service party should be "robbed". This is a service competition model that is truly user-centric, just like the service of a taxi driver. But there are also market adjustment techniques such as subsidies and rewards.

(2) Simplification of service
It is also often said that the user experience is very important (an Internet company last year told the author that they have employed a user experience officer).

For the simplification of the user side, the market space of the platform is determined. We recently came into contact with a "companion robot" (we cannot reveal the name of the company that produced it). An app allows users to directly control the robot to observe the situation of children and the elderly and to talk to them, which is slightly more complicated. Using the same app, children or old people can get some services by talking directly to the robot voice. Although the principle is simple, there is a market for such home services.

(3) Socialization of (local) government functions
The transformation of the functions of local governments has also led to a policy shift. Instead of smart cities, the latest policy promotes new urbanization. It is difficult to adapt to the requirements of the above-mentioned shared economy era by promoting the smart city, which is run according to traditional administrative functions.

Only by gradually transforming the previous administrative functions into "social and service-oriented functions" can the government's management efficiency and social satisfaction be improved, and only then can the position of the producer service industry in the regional economic market be truly shaped.

(4) Distribution of the ecological chain (zero marginal cost sharing economy)

The development of platformization has also benefitted many people. The ecological chain approach seems to be a transition from the farming era to the enclosure movement, and the excessive enclosure is contrary to the WiKIT trend mentioned above. Therefore, the development of the ecological chain will also likely be distributed.

The development of the energy Internet has made it possible for every household in the future to incorporate solar energy and wind energy into a new energy ecology. The large and complete enclosure pattern may change, greatly reducing the marginal cost.

(5) Data availability

This problem is recognized by all parties, but there is still a need to take action in order to produce results. According to the WSS model proposed above, when smart cities are promoted, it is necessary to consider that data must be made available before big data analysis can occur. From the previous four points, it is clear that it is difficult to make data available. The big data trading market is also a solution, but this is not covered here.

(6) Financial generalization

As mentioned earlier, there have been individual companies in the past few years who have cooperated with financial enterprises, which is very far-sighted. The generalization of finance requires us to have a comprehensive investment and financing strategy in the promotion of smart cities.

This can be borrowed from the Big Data Investment Strategy reported by the author to the national ministry not long ago:

The core problem underlying smart city investment and financing is solved by introducing relatively completely social capital into various fields and various links involved in the smart city strategy, and using the market mechanism to decide whether to invest (capital), finance (finance), retreat (get out), or construct (set up, transport (battalion), management (reason) and other aspects, and then form an effective allocation of social resources for the strategic support of smart cities. Specifically, it includes the issuance of special government bonds, smart city guidance funds, local investment and financing platform transformation as well as adoption, which can be carried out by establishing a big data trading market to promote the development of the shared economy.

However, there are great differences in the investment and financing strategies, due to differences in perspective, environment and stage. Only time can prove this.

(7) Normalization of trial and error and fault tolerance (policy)
The transformation of smart cities into new urbanization services requires innovation. The innovation process will inevitably involve the interests of relevant parties and will also have an impact on some old systems.

There is unfortunately a general principle of not crossing the limit of national laws and regulations. If you set the upper limit of innovation, innovation will actually lose its meaning. For example, the "special car" issue that has been hotly debated recently has not been received well by many people. The taxi market has challenged the management's authority, and the special car market has also challenged the taxi market. However, this has reduced the marginal cost in the new urbanization, and adapted it to the development of the shared economy. It has also led to the adoption of the platform, complete with car owners and driving. The staff has created a new ecology, and the corresponding management regulations have been challenged.

"The two evils are taken lightly, and the two interests are taken seriously". A trial-and-error approach to innovation should be normalized. Blocking this will only increase marginal costs and kill innovation.

The companies mentioned above that can undertake local smart city projects, city-level cloud computing and big data projects win because their own companies can keep pace with the times, and also because they take the abovementioned seven aspects into account. Thus we see the big pattern of digital industrialization in action.

3. The Digital Economy Era

The Politburo of the CPC Central Committee conducted the second collective study on the implementation of the National Big Data Strategy on the afternoon of December 8, 2017. At the time of the study, General

Secretary Xi Jinping emphasized that the development of big data is changing with each passing day. We should review the situation, carefully plan, and strive to take the initiative to understand the current status and trends of big data and its impact on economic and social development, in order to analyze the development of big data in China. By taking stock of our achievements in and existing problems with big data, we will be able to contribute to the implementation of the national big data strategy, accelerate the improvement of digital infrastructure, promote the integration and open sharing of data resources, ensure data security, accelerate the construction of digital China, and better serve China's economic and social development. This will result in the improvement of people's lives.

"Digital China" is an ambitious goal. This shows how important the digital economy is in the current stage of social development in our country today. From the relevant reports in the media, we can also see industrial digitalization and digital industrialization occurring, and finally reaching the path of data assetization and resourceization.

According to the definition found in Baidu Encyclopedia, the digital economy refers to an economic system in which digital technology is widely used, thus bringing about fundamental changes in the overall economic environment and economic activities. This is consistent with the operating mechanism of the WSS model proposed in our industry digitalization, and it is also consistent with the basic theory of social economy.

In social economy, there are three basic elements:

(1) Production materials: This also refers to the means of production, which are the resources and tools used by workers for production. They include land, plant, machinery and equipment, tools, and raw materials. The means of production is the sum of the labor data and the labor objects in the production process, and is the material condition necessary for the production of the material. In the bit world, we think that the small data from the server to the Internet of Things and the WSS model mentioned above can be regarded as production materials.

(2) Productivity: According to Engels's point of view, productivity is the ability to transform nature with a combination of laborers and production materials. The emergence of artificial intelligence has enhanced people's abilities with various tools. Therefore, we can use artificial intelligence to improve productivity.

(3) Production relationship: This refers to the social relationship that people form in the production process of material data. It is the social form of production, and includes the ownership of production materials, the status and interrelationship of people in production, and product distribution. Among them, ownership of production materials is the most basic and decisive.

A blockchain is essentially a book. When a commodity, an action, or a transaction begins, a block is created, and its entire life cycle is recorded in detail to form a chain. This account book is subject to multi-party copying on the Internet, so it is called a distributed ledger, and it does not belong to any one individual, organization or institution. Therefore, ownership of "big data" in the bit world is effectively protected and inherited.

The original intention behind the invention of the network car was to solve the problems faced by users of taxis, and the participants involved passengers, drivers and platforms. Network car platforms actually provide two services: one is the automatic generation of a match between a passenger and a driver based on big data; the other is the provision of a payment system that everyone can trust and must respect. The previous relationship between the driver and the taxi company has changed to become a relationship with the platform and the passenger experience. Passengers can also be converted into drivers (who can then be called Prosumers, both consumers and producers). It has become popular, and this change in production relations has brought about a disruptive change in the taxi industry.

However, there have been many problems in the actual operation process. For example, network car drivers used the plug-in to commit fraud, which resulted in many passengers being unable to get the services they deserved. At the same time, due to the pressures of operation (pre-burning subsidy, scale), and after factoring in the costs of technology, marketing, risk control, etc., the final costs are borne by the consumer. So when the new production relationship does not match the rapid development of productivity, changes will need to be made to the platform. Can we incorporate blockchain into the platform to make these changes? If we do, there will be certain implications for the service. First, the formation of the network car ecosystem will no longer belong to an independent company, or an institutional entity, but to the entire Internet (as information will be stored in a public chain). Second, its credit will come from the blockchain agreement itself, and by way of a consensus reached on the Internet. As a result, the intermediary service fees (the amount of commission collected by the platform) will no longer exist. One of the biggest changes is that the new production relationship will become a point-to-point connection.

Of course, such a state is an ideal final state. In fact, there may be many different centers in the evolution process. When different centers are merged with each other, some centers will be gradually removed. The benefits of this change are obvious: first, transaction costs will be reduced; second, the risk of cheating will be reduced; third, the decentralization approach also increases the likelihood that technology will protect data privacy.

Through the gradual iteration of the above production relationship, we have produced the true producer service industry mentioned in the aforementioned "A Panorama of the Industrial Internet" — the blurring of industrial boundaries, the decomposition of production chains, the alienation of organizational forms, and the rise of the network society. This is also the "sharedness" in WiKIT that we proposed earlier — orderly, open, and shared. Through such "sharedness", the "EOP" was established.

We know that "digital economy" refers to a series of economies that use digital knowledge and information as key production factors, modern information networks as an important carrier, and effective use of information and communication technologies as an important driving force for efficiency improvement and economic structure optimization activity. Among them, technologies such as the Internet, cloud computing, artificial intelligence, the Internet of Things, financial technology and blockchain are used in economic activities to achieve flexibility, agility, intelligence and efficiency.

From the case of the network car, we can observe such a phenomenon from the perspective of the digital economy. A large number of heterogeneous enterprises have begun using the Internet and big data through using the blockchain to form a strong correlation, but not confined to a single taxi company. The fusion of relationships, in accordance with a consensus mechanism, has become a new type of industrial ecology.

From the individual management of the farming era to the scale, specialization and corporatization of the industrial era, the focus is on the mining of a company's business potential, as the structural transformation of the enterprise, regional expansion and industrial restructuring across industries is carried out for the benefit of the company (or group). In the development of enterprises, there is control of equity and there is competition for discourse rights, which increases the friction cost of enterprises. Even if a core enterprise builds an ecological platform (like the aforementioned network platform) and reshapes a supply chain, it still cannot solve such friction costs. The synergy between enterprises is because of the sense of participation and presence. The reasons for centralization will also reduce operational efficiency.

The solution is as follows (see Figure 3.4): FEOP: production side, circulation side and trading side.

Production side: The Internet, big data, artificial intelligence and Internet of Things technologies are used in the industry to realize the digitization of the industry, so that data resources can flow between enterprises and the synergy efficiency is improved. In turn, when looking at the panorama of processes and products associated with the industrial Internet, we see that some or all of the non-standard production processes and products are standardized, and then personalized and socialized.

Circulation end: When it comes to the innovation of traditional industries in the field of circulation, the people's vision has turned to e-commerce sales, but this Red Sea has seen very little success. The linkage between the production end and the circulation end, together with the means of Internet finance and financial technology, accelerates the rapid transformation from the production end to the consumption end, and at the same

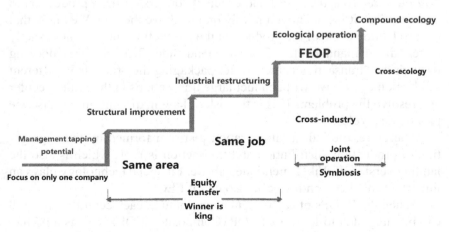

Figure 3.4.   FEOP: production side, circulation side and trading side

time satisfies the demands of relevant enterprises, organizations and individuals.

Example 1: An electronic product manufacturer combines the electronic products he produces with personalized financial wealth management products. After the user purchases a certain electronic product and pays the full amount, the full amount can be returned over a certain period of time, which stimulates the purchase of what the consumer desires. This approach is somewhat similar to that of product crowdfunding, which greatly enhances the attraction of "fans" in the circulation process and increases the conversion rate.

Example 2: A "pig-network" project is one which is initiated by a listed company. Pig farms and farmers at the production end sell the pigs to obtain a share of the "money fund", and these shares are available in the "pig network". Money circulates on the platform, and is used to buy items and services such as breeding pigs, feed and veterinary services. Of course, if you need cash, you can easily redeem the cash. In fact, due to the convenience of use and other incentives such as increasing credit scores, these audiences are still reluctant to redeem, so the share pool is getting bigger and bigger. Some people in the industry call this a "pig" bank. Looking at this model, the stickiness of participants has been greatly improved on the "Pig Network" platform as compared to the traditional method.

Trading side: To achieve fast and efficient conversion from production to consumption, it is not enough to rely on the above method. We know that the production cycle of the products at the production end may not exactly match the demand cycle of our demand side. This requires docking through the "transaction center": after packaging the products in different production cycles, we will conduct large transactions in the trading center and resolve the problem. This is the risk of having discontinuous, discrete production cycles.

Therefore, the industrial operation platform formed by the aggregation of production, distribution and transaction is EOP, which is also the landing version of WikIT mentioned above. Financial technology plays an important role here, and we can also call it FEOP.

When the FEOPs of each segment are mature, each centralized FEOP can be integrated to form a CFEOP (Composite FEOP). This is a perfect ecology.

If the blockchain technology is used to combine FEOP to form a point-to-point smart contract transaction, and a token (timestamp) is implanted in it, the existing currency exchange model can be extended while adhering to the current laws and regulations. The scope of the requirements and upgrade incentives can simplify transaction costs on the transaction side.

In the following chapters, we will look at the application of block-chain in several sub-areas to see how it affects all aspects of the digital economy.

Chapter 4

Relevant Laws, Regulations, Supervision and Application of Blockchain

1. Legal Regulation of Blockchain Technology

1.1. *Technology and legal regulation*

Legal regulation refers to the management, regulation and supervision of things through legal means. Legal regulation in a broad sense includes targeted guidelines and norms such as laws, regulations and policies. For blockchain technology, although there are many different and even opposite interpretations of "decentralization" (or "multi-centered" and "distributed"), it is undeniable that it has a long-standing central organization with human society. Compared with the structure, the matching technology and the thinking mode, the decentralized network built on the blockchain has begun to have an important impact on society in terms of how people think, and in terms of how they draw up business models and organizational forms. The root cause of this conflict is the potential internal cause of the regulation of blockchain technology by law.

However, legal regulation does not mean negative evaluation. The purpose of the legal regulation of blockchain is to make blockchain technology and its related behavior develop in a sound manner within the current legal framework, so as to avoid any adverse impact on the existing social order. On the other hand, regulation is also needed so that we can adapt to the innovative changes brought about by blockchain technology so as to achieve a benign adjustment to the existing legal system.

The above two points will be the two basic forms of the current and future legal regulations on blockchain technology.

Whether technology itself should be adjusted by law is a controversial topic in reality. For example, the "technical innocence" often mentioned refers to the fact that the research and development of the technology itself should not be directly evaluated by law, but should be evaluated in accordance with the specific use of the technology.

In fact, from a legal perspective, the development, research and application of any technology are products of the current legal system. Because technology cannot exist without humans and human behavior, the generation, development, research and application of a technology must be accompanied by human participation and subjective tendencies. In this process, the law plays many roles. It encourages, restricts and regulates.

At the same time, the current and future potential social impact of technology is the logical starting point for the legal regulation of technology, as shown in Figure 4.1. For example, many countries, including China, have currently developed or introduced many laws, regulations or policies for the research and development of technologies such as big data, artificial intelligence and virtual reality. The above legal regulations are based on the current or future impact of such technologies on society, with the aim of standardizing and promoting the development of these technologies. On the contrary, in view of the possible adverse effects on human society, there are also related restrictions or prohibitive laws in the technical fields of nuclear technology, biochemical technology and genetic technology. There are many restrictions on the digital encryption technology closely related to blockchain technology in China and elsewhere, particularly on its development and application, and it is strictly prohibited to apply this technology to the civil field at the beginning of its creation.

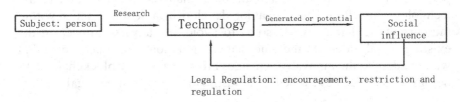

Figure 4.1.   Technical and social impact

1.2. *The dimension of the legal regulation of blockchain*

When many people talk about the regulation of blockchain technology, the related concepts are often confused or vague. These are mainly reflected in the blockchain technology and blockchain technology derivatives (tokens). No distinction is made between the two, just as blockchain technology and its related behaviors are not differentiated. This situation often leads to the inability of the parties to reach a consensus and to engage in debate, because they end up not really discussing the problem. In addition, many people divide the development of blockchain architecture into key periods: blockchain 1.0, blockchain 2.0, blockchain 3.0, etc., but legal regulation does not necessarily correspond to the development stages of the architecture. Rather, it corresponds to the nature of the blockchain and how it behaves. At a macro level, the legal regulation related to blockchain technology is actually multi-dimensional, and should at least include the following three aspects:

(1) Research and development of the blockchain technology itself. This includes the attitudes held towards regulations and policies which apply to blockchain technology, as well as the legal regulation of the technology itself, particularly with regard to issues such as smart contracts, network security, and privacy protection.
(2) Blockchain tokens and related issues of distribution, trading, and circulation. Token-based and token-related behaviors are identified and regulated, as well as taxation and security issues.
(3) Legal regulation of the reconstruction of the business model made available by blockchain technology. This mainly involves the realization of business model reconstruction or organizational structure reconstruction, which has been made available by blockchain technology under the current legal norm system, and how the current law deals with the above-mentioned scenarios based on blockchain technology.

1.3. *The status quo of blockchain legal regulation*

(1) Blockchain technology that is highly valued
Affected by the different attitudes of countries around the world on the issuance and trading of tokens, many people tend to think about negotiating, cracking, observing and other negative or uncertain words when talking about the legal regulation related to blockchain. In fact, if you study it carefully, you will find that, from a macro perspective, many countries in

the world, including China, have a clear and positive attitude toward the research, development and application of blockchain technology.

Blockchain technology has the advantages of security, stability, transparency, efficiency and self-reliance. This is the disadvantage of many centralized organizations or business models. Although from the current point of view, the realization among certain industries of the above-mentioned disadvantages of blockchain technology has not been widely popularized and lauded, but this potential is still valued and welcomed by all countries in the world.

In the United Kingdom, for example, on January 19, 2016, the British government issued a report entitled "Distributed Ledger Technology: Beyond the Blockchain" and included the blockchain in the UK's national strategy. The report mentions that the UK government is analyzing the application potential of the blockchain to traditional financial industry, ownership registration and intellectual property, thereby reducing fraud and costs. At the same time, the UK government is also considering the development of a public platform based on blockchain to connect governments, institutions and the public in order to better provide social services.

Like the UK, most countries in the world are actually encouraging the blockchain technology, and there are no regulations or policies for restricting blockchain technology. Relevant restrictive regulatory policies mainly focus on behaviors such as token transactions, and most of these behaviors belong to areas such as finance and securities that are subject to special regulations by national laws, and cannot be completely equated with legal regulation for blockchain technology.

In China, blockchain technology has also received strong government support. At present, Guangzhou, Guiyang, Chongqing, Suzhou, Hangzhou and other places have issued relevant support policies. Take Huangpu District of Guangzhou as an example. The "Guangzhou Huangpu District Guangzhou Development Zone Promotion Blockchain Industry Development Measures" (referred to as "blockchain ten") is issued by the local government, from the perspective of application, cultivation, growth, platform, application, technology, financial activities and other aspects of the blockchain enterprises or institutions to carry out key policy support, while focusing on the combination of blockchain technology and traditional industrial systems.

(2) Legal challenges of blockchain technology
From the perspective of technology rather than behavior, the blockchain does pose many challenges for the current legal system. Taking smart contracts as an example, the concept of which as proposed earlier

is not unique to blockchain technology, but the highly stable and non-tamperable blockchain system is a "natural harbor" for smart contract practice. Blockchain 2.0 is smart. The introduction of the contract is representative. Many people regard the smart contracts as contracts, but they are not the same. The former is essentially an execution code. When the conditions are met, the program is executed according to a preset path. The latter belongs to the legal concept, including subject, object, rights, obligations and responsibilities. It is precisely because of this difference that the challenge brought by smart contracts is not about reforming the legal service model, but more on how to regulate the ownership of rights, the determination of infringement and the division of responsibilities caused by intelligent and automated execution. This is also a direction for the future. Such issues should be focused on and researched.

In addition, blockchain technology faces some challenges in terms of network security. The "Network Security Law of the People's Republic of China" stipulates: "Personal information and important data collected and generated by operators of key information infrastructures in the operation of the People's Republic of China shall be stored in the territory", and for blockchains, in terms of system, it is a distributed storage solution. Although it can avoid the problem of data storage in the case of private chain or alliance chain, more blockchain systems belong to the open public chain system, in terms of data compliance. The lack of storage is obvious.

(3) Legal attributes of tokens

Token is a companion to the application of blockchain technology. Since the first blockchain technology application, that is, bitcoin, which was created to solve a specific payment problem, people usually refer to the token generated in the actual application process of the blockchain technology as "virtual currency". But the so-called "virtual currency" is not a real currency, both in terms of reality and legally. Since tokens can be circumvented from a centralized organization for peer-to-peer transactions, they are highly private and benefit from the highly stable state of the blockchain system. The tokens also have the attributes or potential to act as tenure, medium or asset. Therefore, how to characterize tokens is often one of the main topics of a country's legal regulation on blockchain. There are currently three views on the qualitative mainstream of tokens:

(i) *Payment medium*

It is recognized that the blockchain token has the payment attribute and even equates to the currency (French currency). Although this is rare, it is also increasing. The German Ministry of Finance has stated that bitcoin acts as a payment method and will treat it as a legal equivalent. But what needs to be clarified here is that even if the blockchain token is equated with currency, it does not mean that the token is the currency. Because the legal currency itself is legal, there is no special reason for the market entity to refuse to accept it in the official circulation jurisdiction. Obviously, in the current state, market entities are not forced to accept the basis of virtual currency payments. Relevant laws or policies usually only emphasize that when paying with tokens, there is no need to pay taxes like for goods, instead of stressing that market players must accept this form of payment.

Of course, it does not rule out the possibility of sovereign countries using blockchain technology to directly issue virtual currency in the true sense. But at least for now, the virtual currency that is widely used by sovereign countries based on blockchain technology has not yet appeared, because it is expected to be accompanied by many risks and challenges. The current common method is to issue a blockchain token based on a specific purpose by the government to solve problems in a certain field or a project. For example, the oil coins issued by Venezuela should be attributed to a variant of futures.

(ii) *Virtual goods*

With China as the main representative, the token is characterized as a virtual commodity, with the attributes of consumer applications. This qualitative distinction has two meanings: First, the token does not belong to the currency; secondly, the token should be regulated by the laws and policies related to the virtual commodity. Specifically, in 2013, the People's Bank of China and other five ministries jointly issued the "Notice on the Prevention of Bitcoin Risk", clearly stating that "in terms of nature, bitcoin should be viewed as a specific virtual commodity, not as a currency. bitcoin does not have equivalent legal status and should not be used as currency in the market". At the same time, "all financial institutions and payment institutions may not use bitcoin as a price for products or services, and may not buy or sell or trade bitcoin as a central counterpart, and may not underwrite bitcoin-related insurance business, which may include bitcoin in insurance coverage, and may not provide other bitcoin-related services directly or indirectly to customers".

In addition, according to the relevant provisions of the Ministry of Culture and the Ministry of Commerce's "Notice on Strengthening the

Management of Virtual Money in Online Games", the market entity must issue the "virtual currency" of the game to the administrative department on a regular basis. At the same time, the corresponding "virtual currency" can only be circulated within the game system, cannot be exchanged for physical objects or flow in reality. For example, the Q coins issued by Tencent, except for the need to regularly report the issuance, can only be used in Tencent's internal ecology, and cannot be directly exchanged for physical objects or transferred from Tencent's internal system. The starting point of such a regulation is actually to prevent the digital tokens in the virtual space from challenging the status of the legal currency in the issuance, circulation and use, or to evolve into a part of the legal currency function.

Blockchain tokens are not necessarily based on game releases, but in fact they have the same characteristics as the game "virtual currency", and they all have the potential to challenge the legal currency system in the areas of distribution and use. On the other hand, for the blockchain tokens, the actual turnover has already broken through, and the exchange and transaction between the different entities for the token itself can be realized. Therefore, under the premise that the virtual goods are not actually changed, the market entity publicly issues the tokens. Even if it is not issued through public offering, it may still violate China's relevant regulations, because it actually challenges the centralized currency issuance system. The "virtual currency" category requires restrictions, which may lead to risks such as pyramid schemes, fraud and illegal operations.

(iii) *Securitization certificate*
The tokens generated by the blockchain technology can achieve quantity and state stability and even if the changes are made, the established rules will be strictly followed. This high degree of stability enables the correspondence and anchoring of tokens to real objects and rights. Many people think that the token itself cannot be divided into dividends, and they can't represent equity as well as rights (such as voting rights, etc.), which is actually a misunderstanding. Technically, blockchain tokens are not difficult to relate to equity or in kind. The reason for this is because securities are strictly regulated on a global scale. From entry thresholds to compliance operations, from day-to-day management to disciplinary measures, there are strict standards and legal regulations. Few blockchain token issuers choose this route. The regulation of the blockchain, as many people call it, actually refers to the current regulatory system.

Whether a token has a securities attribute is usually reviewed and evaluated by the authority, and is not determined by the issuer. For example, the Singapore Monetary Authority (MAS) clearly stated in its "Digital Token Distribution Guide" that "MAS will review the structure and characteristics of digital tokens, including the rights attached to digital tokens, to determine whether digital tokens are A type of capital market product defined in the SFA (Singapore Securities and Futures Act). "If the digital token belongs to a capital market product as defined in the SFA, then the sale or distribution of such a digital token may be subject to MAS Regulatory. Capital market products include any type of securities, futures contracts and contracts or agreements for leveraged foreign exchange transactions".

Like Singapore, although other countries in the world do not explicitly give similar guidelines, the supervision of securities tokens follows the previous legal evaluation system for securities. The token issued by the contemporary currency issuer satisfies the definition of securities in the host country. It is possible to trigger the corresponding regulation.

(iv) ICO related legal issues

ICO is an abbreviation for "Initial Coin Offering". That is, the issuer rewards the participants with the existing digital tokens as the working capital of the project in return for the new blockchain tokens to be issued in the future. As can be seen from the above definitions, the two activities closely related to the existing laws of the ICO are the recruitment behavior and the issuance behavior. Compared with the decentralization of blockchain technology, the ICO of blockchain projects must have initiators and project parties. Therefore, most ICOs are centralized and more easily regulated by the current legal system. Most of the forms of ICO are very similar to crowdfunding, or can be said to be a kind of crowdfunding. But compared with ordinary crowdfunding, the return of ICO to participants is not a real value-for-money product, it is a blockchain token. According to the specific functions of the tokens corresponding to the ICO, the ICO tokens can be divided into the following three categories:

(a) Payment type tokens. This token has no special rights and is only used for functions such as payment, settlement, exchange, etc., and is typically represented by bitcoin.
(b) Functional tokens. This token is not used for settlement of circulation, but for goods that are served or directly consumed. In addition, there tokens are similar to member vouchers.

(c) Asset type tokens. Such tokens can be used as evidence of stocks, options, etc. In terms of economic function, such tokens are similar to securities, bonds or derivatives.

For ICO, the fundraising behavior specifically refers to the collection of "virtual currency", that is, the existing blockchain tokens that are in circulation in the market. Although "virtual currency" is not a fiat currency, in the entire process of collection and use, the tokens raised are essentially used as legal tender, rather than functional consumables.

In most countries over the world, the collection of capital is a strictly restricted behavior. And there will be corresponding regulatory measures for the qualifications, uses and audits of the subject. Obviously, if the fundraising behavior is identified as disguised fundraising (French currency), under the existing legal evaluation system, ICO faces many legal risks. Taking China as an example, ICO will still be suspected of illegally absorbing public deposits even if it does not consider whether the project corresponding to the ICO actually fails. The crime of illegally absorbing public deposits as stipulated in Article 176 of China's Criminal Law refers to the act of illegally absorbing public deposits or disguising public deposits and disturbing the financial order. In the evaluation system of criminal law, the essence is more important than the form. Although "virtual currency" is not a real legal currency, it is not impossible to recognize the public deposit in disguise in combination with the purpose and use of the entire fundraising. When the project fails to land, it is more likely to be suspected of raising funds and other crimes.

Regarding the issuance behavior of ICO, the key point is that the identification of the nature of the token, such as the location of the blockchain tokens as securities, or the ICO project itself is securitized in the token function setting, the relevant issuance behavior will be subjected to local securities laws. For example, the US Securities and Exchange Commission (SEC) has defined tokens in the "The DAO" projects as securities and has accordingly regulated them. In China, the issuance of stocks and other securities needs to be approved by the relevant competent authorities of the State and issued within the statutory scope in accordance with legal procedures. If the market entity issues it arbitrarily, it may violate the 179th Article of the Criminal Law of China, the crime of issuing stocks or corporate bonds. In addition to securities, when contemporary coins are identified as virtual goods or other attributes, they also need to follow the unique legal regulation of the country or region.

ICO is banned in China, because many ICO project tokens almost have no real application scenarios. Even in foreign countries, there are very few scenarios for virtual currency such as trading, and most of them are improper darknet transactions. In order to withdraw from the profit, investors can only hope to speculate on the coins, so that the latecomers can take over. Both the initial investors and the participants who come into the game know this well, but they can't escape the Ponzi scheme. Therefore, how to design a valuable application scenario token prototype or model in combination with the actual application scenario is an important evaluation criterion for whether ICO is legal and compliant.

In addition to the recruitment and distribution activities, ICO still has some other legal issues worth considering. Although most ICO projects only give participants a certain amount of token returns and do not promise the ups and downs of the value of the currency, objectively, if the ICO project party does not implement the project in accordance with the established white paper, or even fraudulently recruits itself, then the probability of a token depreciation in the users' hand will be very large. From the perspective of civil liability, whether the project party bears civil liability, or determining the loss or the fault, is worthy of discussion in the legal profession.

(v) *Legal issues of virtual currency exchanges*
Although tokens issued based on blockchain technology can realize peer-to-peer transactions, they are not convenient to operate and they cannot realize direct exchange with French currency. In this case, virtual currency exchanges have emerged. "Virtual currency exchange" is a popular term. From a legal point of view, such an institution is neither a "virtual currency" nor an "exchange". Blockchain tokens do not belong to the real currency (French currency), which is clearly understood by many people. In the past context, "exchanges" often referred to stock exchanges and stocks established by the authorities, such as exchanges, futures exchanges, etc.

Take China as an example, which has eight transactions nationwide, including three stock exchanges (Shanghai Stock Exchange, Shenzhen Stock Exchange, National Small and Medium Enterprise Share Transfer System, the New Third Board), and four futures exchanges (China Finance Futures Exchange, Shanghai Futures Exchange, Dalian Commodity Exchange, Zhengzhou Commodity Exchange), and a precious metals exchange (Shanghai Gold Exchange). At present, the establishment of the above-mentioned exchanges is approved by the State Council in accordance with the corresponding regulations and policies. The illegal establishment of securities, futures and precious metals exchanges will not only be subject to corresponding administrative penalties, but may also be suspected of infringement of criminal law and illegal business operations.

At the same time, according to the relevant provisions of the "Notice on Preventing Bitcoin Risks" jointly issued by the five ministries and commissions such as the People's Bank of China in 2013, financial institutions and payment institutions may not conduct business related to bitcoin. At this stage, they may not directly or indirectly provide other bitcoin-related services. More directly and rigorously, in the Announcement on the Prevention of the Risk of Subsidy Issuance Financing issued by the People's Bank of China on September 4, 2017, it is clearly stated that any so-called token financing trading platform may not engage in legal currency and generation. Currency and "virtual currency", in their exchange business with each other, may not buy or sell, or as a central counterparty to buy or sell tokens or "virtual currency", may not provide pricing, information intermediary and other services for tokens or "virtual currency". In other words, virtual currency exchanges in China are completely banned and illegal, and futures trading based on virtual currency is not allowed.

Japan, Singapore and other countries have not banned the existence of virtual currency exchanges, but there will be many new legal issues, mainly focusing on anti-money laundering, taxation, user privacy, asset security, etc. These are also virtual currencies. The main risk point of the exchange is that any problem may cause a chain reaction and determine the survival of the exchange.

It can be foreseen that although the supervision of virtual currency exchanges in the world is quite different and still in the exploratory stage, considering the asset attributes of virtual currency transactions, many countries in the future may introduce targeted regulatory policies.

1.4. *The legal issues of the blockchain business model reconstruction*

The reconstruction of business model based on blockchain technology is the specific application direction of blockchain that many people are optimistic about. When new business models emerge, they often mean conflicts with existing business models, such as the emergence of Uber and Didi Travel, which have led to conflicts with the old legal system. Blockchain technology is a decentralized technology. Under the legal system that emphasizes the centralization of regulation, the business model reconstructed by blockchain technology also needs careful consideration.

An example that is worthy of introduction is Kodak. Kodak is a well-known company, mainly engaged in film, digital camera and other related businesses. At the CES Consumer Electronics Show in Las Vegas in early 2018, Kodak announced the entry into blockchain technology and the release of blockchain tokens, also called KodakCoin. For many people, Kodak is focused on the concept of a hot new hype, and does not focus on the whole new set of business models built by Kodak based on blockchain technology. In fact, under the mode of Kodak, products such as digital cameras sold by Kodak are associated with the blockchain platform developed by them, and the timestamp information of photos is extracted while the user is photographing, with the copyright generation record automatically attached to the blockchain. Around the world, copyright is applicable the moment the work is completed. Kodak uses the natural advantages of photos generated in its devices to record copyright information. This generation can directly confirm the attribution, plus the blockchain's unchangeable technology. This way of copyright confirmation is very reliable. If the photographs are separated from the point in time or the copyright information is removed from the device itself, it is difficult to restore the actual elements of copyright and even create unnecessary disputes.

After the copyright record is generated, the photographer can carry out the copyright transfer on the Kodak self-built platform. Since the copyright is reliable, the concern about the source can be avoided. In addition to the transfer of copyright transactions with Kodak, Kodak's original copyright information can help photographers fight infringement or piracy, and the proceeds are shared by the Kodak platform and photographers. As a result, Kodak's main business is no longer just selling physical goods such as digital cameras, but shifting its focus to areas such as digital copyright authentication, circulation and rights protection. In these areas, payments are made through Kodak. Realizing the old, there are changes and restructuring of business models.

The Kodak model is implemented within the existing legal framework system and achieves the protection and use of copyright. Although there are many questions about whether Kodak actually implements the above model, this model is a very classic case for people seeking to restructure their business models through blockchain. Similar to the Kodak model, the Ripple system and the issued Ripple coins are also carried out within the existing legal framework, avoiding the challenge of the legal currency's coinage rights, but only the technical support for remittances and circulation between different currencies between banks. That is, the practical application of many financial institutions.

Not all business model's refactoring will be recognized by the existing legal system like the Kodak model. For example, if Kodak conducts ICO or similar tokens in China, there is obviously a legal dilemma. This has also created new problems, namely, how to balance the boundaries between regulation and innovation, to develop potential blockchain projects, and to curb misconduct such as speculation, which will be many for many years to come, including China. The issues are explored by many countries.

1.5. *Legal extension and improvement of blockchain application*

Blockchain technology can be understood as a low-level technical support, and its value depends on a series of specific applications built on the technology. From the current point of view, the blockchain has immeasurable potential in dealing with digital assets, trading digital assets and reconstructing the digital economy model. But for human society, the digital economy does not mean the economic system in the virtual world, nor does it refer to the digital assets in the virtual world. The real digital economy is bound to run through reality, and is reflected in the real world, in various legal relationships, including subject, property, rights, obligations, responsibilities, etc. Therefore, the specific application of blockchain technology must consider the improvement of the legal structure and realize the connection between the virtual world and the real world. And this kind of perfection mainly reflects the corresponding relationship between the online system and the real legal subject, as well as the embodiment and solidification of the meaning of the legal subject.

The blockchain system itself is a closed system. For example, bitcoin can only be looped in the bitcoin chain, which is a pure online virtual world. Like the bitcoin chain, many other new blockchain systems are also belonged to virtual worlds. In the blockchain system, its only the private key that determines bitcoins' affiliation, which means the private key represents everything. When the private key is lost or stolen, it essentially means that the owner loses the ownership of the bitcoin. This is like if the house key is lost, the owner loses ownership of the house, which is unimaginable or unacceptable in the real world. It can be seen that when the blockchain system or application lacks the mechanism to connect with the real-world legal subject, it can only use the elements in the system (such as the private key) as the criterion for judging, and it is difficult to achieve the connection with the real-world legal sense. In the solution of the legal subject, the technology of connecting the virtual world to the real world is collectively referred to as identity authentication. Therefore, how to apply the identity authentication technology to the blockchain system to realize the binding or correspondence between the identity and the private key is a blockchain technology. One of the key points for further improvement is important for rights recognition, digital asset security, and infringement. In the same way, the realization and expression of the meaning representation on the blockchain application can make the behavior of human beings in the virtual world legal, and give people the ability to process transactions, stipulate rights and obligations, and change legal relationships online. And this depends on the support of digital signature technology and applications such as electronic contracts built on digital signatures.

1.6. *Reflection on the legal regulation of blockchain*

In summary, it can be seen that the legal regulation related to blockchain technology cannot be generalized. The laws and regulations related to blockchain technology and blockchain technology in the world have great differences in legal regulation. However, it can be convinced that in today's globalization, on the one hand, technological progress should help solve the difficulties that cannot be solved by existing technologies; on the other hand, the development and application of technology should be good and beneficial to human beings. If the two bottom lines are crossed, just to be put on the blockchain, then the blockchain technology will become a tool for speculation or utopian ideals, negated by the existing legal system.

2. Application of Blockchain Technology in the Field of Proof-of-Existence

2.1. *The nature of the problem of proof-of-existence*

Notary, the etymology is derived from the Latin Nata, the original meaning refers to the meaning of the record. More than 2,000 years ago, due to the development of the commodity economy, there was already a notary system in Rome. The modern notary system began with the Notarization Law promulgated by France in 1802. Since then, countries around the world have successively formulated a modern notarization system in China. Notarization is a kind of certification activity. The notarization institution recognized by law proves the authenticity of the facts and documents that exist according to the applicant's records as per the legal procedures.

In essence, the notarization solution is to solve the problem of Proof-of-Existence. In legal terms, it is consistent with the "integrity" related to the "authenticity", "consistency", "post-proof" in the three aspects of evidence. Based on this logical starting point, the supporting notarization system is endorsed by the national credibility, carried out by an accredited notary agency, and a strict notarization process has been established to ensure that the proven effect is achieved. Broadly speaking, the current system of accreditation and certification (such as degree certificates, real estate licenses, marriage licenses, driver's licenses, etc.) is also an extension of the "existence proof".

2.2. *The value of proof-of-existence*

The "existence proof" is the cornerstone of the credit system. With the rapid development of the market economy, the credit system has gradually become the "infrastructure" of modern society. Safe, reliable and credible information is critical to reduce resource costs and build a good order. The credit system needed by modern society must not only solve the problems in way that is comprehensive, verifiable, transparent and systematic, but also include elements such as legality, efficiency, economy, reality and reliability. Most of the above must be realized through the "existence proof". In a sense, the implementation, degree, efficiency and cost of "existence proof" determine the degree of development of a country or region's credit system.

2.3. *The macro dilemma of proof-of-existence*

From a macro perspective, the Outline of the Social Credit System Construction Plan issued by the State Council (2014–2020) has a profound summary of the problems existing in the current domestic credit system:

"Although China's social credit system has made certain progress, the contradiction between the economic development level and the social development stage is not matched, coordinated or suitable. The main problems include: The credit service market is underdeveloped, and the service system is not mature. The service behavior is not standardized, the credibility of the service organization is insufficient and the credit information subject rights protection mechanism is lacking; the serious extra-production safety accidents, food and drug safety incidents occur from time to time, commercial fraud, fake sales, fraudulent tax fraud, false reporting, academic misconduct and other phenomena have been repeatedly banned, and there is still a certain gap between the integrity of the government and the degree of judicial credibility from the expectations of the people".

2.4. *The* status quo *in the field of proof-of-existence*

The current "existence proof" system including notarization, certification and certification plays a key role in stabilizing social order and regulating market operations in reality. Its value and merits are indelible, and one-sided negation or evaluation from the objective environment is not advisable. However, it should also be noted that there are some general or partial problems in the above system that are worthy of attention. And with the development of science and technology, many more reliable solutions have begun to appear for many problems.

(1) Low efficiency of proof-of-existence

Intuitively, low efficiency is a common problem in traditional deposits, mainly reflected in the complicated process and cumbersome procedures, which is not the key to the problem. As an important line of defense for the "existence proof", related procedures are indispensable, which is also a necessary process to ensure the authenticity from the process, but the above-mentioned procedures who overall reduced efficiency in many supporting links that have been artificially set.

Take the notarized process as an example. The main links include personal presence, written confirmation, manual review, paper filing and application verification. Each of the above links is actually relatively independent, and it is difficult to fit them perfectly in space and time. The questions that whether the party needs to be present in person when applying for notarization and what if it is difficult to meet the conditions due to personal time or space may cause long delays, which will delay the entire notarization process. Although this concern does not in itself belong to the notary public, it objectively reduces the efficiency of the entire process. In addition, when the notarization enters the manual review process, it also requires a certain period of time, even affected by factors such as the familiarity of the notary public and the amount of business, and other aspects.

(2) High cost of proof-of-existence
The cost of depositing certificates refers not only to economic costs, but also to institutional costs and time costs. Institutional costs are the hidden costs. When a system is established, it will inevitably require many "supporting facilities", such as personnel training, qualification certification, regulatory standards and file management. Take file management as an example, the management of written files has a strict process and requires a lot of manpower, space and facilities. In addition, multiple steps and processes are required for inspection and traceability. This institutional cost is actually reflected in many systems, and there is no room for improvement.

Naturally, the economic cost does not have to be said. In fact, the cost of traditional notarization and deposit is not a small amount. Usually, in a transaction (such as a civil lawsuit), the notarization fee that can be used for notarization and depositing is as small as several hundred yuan and several thousand yuan, sometimes more than 10,000 yuan. On the other hand, the above-mentioned expenses are not used more to improve the system links, or to generate greater economic benefits, but more to spend on labor, file management and other links.

In addition, the issue of time cost is also a common problem. Modern social economy is developing rapidly. The cost incurred in space and time may be much higher than the notarization and deposition themselves.

2.5. *There is a real dilemma in the proof-of-existence*

Whether it is notarization or recognition, certification and other systems are to solve the problem of authenticity. At the same time, verification and traceability are indispensable links in the above-mentioned deposition process. If there is a lack of transparent, rapid and reliable verification, it proves that there are loopholes and defects in the entire proof-of-existence system. But objectively speaking, there are still many academic frauds, marriage fraud, forged identity, commercial fraud, counterfeiting and so on.

In addition, traditional notarization, certification and verification rely on manual review, and subjective judgment factors are difficult to avoid. In the above process, it is not a reliable technical solution to prevent fraud, but a deterrent to the state's regulatory system. That is to say, in theory, there is no technical problem in the fraudulent part of the deposit. Taking the administrative punishment and industry punishment notice published by the official website of the Ministry of Justice of the People's Republic of China as an example, nearly 50 cases have been imposed on notaries in the past six months, among which "the notarization of untrue and illegal matters" was in the vast majority (see Figure 4.2).

Another concern is that with the development of Internet technology, more and more inappropriate behaviors occur in cyberspace, and

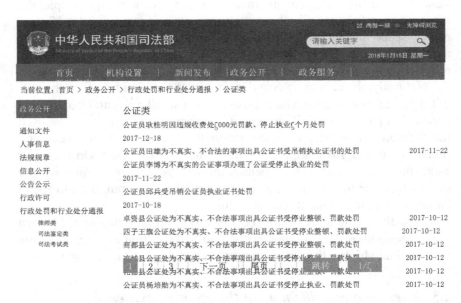

Figure 4.2.　Penalties for notary public or notary public agencies in the past six months

Source: Ministry of Justice of the People's Republic of China official website.

networks are different from traditional paper-based written materials or objective forms, in their presentation forms, operational mechanisms and demand characteristics. There have been significant changes, and it has been difficult for traditional deposit methods to adapt to the forensic and deposit requirements of the Internet era.

In the case of notarization of an e-mail, the final notarial certificate is actually only to restore the e-mail login, review process, and save the visual page at the time of verification. This is not a tampering or completeness of the e-mail itself. Because, if the parties can establish contact with the server provider of the email storage, it is not difficult to modify the content of the email, which is why the notarial certificate does not directly confirm the authenticity of the email but only explains the entire operation process. This also shows that the traditional way of depositing has begun to be out of line with the Internet era.

Another problem brought about by the dilemma of truth is power rent-seeking. When there is the possibility of fraud, there will inevitably be some people taking risks for their interests, and the current findings and traceability are backward. The actual fraudulent acts may be just the tip of the iceberg. For the upstream, notarization, certification and verification can be falsified. For the downstream, the verification party can also easily release water, allowing fake academic qualifications and false identities to run rampant.

2.6. *Feasibility of application of blockchain technology in the field of depository certificates*

Blockchain technology has the characteristics of being non-tamperable, time-series irreversible and highly transparent. For the certificate, the purpose is to ensure that the elements have not been tampered with. Time is determined, and it is convenient to check. It can be said that the existence proof has a higher degree of fitness than other industries or applications and blockchain technology. Therefore, applying blockchain technology to the depository field has always been an important direction for the development of blockchain technology.

Through the blockchain technology, documents, protocols, audio–visual materials and data materials that need to be verified can be hashed, the corresponding data fingerprints are obtained and are permanently written into the blockchain in the form of transactions or states. This forms the proof that it is untamperable, highly secure, and accurately identifiable. This online depository operation can be completed in a very short time. At the same time, combined with electronic signature technology, online deposit verification can realize the authenticity of the subject, greatly saving the applicant's time and economic costs. In addition, with the development of information technology and Internet of Things technology, more and more data and real-life items can be digitally processed, which will greatly expand the space for using blockchain technology for depositing certificates.

Many problems will be solved by depositing blocks through the blockchain. Because the blockchain has the characteristics of being non-tamperable and time-series irreversible, the possibility of illegal deposit and verification in the upstream of the deposit will be greatly reduced. With the characteristics of accurate traceability of the blockchain, fraud and power rent-seeking can also be effectively curbed and disciplined. In addition, because the blockchain itself is highly transparent, enterprises and individuals can more easily conduct information verification for the downstream of the deposit, and academic fraud, identity fraud and false proof will be difficult to survive.

2.7. *The necessity of applying blockchain technology in the field of depository certificates*

Openness, transparency and reliability are the common pursuits in many fields. The characteristics of blockchain technology have made many industries eager to try it and it has been called "potential technology that subverts all industries". However, it should be noted that the feasibility and necessity are two separate concepts. As the saying goes, "killing the chicken and using the knife" is the best interpretation of feasibility and necessity. Since the blockchain technology itself has a high technical threshold and is criticized in terms of energy consumption and transaction time confirmation, it is necessary to consider the situation in which the prior art is difficult to solve and must be completed by blockchain technology. Deposit is one of them.

The traditional method of depositing is a centralized method, which is carried out independently by a third party. Technically, as long as there are sufficient server and database permissions, it is not difficult for the organization to change the results of the deposit. When the benefits or pressures are large enough, tampering is unavoidable. That is to say, the traditional method of depositing cannot achieve the immutability in the absolute sense, that is, the so-called "relative credibility". The emergence of the blockchain has brought about a new possibility of the depositing method. The depositing of the chain can realize true immutability, because it takes a lot of effort and expertise to change the blockchain. The possibility is extremely low and negligible, thus achieving "strictly credible" or "absolutely credible".

2.8. *The solution case of blockchain technology applied in the field of proof-of-existence*

Due to technical barriers, chain-hanging costs, market-oriented applications, etc., the application of blockchain deposits that can be truly implemented in China is extremely rare. Beijing Fengyu Technology Co. Ltd. has made unremitting exploration attempts since its inception, and finally developed and completed the blockchain storage products that can be used for market application.

The "proof-of-existence BAOBAO" is the longest running and most reliable bitcoin chain from the current point of view. As a chain carrier, combined with its own patented technology, it can provide low-cost and efficient chain-storage services for individuals or enterprises. The identification center cooperates to ensure the legality and reliability of the deposit information in the aspects of evidence collection, verification and certification. In addition, "the Deposit BaoBao" provides different solutions for different deposit scenarios, as shown in Figure 4.3.

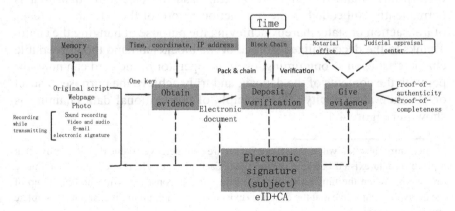

Figure 4.3. Complete flow chart of the certificate of "the Deposit BaoBao" blockchain

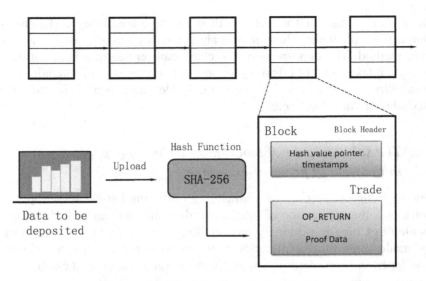

Figure 4.4.   Principle of regular data chaining

(1) proof-of-existence of conventional data

The verification of regular data refers to the integrity and consistency of electronic data such as web pages, photos, audio recordings, videos and documents. In addition to the typical traditional notarization method, there is also a way of depositing timestamps for electronic data. However, whether it is a traditional notarization or a timestamp by a third party, it is a centralized way of depositing, there is no way to ensure that the data is not tampered at all. Different from the above method, the timestamp[1] (data fingerprint) obtained by the server can hash the electronic data that is permanently embedded in the transaction record of the bitcoin by means of transaction or state, thereby achieving the purpose of hanging the chain. Thanks to the decentralized storage of the blockchain and the irreversible characteristics of strong timing, even the operator of the card can not tamper with the contents of the deposit, and truly achieve the purpose of strict or absolute authenticity. The principle of conventional data chaining is shown in Figure 4.4.

---

[1]Timestamps, also known as data fingerprints, are complete, verifiable data that prove that a piece of data existed before a certain time. Each piece of electronic data has a unique timestamp. When the timestamp of the existing data is consistent with the timestamp of the deposit, it can prove that the data does exist at a certain point in time, and it is complete and tamper-proof.

(2) The proof-of-existence of special data such as trade secrets

Depositing, in general, includes preservation, that is, the object that needs to be proof of existence is kept by a third-party depository institution, and the authenticity is confirmed. As the conventional data mentioned above, the user uploads the corresponding data to the card baby server, and the baby performs a hash operation to obtain a timestamp, and then performs a certificate hanging chain. But for some special documents or data (such as trade secrets), once it is disclosed or known to others, it can cause huge losses. Therefore, whether it is a credible notary public or a third-party depository institution, it is difficult for the applicant to disclose the information and keep it safely. Therefore, the baby has a good solution.

When depositing such special data such as trade secrets, personal works, important documents, etc., the baby does not require the user to directly upload the file, but the timestamp (hash value) of the data obtained by the user himself to perform the hash operation. Then just upload the timestamp to the card baby. When needed, you only need to re-acquire the timestamp in the same way locally, and compare it with the data fingerprint mounted on the blockchain. When the two are consistent, you can confirm that the special file already exists at the time of deposit, complete and without tampering. This not only ensures that the trade secret itself does not remain in any other institution, but also achieves the effect of holding a non-tamperable deposit. The principle of special data hanging chain is shown in Figure 4.5.

In addition to the above-mentioned electronic data deposit scenarios, the baby can help the government, enterprises and institutions achieve the chain-keeping services of important information in different industries and fields.

(3) Other proof-of-existence scenarios

Thanks to the rapid development of information technology, all kinds of information and affairs in today's society are developing in the direction of electronics and data. Common data such as electronic contracts, medical records, production links, anti-counterfeiting information, logistics records, files, identity authentication, document information, academic qualifications, wills arrangements, etc. can achieve data management. And without exception, these data must be guaranteed to be tamperproof, highly secure and easy to verify. Through the baby's customized service interface, the government and enterprises can achieve a large number of

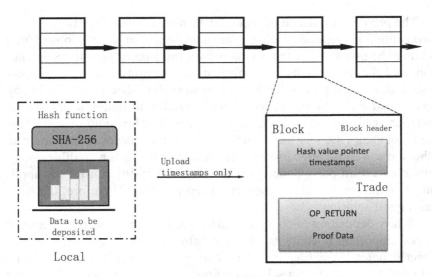

Figure 4.5.   Principle of special data hanging chain

data deposits in the above scenarios, and the whole process is efficient, inexpensive and reliable.

2.9. *The development trend of blockchain in the field of notarization and proof-of-existence*

Judging the development direction of a field always returns one to the starting point of the entire field. The starting point of proof of existence is to ensure the integrity and consistency of the subject. From the ancient times to the present, the proof of existence has experienced the relative stage of authenticity such as endorsement by authoritative persons and endorsement of national credibility. With the development of information technology and the mature application of blockchain technology, the existence proof will eventually move closer to the authenticity in the absolute sense. This kind of authenticity does not rely on third-party endorsement, and there is no possibility of being tampered with by a third party. It is a reliable deposit in the true sense.

It can be foreseen that with the development of information technology such as big data, Internet of Things, cloud computing, etc., data will be connected to everything, and the application scenarios of blockchain deposits will be gradually expanded. Deposit certificates will no longer be limited to legal notarization, but will be used as a cornerstone of the entire social credit to all walks of life. In addition, it is not excluded that a new blockchain carrier with multiple institutions and multiple government and enterprise participation on the chain carrier can meet the need for more efficient and economical certification.

Chapter 5

Blockchain + Local Government Innovation

1. The Central Role of the Government in the Development of Blockchain Innovation

1.1. *Government innovation based on blockchain is the key to seize the commanding heights of competition*

"Missing the Internet, don't miss the blockchain", is a popular phrase in the IT industry, reflecting the important position and significance of the blockchain. The combination of blockchain and big data, artificial intelligence, and Internet of Things (IoT) can greatly enhance national innovation and competitiveness among countries. As the leading force for promoting economic and social development, the Chinese government's understanding and application ability of blockchain technology will directly affect the application and promotion of the technology in various industries and the construction and development of the industrial ecosystem, thus affecting China's global strategy. The status is in the system.

At present, many countries around the world have realized that the blockchain technology itself and its integration with other technologies could bring great value to the economic and social development. They have formulated relevant strategic norms to support the research and application of their own blockchain technology to seize the commanding heights of future national competition. For example, the Australian government hopes to enhance its international competitiveness through efforts in blockchain technology. To this end, a number of measures have been taken to accelerate the application of blockchains in different industries in the country and to gradually improve its relevance. Institutional standards, etc., as early as 2016, explicitly invested more than $300,000 to fund blockchain standard research to achieve the goal of "consolidating and enhancing the country's position as the global center of distributed ledger technology (DLT)". China also attaches great importance to the development of blockchain technology. In December 2016, China officially included blockchain technology in the national informatization plan for the first time in the 13th Five-Year National Informatization Plan. On the one hand, it is positioned as one of the key technologies to provide digital, networked, and intelligent services in the next five years, and on the other hand, it is positioned as a long-term strategic cutting-edge technology.

1.2. *Government innovation based on blockchain is a powerful guarantee for the development of digital economy*

In recent years, with the rapid development of the digital economy, it has become one of the most important components of the modern economic system, both in terms of development scale and growth rate, and in terms of contribution and influence. At the same time, the problems in the development of the digital economy have become more and more prominent. For example, in the process of digital economic transactions, the transaction cost is increased due to the lack of reasonable trust mechanism. How to ensure the safety and effectiveness of a large amount of transaction data and behavior data generated in the transaction, etc.? The solution to these problems is inseparable from the support of blockchain technology. On the whole, the application of blockchains in practice in China is still in the exploratory stage. The related legal systems and standard systems are not perfect, the industry application is shallow, and the industrial ecosystem is not yet formed. Its future development is inseparable from these as the society works together, with the government playing a special role. The government must speed up the formulation of a perfect legal system and standard system related to the blockchain, and comprehensively strengthen the supervision of new formats and new things arising from the application of blockchain technology, thereby laying a good market environment for healthy and orderly development of the digital economy.

1.3. *Government innovation based on blockchain is an objective requirement for the government to adapt to new developments*

On the one hand, innovation is the source of power for the development of modern government. As a modern social and economic manager, the government's advanced nature of its governance concept and the innovation of its governance methods will directly affect its governance capabilities. In recent years, with the rapid development of new generation information technology represented by big data, IoT, artificial intelligence, etc., the government's existing governance capabilities and public service capabilities found it difficult to adapt to the development needs of the new era. How to use these technologies to improve government innovation and adapt to the new developments in the new era have become an objective issue for the government. With the expansion of the blockchain technology in the industry, the government departments found that the technology cannot effectively be tamper-proof and traceable, which could effectively solve the government's low administrative efficiency, poor supervision, lack of innovation, and transparency. On the other hand, driven by a new generation of science and technology, the new economy with digitalization is booming, and many new formats and new things have emerged under its influence. Traditional government governance models and regulatory models find it difficult to adapt to the new. The new requirements for the development of economy and new business must transform government functions and innovate government governance models in light of real needs.

2. Government Innovation Application Scenarios and Practice

2.1. *Blockchain + targeted poverty alleviation*

2.1.1. *Introduction*

Poverty alleviation has always been a focus of government work, as the General Secretary Xi Jinping said in his 2018 New Year message, "there are only three years till 2020. The whole society must act, fight sharply, make precise decisions, and constantly win new victories. After three years, we should win the battle against poverty as planned, which would be the first time in thousands of years in the Chinese nation to completely eliminate absolute poverty. Let us work together to complete this 'great cause' that is of great significance to the Chinese nation and to the entire human race. It is not easy to let poor households really get rid of poverty. Poverty alleviation is a systematic project. With the support of the government, multi-party synergy can truly achieve the goal of poverty alleviation. Poverty alleviation is not only to support the economy, but also to support the spirit. The government's poverty alleviation work needs to establish a good poverty alleviation orientation from the system and form a positive set in the whole society. The feedback mechanism enables the labor ability of the difficult households to be cultivated effectively, and the employment environment is built up. The spirits of the hard-working households who have been lifted out of poverty will cheer up and will not return to poverty again after getting rid of poverty".

Poverty alleviation is a big issue. This section introduces blockchain + targeted poverty alleviation by using blockchain technology to help poor herders get rid of poverty.

2.1.2. *Background knowledge*

The aquaculture industry is one of the pillar industries that increases the income of the farmers. It is highly valued by the government. However, the aquaculture industry faces the dilemma of "peasants have no money to invest, banks are afraid to invest, and the government is helping the poor". For "peasants have no money to invest", take beef cattle farming as an example, where the price of imported cows is 10,000 yuan. The breeding cycle of beef cattle is close to one year, and the investment return period is about two years. As a farmer is usually under financial stress, it is impossible for him to generate such funds by himself. In order to maximize the limited funds for poverty alleviation, appropriate financial leverage can help farmers apply for loan support from financial institutions, so that they can obtain sufficient funds to purchase beef cattle for breeding.

On the other hand, due to the concentrated risk of beef cattle breeding, and as farmers have poor anti-risk ability, the risk of credit default is high. As a collateral, beef cattle are used to finance movable assets. There is no effective post-loan tracking method. It is difficult for financial institutions to control risks. This has led to the statement that "the banks are afraid to invest and the government is helping the poor". In order to meet the bank's requirements for risk control, insurance companies were also invited to join the poverty alleviation project to provide agricultural insurance that is urgently needed for the project. The quasi-commercial insurance business model supported by the government is a common mode of agricultural insurance. This model is formed by a commercial property insurance company that establishes a department that specializes in agricultural insurance on the basis of self-employed general property insurance, implementing internal accounting, and seeking financial support from local governments. This model is characterized by commercial insurance companies taking the initiative to carry out agricultural insurance business and assuming social responsibility. In the process of operating agricultural "risk insurance", the company should make up for the potential losses of agricultural insurance with other insurance business profits, and strive for the government to grant farmers premium subsidies and business tax concessions.

The beef cattle industry value chain is shown in Figure 5.1. Throughout the entire value chain, risk monitoring in the beef cattle breeding process is the key to forward.

2.1.3. *Solution*

Based on the risk monitoring objectives in the process of poverty alleviation, blockchain is used as the underlying platform, and APP is used as the front-end display of the aquaculture industry chain. Combined with the IoT equipment, the whole process of beef cattle breeding is recorded, as well as the loan financing for beef cattle breeding. The disaster prevention and loss of the breeding insurance and the fixed loss of claim settlement provide a reliable basis. The data items collected by the blockchain platform involve financing parties, insurance parties, farms, veterinary bureaus and other related parties. The main business functions of the blockchain platform include:

(1) Pre-lending risk assessment for financiers: Provide basic information on aquaculture projects, such as update and review of farm assets, scale, historical financial statements, land certificates, etc., to assist the financier in risk assessment.

(2) Post-lending risk tracking for financing parties: The design process and rules are mainly focused on real-time or quasi-real-time tracking of the quantity and value of collateral live animals, and are used to complete risk tracking and early warning after loan.

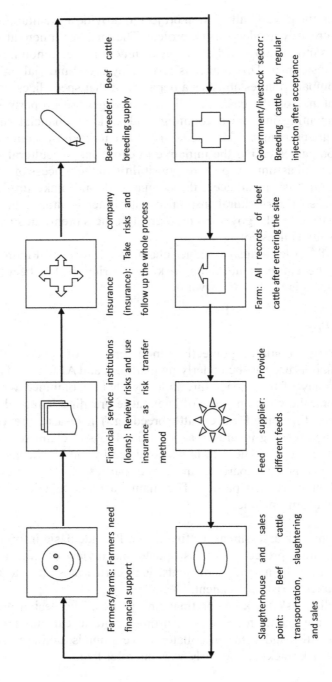

Figure 5.1. Beef cattle industry value chain

(3) On-site inspection and assistance for insurers: Provide information inquiry and insurance proofreading and status services for insurers' on-site inspection.

(4) Business risk warning for insurers: Provide early warnings on the risks of insurance in the process of breeding or insurance services (such as the matching of the number of insured and the number of stocks, the number of risks and the number of deaths).

(5) Poverty alleviation effect for relevant government departments: Collect information on poverty alleviation of farmers and breeding returns driven by the farms by region for the relevant government departments to check.

(6) Viewing the *status quo* of the relevant departments of the government: Collect information such as the scale of the farm by region for the relevant government departments to view.

(7) Auxiliary functions: Provide an update of the farming status and review of loan business. The blockchain alliance with multiple parties is shown in Figure 5.2.

2.1.4. *Revelation and meaning*

Based on the characteristics of blockchain technology, applied to the poverty alleviation scenarios, it is expected to introduce four aspects of value to all parties involved:

(1) Bringing together the stakeholders in the poverty alleviation project to build a safe, open and credible information network for beef cattle breeding, expand information sharing and reduce the one-way transmission of information among relevant parties.

(2) Information recorded on the blockchain (such as farming information, loan information, insurance information, etc.) cannot be tampered with and traceable to reduce disputes or misunderstandings caused by inconsistent information or moral hazard.

(3) Mutual verification of the information of all parties ensures that the information is highly credible and inhibits the generation of financial risks.

(4) Provide real-time monitoring and early warning to relevant parties through intelligent contracts on the blockchain to ensure that contracts agreed in advance are fulfilled in a timely and correct manner.

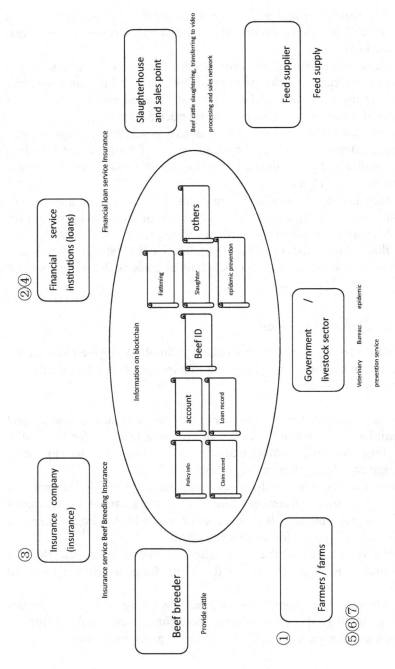

Figure 5.2.   Multi-participant blockchain alliance

Notes: (1) Cattle admission; (2) Due diligence; (3) Insurance; (4) Lending; (5) Cattle death; (6) Cattle out of the bar; (7) Cattle birth.

In summary, through the multi-party collaboration represented by the government, banks and insurance, the trust platform built with the help of blockchain technology is expected to solve the dilemma of "peasants have no money to invest, banks are afraid to invest, and the government is helping the poor". Work contributes strength.

2.2. *Blockchain + food and drug supervision*

2.2.1. *Introduction*

The safety of food and medicine is related to the national economy and people's livelihood. The human race is highly concerned about any safety issues related to food and medicine. With the development of society and the improvement of living standards, people have put forward higher requirements for the safety and effectiveness of food and medicine. In order to improve the level of food and drug supervision, the state has implemented unified supervision over food and drugs.

Safety issues such as counterfeiting of food and medicine may exist in all aspects from production, circulation to final sales. These links are widely distributed and involve many participants. Compared with the production lines of common foods, medicines, Chinese herbal medicines, vaccines and fresh foods, the safety involved in the process is more complicated, or involves agricultural production activities in the production process, or cold chain in the circulation or in the sales process. It involves special storage requirements and strict time limits. All these links and participants are within the scope of food and drug regulation.

Food and drug supervision is a big issue. This section introduces the blockchain + food and drug regulation in the case of a main grain producing area that traces the circulation and sales of rice through the whole life cycle of blockchain technology.

2.2.2. *Background knowledge*

Food and drug regulation faces a full range of pressures and challenges. Taking agricultural production as an example, the cost of establishing mutual trust between upstream and downstream is high. For example, in the purchase of agricultural products produced in a specific area, due to the downstream circulation and sales links, the information records of the logistics companies and the information records of the origin of the agricultural products may not be consistent, just as the information records of the logistics companies and the supermarkets are not the same. Lack of interconnection and interoperability among the parties makes it difficult to overcome the inconsistencies. In the case of flower trade, for example, the global trade volume of flowers is as high as $105 billion per year, and 700,000 tons of flowers are distributed through logistics. A complete distribution process, from origin to the sales terminal, requires about 30 organizations to communicate for up to 200 times for more than one month. Although flowers are not food and medicine, through the whole logistics process of flowers we can feel the pressures and challenges faced in the food and drug supervision. Heilongjiang Wuchang rice is a well-known rice in China. The data from the place of origin show that the annual output of Wuchang rice is more than 1 million tons. However, if the total sales of Wuchang rice in various stores and supermarkets in the country are aggregated, the total amount is more than 10 million tons. This extra millions of tons of green organic rice out of thin air reflect the enormous challenges in the current food and drug supervision.

In summary, in the whole process of food and drug production and distribution, the complete and true traceability of information records throughout the life cycle has become an important requirement in food and drug regulation. As long as the integrity and authenticity of the information are guaranteed, the behavior of counterfeiting, fraud and sale of fakes is largely shaken, and the original intention of supervision is to prevent it from happening. Let the true information be complete and transparent, so that the acts of counterfeiting and selling fakes are nowhere to be seen, and so that no one dares to make or sell fakes. Let the people have peace of mind in the supply of food and medicine.

2.2.3. *Solution*

Many people think that the scientific and technological content in traditional agriculture is low. In fact, with the development of agriculture and the progress of agricultural production, some farmlands have deployed IoT equipment, such as sensors, established agricultural production data collection systems and compiled relevant data. This lays the foundation for the subsequent recording and traceability of these basic data through blockchain technology. The irreversible modification of the blockchain ensures the reliability of the original information recorded by the blockchain. When the crops in the farmland have been initially processed and packaged into bags in the form of rice, each bag of rice will be labeled with an electronic anti-counterfeiting seal based on the IoT technology. This one-time electronic seal becomes the identity of rice. The identification is recorded on the blockchain. The parties can find out the basic information of rice in the production process by checking the seal information on the blockchain.

After the rice has been packaged with anti-counterfeiting labels, it enters the circulation and sales links. Facing the numerous participants in the logistics process and the various information systems of different parties, the interconnection and intercommunication of various information systems is completed through blockchain technology. With the consensus nature of the blockchain itself, all parties have the circulation-related information on the blockchain, and the participants endorse the information through consensus. Participants with strong technical strength independently hold a complete copy of the distributed ledger, and the participants with relatively weak technical strength hold a complete copy of the distributed ledger with the credible blockchain cloud service platform, ensuring that no party can tamper with it, hide or falsify data. This ensures that the process information of the entire circulation link is true, complete and traceable.

The customer sales terminal units in shopping malls and supermarkets can retrieve the rice origin information and complete circulation information on the blockchain through the easy-to-use client application: the data is both true and recognized by many parties. The food and drug regulatory agencies can also easily sample and trace the items.

2.2.4. *Revelation and meaning*

There are three main types of food and drug traceability approaches currently using technical means:

(1) It is the trading platform itself, and does not participate in the specific work of traceability. Instead, the supplier on the platform provides relevant traceable data.
(2) The traditional method itself, where the process followed involves stamping and entering the information system of the party, and querying multiple information systems, to obtain traceability-related data.

(3) The blockchain traceability platform on the pure line traces the data, and the blockchain record on the line shows its origin, sales and transfer process. Each link is manually recorded by the offline staff.

None of the three aforementioned can be singularly called an end-to-end traceability solution. Whether it is the traditional way, the middle-man platform approach or only the blockchain method without offline is flawed. The approach introduced in this section relies on the organic combination of IoT technology and blockchain technology to truly achieve end-to-end real, complete and traceable data, thus eliminating information fraud. When the people can easily distinguish between Li Wei and Li Gui, and when fake goods are nowhere to be seen, the essential purpose of food and drug supervision can be realized.

2.3. *Blockchain + digital identity*

2.3.1. *Introduction*

As a provider of social public services, a representative of social public interests, and a maintainer of social public order, the government is committed to building a social public order with the lowest cost, highest efficiency and minimal friction. It is not easy to construct such an order. It is necessary to construct a true and credible, comprehensive credit system between people, between enterprises and between groups in order to achieve such a state.

For example, in the case of simple administration and decentralization, the traditional process requires the enterprises and the masses to find approval nodes according to the process and find different departments, different institutions and different people. This not only makes the work efficiency relatively low but also results in social feelings that are extremely low. With the establishment of the administrative service center, the external window services of the government's multiple commission offices are concentrated in one service hall, which enables the masses to complete all the things once they come to the administrative service center. The simple decentralization of power from the original multiple doors, multiple mouths, multiple people to "one", is to achieve an efficient and good social response.

In order to further improve efficiency and social experience, the "one" was further simplified to "zero", and the administrative examination and approval work was transferred from offline to online. Building a credible digital identity for citizens is a key step forward.

2.3.2. *Background knowledge*

To achieve "one" to "zero", the following two basic conditions need to be met:

(1) In view of the fact that the staff member does not need to visit the administrative service center in person, how do we confirm the service information submitted has been provided by him personally?

In terms of authenticity protection, most administrative services require the staff member or the agent authorized by him to provide identity documents (identity cards, military officers' cards, household registration books or passports, etc.), and corporate services are often required to provide corporate licenses (business license, account opening permit and corporate legal person ID card, etc.). The staff member verifies the authenticity of the identity of the staff in person. When the process is translated to online, the issue of authenticity protection becomes prominent.

(2) Based on the conditions of the existing Internet, the challenges are how to maintain information security and how to protect personal privacy?

The government has a responsibility to maintain its security against these private data.

Information security and privacy protection are important issues in the Internet space. The computer of the administrative service center accesses a proprietary network, and the public servants providing administrative services perform information entry, modification and extraction according to the contents of the service. Some proprietary networks are not connected to the Internet, and those that are connected to the Internet also provide strict protection against Trojans, viruses, and malicious programs circulating on the Internet through firewalls, making it difficult to access. Also, when the process is translated online, information entry, modification and extraction of personal privacy data occur on the Internet, and security maintenance becomes difficult.

Only when the authenticity of the information is met can the online process have legal and compliance guarantees. And only by protecting the security of information can the people use the service with confidence. However, the challenges of authenticity and security are prevalent in all aspects.

2.3.3. *Solution*

The so-called digital identity is the information technology that breaks away from the identity document of the entity in the virtual Internet world. Since the hardware configuration of today's desktop computers, portable computers or smart phones is already quite rich, the camera and fingerprint recognition module have been popularized on personal terminal devices, and the digital identity construction time using face recognition technology and fingerprint recognition technology has matured. The digital identity can be confirmed by comparing the face recognition information or the fingerprint identification information collected on the personal terminal device with the information held by the government. The problem of authenticity is solved.

In view of the fact that the aforementioned information is transmitted in relation to personal privacy data, in order to ensure information security, blockchain technology can be considered for introduction. The government's subordinate bureaus act as participants to form a peer-to-peer alliance blockchain network. Each administrative service process corresponds to a smart contract in the blockchain network, which is initiated by the staff at home or at any place where the network can be accessed, based on the digital identity. The service personnel or approvers of the relevant departments are required by the smart contract. Smart contracts ensure rigorous, compliant and traceable processes, and blockchain platforms protect personal privacy from disclosure.

Based on blockchain technology, in June 2017, the government of Chancheng District of Foshan released a digital identity authentication platform, becoming the first region in the country to explore the application of blockchain by the government. Through the digital identity authentication platform, the people in Chancheng District can enjoy the convenience of small-scale allowance, certificate processing, certificate issuance and qualification confirmation in four categories and 20 matters. The 20 items cover a wide range of issues, such as the application for senior citizens' allowances provided by the District Civil Affairs Bureau, the National "Certificate of Marriage and Childbirth of Floating Population" handled by the District Health and Safety Bureau, the personal income tax payment certificate issued by the District Tax Bureau, and the certificate issued by the District Social Security Fund Administration. Personal participation is guaranteed.

2.3.4. *Revelation and meaning*

Based on the digital identity authentication platform, the government's various bureaus can work together to create a "personal information file" based on the blockchain. The "archive" takes the individual subject as the object, and constructs the encrypted data set of the personal subject-related information and its historical record around the three dimensions of personal basic information, business processing record and privacy information security. The "personal information file" is called "archive" and the key lies in the protection and authorized access of private data. Blockchain technology solves the problem of unclear data sovereign boundaries in traditional big data systems, as well as the problem of low data confidence and the problem of unsuccessful information security and hierarchical protection. Providing high-level personal information management capabilities, high-security private data protection capabilities and high-quality multi-dimensional data sharing capabilities will promote the modernization and digitization of social public services.

Blockchain technology is reshaping the ecology of the digital economy. Banks and other financial sectors have taken the lead in applying blockchain technology. The application potential of blockchain technology in e-government is also huge, and it is expected to effectively improve government service levels in the near future.

2.4. *Blockchain + tax management*

2.4.1. *Introduction*

In 2017, the Department of Taxation and Science and Technology Development of the State Administration of Taxation established a blockchain research team and held seminars on "blockchain technology and taxation management" to analyze the impact of blockchain technology on tax management and policies. The development of blockchain technology, the opportunities and challenges are brought about by tax collection and management. Two research reports show that the central government pays attention to and attaches importance to the use of blockchain technology in tax services and at the national level.

With the realization of "reform of the camp", the coordination of national tax, local tax and even other relevant departments such as industry and commerce, and financial institutions has become a trend and is inevitable. The biggest change in "reform of the camp" is avoiding the drawbacks of repeated taxation, irreducible deduction and difficulty in refunding taxes, effectively reducing the corporate tax burden and forming a deductible relationship between VAT input and sales. At the same time, the "reform of the camp" has a higher level of refinement requirements for tax source monitoring and taxation. When working together, data privacy protection has higher requirements. Even the legislation on relevant rules and regulations has higher requirements.

2.4.2. *Background knowledge*

In the face of increasing requirements, the electronic conversion of paper invoices promoted in parallel with the "camp reform" has become an important research direction of fiscal and taxation technology. In the context of the steady advancement of the national big data strategy, electronic invoices have the natural convenience of big data analysis compared to traditional paper invoices. The data required for the analysis are from the national tax and local tax collections and management systems, and are also distributed in the external systems such as the industrial and commercial departments and financial institutions, forming a scattered data island. Cross-system big data analysis requires close collaboration between different departments. Simply converting paper invoices into electronic computer files does not solve the problem of coordinated taxation that has plagued the tax authorities. The tax authorities urgently need smarter digital means to better serve the tax governance.

The implementation of coordinated tax governance is not an easy task. National tax, local tax, industrial and commercial, and financial institutions belong to peer entities that are not affiliated with each other. There is currently no legal requirement for the definition of tax-related data and the tax-related data provision process. On the other hand, various types of regulations of financial institutions also constrain the behavior of financial institutions' external data. Under traditional technical conditions, refined management and privacy protection often appear as two aspects of contradiction. Management is refined, and privacy is often violated. The privacy protection has improved, and the resulting management granularity has become extensive.

How to use more advanced technology to coordinate and reciprocate multiple government entities and financial institutions to meet the granularity requirements of refined management without infringing or revealing private information, without the relevant regulations being perfected, is a problem that needs to be solved urgently.

2.4.3. *Solution*

Distributed encrypted ledgers based on blockchain technology are naturally applicable to data sharing between multiple peer government entities and financial institutions. Through authorized access, while protecting privacy, the degree of sharing of tax-related data and the degree of refinement is greatly enhanced, thereby improving management.

Defining the scope of tax-related data is the first step of the entire work. The start of the work requires the government to take the lead in establishing a joint meeting mechanism between the national tax, local tax, land, development, finance, municipal, housing construction, industry and commerce, etc., at the joint meeting. The parties confirm the scope of the tax-related data, and the online approval process for the parties to provide tax-related data is based on current laws and regulations.

Next, the parties set up a peer-to-peer alliance blockchain network. Each participant is a node in the blockchain. According to the confirmation of the joint meeting, the parties encrypt the tax-related data that they have mastered and record them in the blockchain. Thanks to the innate technical characteristics of the blockchain, once the tax-related data is registered on the blockchain, it has traceability and non-tamperability, and the data quality is greatly improved. At the same time, according to the agreement of the joint meeting, the parties develop and deploy smart contracts on the blockchain, and complete the approval process of data acquisition through smart contracts. When the process is approved, the applicant can obtain high-quality credible tax after decryption of data. It not only protects user privacy but also greatly improves the level of management refinement.

By extension, the same working mechanism applies to data sharing mechanisms in other government departments. For example, financial data, national land information, business information, etc., which need to be consulted across departments, can confirm the data scope and online approval process by establishing a joint working group, and then relying on blockchain technology to realize authorized access to shared encrypted data.

2.4.4. *Revelation and meaning*

The tax-related data sharing mechanism based on blockchain technology has the characteristics that the data record can be traced, cannot be falsified, and the identity of the subject is authentic. While ensuring data privacy and security, the blockchain further ensures the legality and compliance of the process. The practical significance is not limited to the tax-related data sharing of the taxation department. It is widely used and has important significance for the entire government information disclosure system.

Moreover, with the gradual improvement of the system, through the advantages of interconnection and intercommunication, the alliance chain formed by these parties can truly integrate the data originally distributed in the information islands of all parties. At the same time, it provides a secure and distributed storage solution for all data in the blockchain. Moreover, the data on these chains have accumulated more and more statistics over time. When authorized, tax-related big data analysis and future tax source trend prediction can be carried out to fully integrate blockchain and big data. Together, they can play a greater role.

2.5. *Blockchain + city management*

2.5.1. *Introduction*

The United Nations Human Settlements Programme (UN-Habitat) gives some reference to urban management in the Urban Topics section of the official Chinese website: "Urban Governance is software that helps urban hardware work. Urban governance can be defined as institutions and individual organizations. There are a variety of ways in the day-to-day management of cities as well as processes for realizing the short-term and long-term agenda of urban development. Good governance can lead to an enabling environment that requires an appropriate legal framework, effective political, managerial and administrative processes, and mechanisms, guiding principles and tools to enable local governments to meet the needs of citizens".

Combined with China's national conditions, the rapid urbanization process in the past few decades has made the hard facilities (infrastructure construction) of most cities progress rapidly, and the supporting soft power (city management level) often fails to follow up. How to strengthen urban comprehensive management and comprehensive coordination while strengthening urban professional management, and how to deal with the decentralization and concentration of urban management, as well as the relationship between professional lines and the system as a whole has become a desk problem for urban managers.

2.5.2. *Background knowledge*

With the steady development of the economic level, China's urban built-up areas have gradually expanded, the resident population and the floating population have increased substantially. Urban management work has become increasingly complicated. Cities are increasingly relying on professional city management institutions to address the various aspects involved in urban operations. Professional subsystems for scientific management with further complication of urban management, urban operations and their governance methods increasingly reflect the characteristics of complex giant systems involving multiple parties and processes. Traditional methods are used to emphasize decomposition and simplification. The complex and huge urban system is artificially divided into several independent subsystems. The way to strengthen professional operation management, with a single professional line as the basic unit, is increasingly unable to adapt to the development of the times. Take the operation and management of urban water system as an example. It is connected with urban infrastructure systems, urban rivers and lakes ecosystems, public utilities systems, and various underground power lines such as electric power, communication, and heat, and roads along with water supply and drainage systems. Traffic is organically integrated, and it is increasingly futile and purposeless to solve the complex problem of urban management only through decomposition and simplification.

In addition, the relevant departments of urban management urgently need to rationalize the relationship among management, law enforcement and services. In the process of urban management, comprehensive supervision of administrative management, administrative law enforcement and public services clears the boundaries of responsibility to implement of all parties. It is necessary to avoid the problem of multi-long water management, the lack of responsible persons, and problems such as simple management methods, extensive law enforcement behavior, and weak service awareness. Putting an end to these is necessary to prevent chaos and inaction. How to use scientific and technological means to do a good job in multi-party coordination, improve work efficiency and people's satisfaction has become an important topic in urban management.

2.5.3. *Solution*

Considering the wide variety of urban management work, this section takes a seemingly small transaction as an example to show the complex departmental synergies that may be involved in the background, trying to improve the efficiency of collaborative work with blockchain technology. For example, the implementation rules for parking management around residential areas promulgated and implemented by a central urban management committee are based on the principle of "government-led, multi-pronged measures, local conditions, and consultation", in view of the serious shortage of parking spaces in residential areas of the central city. It has allowed the use of roads around the residential areas to set up temporary parking spaces for residents.

In the actual operation, there are four aspects: the definition of the parking area around the residential area; the qualification of the temporary parking lot user; the application approval process; the charging standard and the charging unit. The units involved include: street offices, community workstations, parking management companies, district development and reform commissions, district traffic detachments, district urban management law enforcement bureaus, and district municipal councils. Applying for a parking space in the traditional way requires residents to go to multiple departments to complete the process. The striving for convenience of a person has greatly reduced the satisfaction of the masses because of the complicated process.

Combining the digital identity and multi-party collaboration system discussed earlier, a multi-participating alliance blockchain network is built and provides online services to residents through the government website. In areas where digital identity has not been completed, a station can also be provided by the administrative service hall to provide service. In the subsequent law enforcement and management process, the parking management company, the transportation detachment or the municipal city appearance committee can automatically obtain the data registered by the relevant department from the blockchain according to the procedures agreed in the smart contract. It facilitates law enforcement and management, and also reduces misunderstandings and contradictions in law enforcement management that are caused by misinformation. It has improved the level of urban management and increased the satisfaction of the masses.

2.5.4. *Revelation and meaning*

Most of the urban management work is closely related to the people, and it always affects the daily life and traffic of the people. Overall, city management staff are very hard-working as first-line staff, and often do not have the understanding of service, management and law enforcement objects. Using blockchain technology and other related new scientific and technological means to effectively improve the synergy between the first-line urban management staff and the relevant departments in the background can greatly enhance the feelings and experience of the people, thereby enhancing the satisfaction of the people and reducing misunderstandings. On the other hand, by virtue of the blockchain's inherent tamper-proof, traceable nature, it also facilitates the necessary justice after disputes by recording key information of the service, law enforcement and management processes on the blockchain. The proof will help clarify the truth and provide necessary support and convenience for subsequent judicial intervention.

In general, the blockchain technology is of great benefit to the improvement of the soft power of urban management work. Due to the complex content of urban management, it needs to be carefully evaluated in the specific implementation process to achieve good social benefits.

2.6. *Blockchain + education governance*

2.6.1. *Introduction*

Internet + education is a major trend in the development and transformation of education worldwide. With the reform of the education system, the in-depth advancement of the revolution and the continuous enhancement of the influence of the new generation of science and technology on the education industry have led to profound changes in modern education management and teaching models and educational resources. Especially in recent years, with the in-depth promotion of the concepts of "Internet + education" and wisdom education, the degree of informatization of the teaching environment has been significantly improved. The individualization and interaction of the teaching management model have been significantly enhanced, and the forms of educational resources have become more diversified and decentralized. The scale of the online education industry continues to expand. Blockchain technology is expected to play an important role in the construction of the Internet + educational ecology. The White Paper on China's Blockchain Technology and Application Development (2016) issued by the Ministry of Industry and Information Technology clearly states that "the transparency of the blockchain system and the inability to tamper with data are fully applicable to student credit management, careers, and employment. Academic, qualification certificates, industry-university cooperation, etc., have important value for the healthy development of education and employment".

2.6.2. *Background knowledge*

As a key part of the national development strategy, education is faced with historical difficulties such as the rigid management of education, the uneven allocation of teachers, the asymmetry of educational information, the phenomenon of academic fraud, and the cost of education informatization. New problems such as low integration of high- and online education resources and low interaction are also prevalent in the teaching process.

Specifically, at present, most of China's educational resources are still scattered among different entities or different platforms. Due to the lack of a reasonable exchange and sharing mechanism, the cost of acquiring educational resources is relatively high. Affected by many factors such as the education system, technical conditions and security privacy, the more standardized digital files of students nationwide have not yet been completed, which provides an opportunity for academic fraud, etc., which has invisibly increased the education management cost. Under this circumstance, how to effectively deal with the problems of education development and innovative education management has become an important issue facing the development of education in various countries.

2.6.3. *Solution*

(1) Integration and sharing of educational resources based on blockchain enhancement: More educational resources can be released based on the blockchain decentralization model, which would help reduce the cost associated with learning resources for learners and improve the efficiency of learning resources. Based on its distributed ledger

technology, the direct connection between users and resources can simplify the operation process and improve the efficiency of resource sharing, so as to promote the open sharing of educational resources and solve the problem of resource islands. In addition, blockchain is a global technology that can better realize the cross-border sharing of quality education resources at home and abroad. For example, Delft University of Technology, the Federal Institute of Technology in Lausanne, Boston University, the Australian National University and the University of British Columbia have formed a code-sharing certification protocol based on blockchain technology to share educational learning resources among different universities.

(2) Construct a student credit file based on the blockchain: The first is to build a learning file covering the whole life cycle based on the traceability and anonymity of the blockchain. The government education department can store the information of each stage of each student (including basic personal information, academic achievement and academic certificates) in the blockchain to prevent information loss or malicious tampering, and build a safe, credible and unchangeable student credit. The system helps solve problems such as the current lack of student credit and global academic fraud. At present, there are many national education departments and universities such as MIT, Hobart School, and Kenya Information and Communication Technology Department trying to introduce blockchain technology and build a new degree certificate system to realize the integrity of academic information. And keep credible records to effectively address academic fraud. For example, the Kenyan government has tried to establish a network publishing and management platform based on blockchain-based academic credentials, so that all schools and training institutions can issue academic certificates on the blockchain network to achieve transparent production, transmission and inspection of the certificates.

(3) Enhance the protection of intellectual achievements based on blockchain: The infringement of educational assets and intellectual achievements is a common problem faced by many countries in the digital age. The copyright information protected by asymmetric encryption algorithm has higher security and reliability. At the same time, given the open and transparent characteristics of blockchain technology, it can solve the intellectual property disputes from the source and realize the copyright protection of educational assets and

intellectual achievements. Any resource information created based on the block (including resource creator, creation time, resource type, etc.) can be queried, tracked, obtained and validated by the user, thereby helping to solve the copyright attribution problem from the source.

(4) Reduce the learning cost of learners based on blockchain: At present, China's quality education resources are still inadequate. Due to information asymmetry, students and parents often need higher information costs and transaction costs in order to obtain quality education resources. To this end, relevant government departments can encourage the educational learning platform and the educational resource exchange platform to introduce blockchain technology. Based on the technology, users can directly share resources through peer-to-peer communication, thereby reducing R&D management and maintenance on a large number of intermediary platforms. Moreover, all kinds of learning resources can be completed based on the intelligent contract mechanism. The purchase, use, payment and other work of various services are all automatically completed by the system, no manual operation is required, and as the purchase record cannot be tampered with, it is credible and effective, and all transaction and contract data will be saved permanently.

2.6.4. *Revelation and meaning*

Blockchain technology, with its unique decentralization, traceability, non-tamperability and anonymity, will have a very broad future in the education industry. Governments, enterprises and various types of schools can build alliance chains according to actual needs and provide a more developed blockchain underlying architecture system for their business development. Based on the framework, encrypted transmission, secured sharing and permanent storage of basic information, educational learning resources, etc., on different subjects or different platforms in the region can be realized, and more people can be queried and obtained through authorization.

At the same time, under the decentralization mechanism and the intelligent contract mechanism, all kinds of educational data resources scattered in different hands and platforms will be fully shared, online education resources sharing and interaction are more convenient, traceable and non-tamperable, etc. Under the influence of the mechanism, the data generated by the students' educational process will not be freely modified, so that students' academic falsification will be effectively controlled. The record and assessment of students' academic level will be more accurate and effective, aiding in innovating teaching methods and improving students' comprehensive quality. At the same time, it also contributes to the reduction of education management costs. In the future, with the deep application of blockchain technology in the teaching field, and organic integration with big data, artificial intelligence and other technologies, it will inevitably bring revolutionary impact on school management and teaching modes.

2.7. *Blockchain + customs border inspection*

2.7.1. *Introduction*

According to Xinhua News Agency's report in early April 2018, Sinochem Group successfully completed the pilot export trading of blockchain applications for a gasoline export business from Quanzhou to Singapore. This is the world's first energy trade blockchain application project involving government departments. It is also the world's first blockchain application that includes all key players involved in the commodities trading process.

According to the relevant person in charge of Sinochem Group, the pilot participants include Quanzhou Petrochemical and Petroleum Company, Xiamen Customs, China Inspection Group, HSBC, and shipowners and freight forwarding companies under Sinochem Group. The spot market completed the sales bidding.

The pilot digitizes the core documents of key links in cross-border trade, and records transaction information such as contract signing, payment remittance, bill of landing, customs supervision, etc., in the trade process, improving contract execution, inspection, cargo clearance and settlement and delivery of goods. The efficiency of each link reduces the trading risk. Compared with the traditional method, the blockchain application can improve the time efficiency by more than 50% and reduce the financing cost by more than 30%. The participation of Xiamen Customs indicates that the application of blockchain in this field has entered a higher stage, and will help energy and chemical trading enterprises to improve transaction execution efficiency in the future.

2.7.2. Background knowledge

In July 2014, the Sinochem Quanzhou project was completed and put into production. In the year of production, the Sinochem Quanzhou project imported 6.5 million tons of crude oil. In 2015, the import of crude oil was 10 million tons, an increase of 53.8%. The commissioning of the Sinochem Quanzhou project made the import of crude oil at the Xiaoyu Port of Quanzhou Customs create a new record.

For customs, inspection and quarantine, border inspection and other import and export trade inspection units, the surge in trade volume also means that the workload has increased sharply and the difficulty of work has been rising. The docking time of the cargo tanker is not fixed, and the connection of business work is extremely difficult. In order to ensure the normal production of enterprises, the port office should take the initiative to follow up and coordinate the inspection units to solve the difficulties and problems one by one. Under the coordination of the port office, the Maritime Safety Administration held a pre-flight meeting to formulate a plan, dispatched sea patrol boats and law enforcement personnel to participate in on-site escort, and implemented on-site safety supervision during the ship's presence in Hong Kong. The border checkpoint overcame the difficulties of insufficient police force and practiced "5+2" "White Plus Black", and 24 hours monitoring. Inspection and Quarantine Bureau implements full-scale supervision of the quality of imported crude oil, and provides "instant inspection, stop and check" services. Customs establishes a liaison system for enterprises and develops individualization service initiatives. In each collaborative work overtime, each inspection unit has also formed a cooperative tacit agreement: as long as the enterprise makes an appointment in advance, the ship has not yet been docked, and the staff of each unit has already waited on the shore to ensure that the tanker "is on the way. Just put it on the unloading and unload it".

On the other hand, in order to guarantee the export of refined oil products, the Inspection and Quarantine Bureau has specially formulated inspection and supervision programs, and has done a quick test of the whole project to ensure that the exported refined oil meets the national compulsory standards and environmental protection requirements. The first batch of exported gasoline was certified from the sampling to the inspection. It took 4 days alone. The Customs had not been able to send customs declaration data through the arrival reporting system, and the ship carrying the exported goods had already arrived at the anchor. In order to ensure that the processing trade refined oil was exported as scheduled, the Customs had to send a special person to follow the whole process and review the customs declaration materials in advance. So the Customs could, for the first time, use the special channel of the on-site audit to help complete the export declaration. After continuous efforts, today, a 300,000-ton large tanker only requires 48 hours from inbound and unloading operations to normal departure, saving a lot of cost for both Hong Kong and the ship.

How to further strengthen the synergy efficiency of the inspection units, further shorten the customs declaration time, and save the capital cost of enterprises through the power of science and technology has become an important issue for the Customs in the field of energy and chemical trade.

2.7.3. *Solution*

In the aforementioned multi-party blockchain pilot project, the involved parties include entity enterprises (such as Sinochem Group), financial institutions (such as HSBC), and government agencies (such as Xiamen Customs). Such a scenario is naturally suitable for building distributed encrypted books based on blockchain technology. All parties share key data through encrypted data on the chain, and through authorization access and privacy protection the efficiency and level of Customs supervision are greatly improved.

The carding process is the first step in the entire work, based on the current refined oil export process to build the basic logic of the blockchain smart contract. At the same time, according to the sensitivity of the data and the scale of the data volume, the comprehensive evaluation is to encrypt the data directly after the link, or to hash the data. The database structure of the parties is then designed to ensure that the unwinded data are properly stored in a database that is operated independently by each party, while ensuring that all data are authenticated by the data or hash of the chain. After the data layer design is completed, the internal business processes and intelligent contracts of the parties are organically combined to complete the design of the business logic layer. Finally, the design of the presentation layer is carried out.

As a pilot project, some business processes and operational requirements were moderately simplified in order to achieve proof of concept as soon as possible. Based on its own cloud platform, Sinochem Group, based on the Linux Foundation's open source blockchain project Hyperledger fabric, built a Blockchain as a Service (BaaS) platform for use by all parties. According to the plan for formal production in the future, the blockchain network deployment across the computer room, across regions and even across borders will be standard. That there is no single central node is one of the core concepts of the blockchain. In the blockchain network that will be officially put into operation in the future, Sinochem Group and some of the custodians will continue to deploy blockchain nodes on the BaaS platform located in Beijing; Customs and other government agencies may deploy their own blockchain nodes in government data centers in Fujian; HSBC and some foreign institutions may deploy blockchain nodes in data centers in Singapore.

In the cross-border deployment environment, technical topics such as information security and transaction throughput on the chain need to be considered. Different laws and regulations of various countries have also become factors to be considered. The pilot project proved the important value of the blockchain in government innovation, while leaving more operations for customs, enterprises and banks to complete in the future. As an emerging technology, blockchain is expected to play an increasingly important role in e-government in the future.

2.7.4. *Revelation and meaning*

In this pilot, both the government agencies such as the Customs State Inspection and the commercial institutions such as bank inspections are deeply involved. All parties indicated that this application pilot has brought more help to the field.

Xiamen Customs stated that the blockchain technology can bring the following three advantages to the Customs in terms of supervision:

First, the way the digital documents pass through the whole network by point-to-point transmission enables Customs to receive customs declaration documents faster, which can improve customs clearance efficiency;

Second, both import and export parties and other related entities initially engaged in the operation of contracts, chartering and letters of credit on the blockchain system, ensuring that materials were taken from the source, and that the materials used in the blockchain technology could not be tampered with, thus making it more secure and reliable;

Third, each transaction entity transmits data in the system by means of digital signature. By means of asymmetric encryption, the authentication of the transaction subject is more effective, which reduces the difficulty of customs supervision of related subjects.

HSBC said that blockchain technology has brought great advantages to banks in international settlement and trade finance in the following ways:

First, the import and export parties conduct business contract links and customs logistics operations on the blockchain system to make the documents more realistic, thus reducing the risk of bank trials and audits;

Second, the blockchain network broadcast and the confirmation of the parties have greatly improved the efficiency of the issuance and delivery of letters of credit. Compared with the traditional process of modification and comparison, the speed is faster and the cost is lower;

Third, the way of digitizing documents allows banks to confirm the ownership of goods more quickly and accurately, and to reduce the risk of repeated pledges and document forgery that banks often worry about.

China Inspection and Certification Group (CCIC) said that blockchain technology can bring many advantages to third-party inspection in international trade. For example, the authenticity of the documents required for the loading instructions is improved, and the trust mechanism can effectively form a digital commodity inspection report, thereby reducing the circulation time of the documents, and the chain recording makes the forgery of the commodity inspection documents more difficult.

Sinochem Group said that through this cooperation with Xiamen Customs, State Inspection, HSBC, China Inspection Group and various institutions, in the future they will promote the application of blockchain technology in the petrochemical industry and the development of new business models. It is faster and better, and it also provides a better boost to China's energy industry to compete for global pre-emptive rights and rule-making rights in blockchain applications.

3. Governments have Issued Blockchain-Related Development Policies

The development of blockchain technology and industry is inseparable from the support and guarantee of relevant policies. In recent years, the

Chinese government has attached great importance to the development of blockchain, and has introduced relevant policies to accelerate its development. Many provinces and cities have developed blockchain technology for "13th Five-Year" development plan, including Guizhou, Chongqing and other provinces and cities. A special policy to promote the development of blockchain has also been developed. The following is a summary of the policy papers of national and local provinces and municipalities in promoting the development of blockchain (see Tables 5.1 and 5.2).

On the whole, since 2016, the provinces have increased their emphasis on blockchain technology and industrial development, and have issued relevant policy documents to strategically organize them.

From the perspective of regional policy release, only Heilongjiang Province in the Northeast region has increased the development of blockchain technology for 13th Five-Year Plan of the national economy, but it has not issued specific implementation rules; many provinces and cities in North China are in The relevant policies mentioned the need to develop blockchain technology, but no specific guidance was issued. Tianjin is the only city among the four municipalities directly under the central government that has not explicitly proposed to develop blockchains in relevant policy documents; Shanghai, Zhejiang and other provinces and cities in East China are the gathering places for the innovation and development of China's blockchain, although they have not formulated special guidance. However, the topics have been mentioned in several policy documents to vigorously promote the development and application of blockchain, and the related policy measures are more operable; Guizhou and Chongqing in the southwest have issued special guidance about blockchain

Table 5.1.   National level policy documents

Policy release date	Policy document and content
October 2016	The Ministry of Industry and Information Technology officially released the White Paper on China's Blockchain Technology and Application Development (2016).
December 2016	The blockchain technology was first mentioned as a strategic frontier and disruptive technology in the Notice of the State Council on Printing and Distributing the National Informatization Plan as a part of the 13th Five-Year Plan.

Table 5.2. Provincial level policy literature

Region	Province	Policy documents and basic content
Northeast	Helongjiang	In August 2017, the "13th Five-Year Plan" for informatization of national economic and social development in Heilongjiang Province clearly stated that it should "enhance quantum communication, artificial intelligence, virtual reality, big data cognition analysis, unmanned vehicles, blockchains, etc., new technology basic research and development and cutting-edge layout".
North China	Beijing	In August 2016, the "2016 Financial Performance Bureau 2016 Performance Tasks" clearly stated that in order to promote the construction of Beijing's financial development environment, the establishment of the Zhongguancun blockchain alliance was promoted.
		In December 2016, the "Financial Industry Development Plan of the "13th Five-Year Plan" in Beijing" proposed "encouraging the development of blockchain technology, credible timestamp identification and other Internet financial security technologies to protect consumer rights and enhance Internet finance safety".
	Hebei	In February 2018, Hebei Province officially issued the "Notice of the Hebei Provincial Government on Printing and Distributing the Three-Year Action Plan for the Development of Strategic Emerging Industries in Hebei Province", which was clearly stated in the "Special Implementation Plan for the Development of Big Data and Internet of Things Industry" in the Action Plan. "Support the development of cutting-edge technologies such as massive data storage, cluster resource scheduling, computing resource virtualization, blockchain, virtual reality, etc".
	Inner Mongolia	In June 2017, the official office of the Inner Mongolia Autonomous Region People's Government officially issued "Notice on Printing and Distributing the Key Points for the Development of Big Data in the Autonomous Region" (Internal Office), of which No. 116, clearly proposed "strengthening data sensing, data transmission, computing processing, basic software, visual display, blockchain and information security and privacy protection technology, and product research and development".

(Continued)

Table 5.2. (*Continued*)

Region	Province	Policy documents and basic content
East China	Shandong	In July 2017, the People's Government of Shibei District of Qingdao officially issued the "Opinions of the Municipal People's Government of Qingdao Municipality on Accelerating the Development of Blockchain Industry (Trial)", clearly stating "Strive to form a blockchain by 2020. Visualize standards, ... strive to build a blockchain industry highland, blockchain + innovation application base, based on Qingdao".
	Zhejiang	In September 2017, Xihu District of Hangzhou issued the "Policy Opinions on Building the Blockchain Industrial Park in Xixi Valley (Trial)".
	Jiangsu	The Nanjing Municipal Government issued the "Notice of the General Office of the Municipal Government on Printing and Distributing the Development Plan for the Financial Industry of the 13th Five-Year Plan in Nanjing"; "The Office of the Municipal Government Forwards the Municipal Economic and Information Committee to Accelerate the Implementation of the Integration of Manufacturing and Internet in Nanjing — The Notice of the Program"; "Several Opinions of the Municipal Government on Accelerating the Construction of the Science and Technology Financial System to Promote Science, Technology, Innovation and Entrepreneurship" — all mentioned blockchain technology.
East China	Jiangxi	In September 2017, the People's Government of Jiangxi Province issued the Notice of the General Office of the People's Government of Jiangxi Province on Printing and Distributing the Plan for the Construction of the Green Finance System of the 13th Five-Year Plan of Jiangxi Province, "Encouraging the Development of Blockchain Technology, Trusted Timestamping, Internet financial security technology, etc., applied to financial business scenarios".
	Fujian	In February 2018, the General Office of the People's Government of Fujian Province officially issued the "Opinions on Accelerating the Innovation and Development of the Industrial Digital Economy of the Province" (Zhu Zheng Ban [2018] No. 9), and will explore blockchain technology innovation as an accelerating local emerging information technology, to promote the important content of industrialization development.

Central China	Henan	In May 2017, Henan Province clearly stated in the "Implementation Plan and Several Opinions on the Construction of National Big Data Comprehensive Experimental Zone in Henan Province" to "encourage financial institutions to use big data to innovate financial products and services and explore the establishment of big data-based, cloud computing. New technologies in the new financial model of technologies such as blockchains".
	Hunan	Blockchain research and application test area set up in Loudi, Hunan.
South China	Guangdong	In November 2016, Shenzhen City proposed in the Shenzhen Financial Industry Development "13th Five-Year Plan" to "support financial institutions to strengthen research and exploration of emerging technologies such as blockchain and digital currency". In September 2017, the "Notice of the Shenzhen Municipal People's Government on Printing and Distributing Certain Measures to Support the Development of the Financial Industry" was issued, which clearly states that it is necessary to "focus on outstanding projects in the areas of blockchain, digital currency, and financial big data applications". The annual award quota is controlled at 6 million yuan. In December 2017, the "Measures for Promoting the Development of Blockchain Industry in Guangzhou Development Zone of Huangpu District, Guangzhou" were issued.
Southeast	Guizhou	At the end of 2016, the Guiyang Municipal People's Government Press Office officially released the White Paper on the Development and Application of Blockchains in Guiyang. In May 2017, Guiyang National High-tech Zone issued the "10 Policy Measures for Promoting Blockchain Technology Innovation and Application Demonstration in Guiyang National High-tech Zone (Trial); in June 2017, the General Office of the People's Government of Guiyang issued a notice on "Some Policy Measures to Support the Development and Application of Blockchain (Trial)".
	Chongqing	In November 2017, Chongqing issued the "Opinions on Accelerating the Cultivation and Innovation of Blockchain Industry", clearly stating that by 2020, Chongqing will build 2–5 blockchain industrial bases, and introduce and cultivate blockchain domestic files, more than 10 leading enterprises in the field, with more than 50 core technology or growth blockchain enterprises, and more than 500 senior talents in the blockchain and strive to build China's important blockchain industry highland and innovative application base.

technology, and strive to be at the forefront of the country in the development of blockchain.

Judging from the policy release method, the number of provinces and cities that have introduced special policies for promoting the development of blockchain is relatively small. The cities that have developed special policies to promote the development of blockchains include Chongqing and Guiyang. According to some provinces and cities, the blockchain is the key content of the development of the Internet finance field, and it is clearly stated in relevant policies that blockchain technology should be vigorously developed. The more representative cities include Beijing, Shenzhen and Nanjing; in some provinces and cities, blockchain is promoted as the content or supporting technology of big data construction and application. For example, Hebei or Inner Mongolia provinces or autonomous regions have mentioned in the big data special promotion policy that they should accelerate the development of blockchain. Some provinces and cities have explored and adopted the development of the blockchain in the region, promoted by the development model of "point-to-face, pilot demonstration". Guangdong, Zhejiang, Shandong and other provinces will develop special blockchain development policies based on prefecture-level cities and development zones, such as the official release of the Municipal People's Government of Qingdao City's "Opinions of the Municipal People's Government of Qingdao Municipality on Accelerating the Development of Blockchain Industry (Trial)" item policy.

From the perspective of the operationality of the policies, cities such as Beijing and Shenzhen have given more practical support to the development of blockchain in their policies, and have clarified the specific amount of support for the development of blockchain enterprises. For example, Beijing can provide 5 million yuan financial support for enterprises. Shenzhen supports the companies through Fintech special funds.

From the perspective of future policy trends, in February 2018, Hebei and Fujian provinces mentioned in their published policy documents that they would increase the development of the blockchain industry. It is expected that local governments will continue to increase policy support for the development of blockchain industry, and the intensity of policy introduction will be greater than the previous years. At the same time, with the gradual maturity of blockchain technology and the enhancement of integration with other industries, the possibility of developing special guidance opinions will be increased in order to better guide the local development of the technology and related industries.

Although blockchain technology has broad prospects for innovation and application in government management and service, there is still a long way to go in how to conduct scientific regulation and standard development.

4. Suggested Measures to Promote Healthy Development of Blockchain Applications

4.1. *Strengthen the top-level design of blockchain development*

Blockchain technology is considered to be the fifth subversive innovation following large computers, personal computers, the Internet and mobile technology, as well as the fourth milestone in the evolutionary history of human credit following blood credit, precious metal credit, and central banknote credit. It is expected to completely reshape human social activities like the Internet. To follow the current transformation of the information Internet to the value Internet: First, develop a special strategic plan for blockchain technology and industrial development, form a top-level design to promote the development of blockchain, and promote the integration of blockchain with national strategies such as big data and artificial intelligence; second, clarify the key tasks, key directions and safeguard measures for blockchain technology and industrial development, support the development of key technologies such as blockchain basic software and hardware, storage management and computing platforms; third, accelerate the construction of blockchain infrastructure, cultivating a number of blockchain backbone enterprises and specialized and innovative SMEs; fourth, formulate and improve relevant laws and regulations, guide and constrain the underlying technology and application level of the blockchain from the legal level, and combine the blockchain as a whole system to operate features from software security, storage security, business security, etc., and address introduction of laws and regulations to prevent the potential risks posed by new technologies.

4.2. *Enhance support for core technology research*

At present, the blockchain field has shown obvious development trend driven by technology and industry innovation, but the blockchain technology is still in its initial stages. Relevant academic research is seriously lagging behind and urgently needs to be followed up:

First, establish a linkage mechanism among the industry, academia and research to promote domestic key enterprises, scientific research, universities and user units to strengthen alliances, accelerate the key technologies of consensus mechanisms, programmable contracts, distributed storage, digital signatures, etc.

Second, promote the establishment of blockchain open source communities, strengthen cooperation through forum members, and improve the safety and reliability level of blockchain technology that supports the development of small and medium-sized enterprises at all levels of government.

Third, promote the integration of blockchains with new technologies such as big data and artificial intelligence to improve the perception, prediction and prevention of risk factors.

Fourth, promote mutual penetration and cooperation between domestic and foreign industries, promote technical exchanges and platform cooperation between countries and relevant institutions, establish various forms of international non-governmental exchanges and cooperation mechanisms, and actively promote China's competitive blockchain technology.

4.3. *Select key industries to demonstrate first*

The successful experience of China's high-speed railways tells people that application of technology is conducive to accelerating technology maturity and industry leadership, as well as the development of blockchain technology:

First, focus on typical application needs, around smart manufacturing, new energy, and supply chain management in the field of digital asset management. The blockchain technology will lead the supply-side structural reform, supporting large enterprises to take the lead, combining production, study, and research, developing blockchain application demonstrations, exploring the formation of blockchain application promotion model, and creating an application environment;

Second, build a blockchain comprehensive experimental zone and a blockchain industrial agglomeration zone in a place with good basic conditions, to encourage local integration of its own advantages to promote the development of blockchain industry agglomeration;

Third, build a blockchain general development platform to reduce blockchain technology R&D and application costs, to provide entrepreneurial innovation services for small and medium-sized enterprises;

Fourth, in conjunction with national major project construction, build a number of demonstration projects to drive and guide the industrial application of blockchain technology.

4.4. *Strengthen supervision of industrial development and application*

Excessive use or abuse of the blockchain is not only not conducive to its application in industry, but also to the country in seizing the future high-information strategy. This requires the relevant government departments to attach great importance to and strengthen the supervision of the blockchain industry and applications:

First, strengthen the formulation of regulatory policy documents related to the development and application of blockchain technology, and provide the necessary legal basis for its supervision. As a new technology, blockchain is in a state of missing or lagging behind in terms of the legal system and supporting documents. From the current majority of policy documents, it can be determined that there is still only partial encouragement. No relevant measures are proposed on how to effectively regulate the development and application of the blockchain industry. For this, the relevant ministries and commissions can take the lead in formulating a special blockchain industry supervision pilot policy.

Second, strengthen supervision of key industry sectors in the application of blockchain technology. It is necessary to organize relevant departments to strengthen supervision over the application of blockchain technology in industries that are of high concern to society, closely related to public life safety and national information security. The central and local departments are divided and classified according to their business scope to strengthen the supervision of the application development of the blockchain industry and ensure the standardized and orderly development of the application of the blockchain industry. Third, explore new modes of supervision, actively learn from the experiences of other countries, try to implement functional supervision or "sandbox" supervision, change passive supervision into active supervision, and post-event supervision to pre- and post-regulation, and comprehensively improve supervision efficiency, to effectively avoid risks in the development of the industry.

5. Actively Promote the Construction of Standards and Norms

The development and application of the blockchain industry cannot be separated from the establishment and improvement of relevant technical standards and normative systems. To this end, relevant government departments are required to organize relevant forces to accelerate the construction of the blockchain standardization system and promote the standardization and sustainable development of China's blockchain technology.

Development direction:

First, accelerate the construction of the blockchain standardization system, and speed up the establishment and improvement of data standards, application standards and algorithm mechanism standards related to blockchain technology; actively participate in the international standardization organization of blockchain field; strive for more discourse power; speed up the formulation of reference standards; block data formats and other basic standards; lead or substantively participate in the development of blockchain international standards and promote the transformation of China's superior technology into international standards.

Second, give full play to the role of social forces such as industry associations and industry alliances. All localities should establish industry associations and industry alliances according to the development needs of the blockchain industry in the region, and strengthen communication with the competent government departments while giving full play to the professional and technological advantages of these social organizations. And assist government departments to develop local industry policies, industry standards and industry norms.

6. Promote Industrial Chain and Ecosystem Construction

A typical blockchain system consists of data layer, network layer, consensus layer, incentive layer, contract layer and application layer. The main focus of current blockchain technology is application. China should accelerate the promotion of blockchain industry chain. The improvement and the construction of the ecosystem can be accomplished through the following measures:

First, improve the blockchain industry support system, rationally lay out the blockchain infrastructure construction, accelerate the construction of the blockchain industry development public service platform;

Second, combine the actual application scenarios and needs, promote the public chain (Public Blockchain), Consortium Blockchain and Private Blockchain construction and application;

Third, accelerate the training of professional talent, encourage and support key universities to set up blockchain professional courses, promote the joint venture of key enterprises and universities, and build the blockchain talent training base that will accelerate the cultivation of professional talent in the blockchain.

Chapter 6

Promoting the Big Data Industry, the Internet of Things and Artificial Intelligence

1. Application of Blockchain in Big Data Industry

1.1. *The problems encountered in the development of big data*

With the rapid development of the big data industry, the value of big data itself is being paid more and more attention by people. Some industries with rich data resources and relatively high degree of informatization such as finance, logistics and Internet have used big data to achieve a more significant application effect. While people are strongly encouraging the development of the big data industry, they are also constrained by the problems brought about by big data itself.

(1) The problem of data islands is outstanding, and the data information is not comprehensive

Due to the imperfect mechanism, the current data is open and shared to a lesser extent. Government agencies with large amounts of data are concerned about data leakage and information security, and are subject to certain restrictions on data sharing; enterprises are concerned about data openness in order to protect commercial interests and competitive advantages; individuals are worried about privacy exposure and are often reluctant to take the initiative when the public or agencies collect personal data. At the same time, government agencies, industry leading enterprises, especially a small number of Internet companies have mastered most of the data resources, but because the definition is not clear, the data attribution and legal provisions are not clear. The two-way sharing of government and enterprise data resources is low, and the information represented by the data is not comprehensive, leading to the results of data analysis, the reference value is not large.

(2) The data standards are not uniform and the quality is uneven
On the one hand, government agencies and enterprises have a large amount of data resources. But because the data format is not uniform, they cannot be integrated and used directly, and need to be converted and cleaned. In addition, the information format of a single data is not uniform, besides being incomprehensive, so the data information cannot be used. On the other hand, because the data collection standards are not uniform, data collected by different data sources have great differences in format, semantics, and weights and measures. Fast and accurate interpretation cannot be achieved when data is fused. At the same time, we have seen that the credibility of the dissemination of data from the prevailing media, WeChat, Weibo, etc., cannot be considered, to a certain extent affecting the quality of the data.

(3) Data security and privacy issues have not been effectively protected
Through data analysis, we can not only understand individual behavior habits, the company's operational status, but also predict future behaviors and decisions. In this case, data collected, used or even flowed into the data black market without the consent of the production entity may cause serious security and property damage to individuals, businesses and even the country. With the deepening of big data applications, some lawless elements, in order to obtain the great value brought by the data, indulge in private data reselling, information leakage, resulting in damage to the interests of the state, business or personally, which hinders the development of big data.

(4) Unclear data ownership, confusion in circulation and utilization
If the data property rights are not clear, the data owners cannot protect their own interests. In the process of circulation, data is transformed into the owner of information through "seeing, copying and pasting". It is impossible to define who is the true owner of the data. And in the process of using the data, there will be deviations and misinterpretation of

information transmission. The emergence of these problems harms the interests of information owners and greatly reduces the power of data sharing. In addition, in the data circulation management ecosystem, data generation of owners, cloud computing service providers for data cloud access management, data laws and administrative regulatory agencies exists with the legal rights and responsibilities of property rights, property rights definition and security protection. Complex powers and responsibilities are not clearly defined.

(5) The value of data cannot be accurately measured, and the pricing of data transactions is difficult

Data is an intangible asset that has gained wide consensus. At present, the data transaction system is still not perfect. As a virtualized digital resource, the pricing standard needs to refer to the data popularity, data utility, data scarcity and the estimation of the value generated by the specific application scenarios of the data. In addition, data with information attributes also need to consider the problem of time decay, and the difficulty of the data pricing system is obvious. Although a large number of different types of data have been realized in the data trading market, the deviation between data price and value is large, and the normative nature of the big data transaction market needs to be strengthened, which affects the development of data transactions.

1.2. *The application of blockchain in the big data industry*

Although big data is still in its early stages of development, its technology has evolved into a relatively mature Internet technology after a period of precipitation. Therefore, the integration of emerging blockchain technology into big data based on big data as a carrier will have a positive impact on the big data industry that is currently facing bottlenecks in development.

(1) Decentralization and autonomy of blockchain to solve the problem of information island

Data circulation is the key to the development of the big data industry. The blockchain does not depend on the decentralization characteristics of third-party management organizations or hardware facilities, and the trust problem of "people" is changed to the autonomy feature of machine trust, which effectively solves the problem of big data information islands.

Information can be communicated transparently. The blockchain can regulate the use of data, clarifying the scope of data authorization. And data desensitization will reduce the concerns of data owners to some extent, with the result that it is easier to open the data.

(2) The accounting characteristics of the blockchain multi-party consensus enhance the data storage quality

A blockchain is a distributed database that is jointly recorded and maintained by multiple parties. The recording and storage of data is jointly maintained by each transaction node. The unanimous consent of all participants means that the information is verified through verification in the network. The decentralization of the blockchain makes it impossible for a single node to modify and adjust the data at will, reducing the possibility of manufacturing erroneous data. The blockchain makes the data quality an unprecedented endorsement of strong trust, greatly improving the correctness of data analysis results and the effect of data mining, so that the predictive and analytical capabilities of big data can be fully utilized.

(3) Blockchain uses cryptography and distributed technology to protect users' privacy

On the one hand, the blockchain's trustworthy, secure and non-tamperable features allow more data to be liberated and more secure. On the other hand, blockchain-based data desensitization technology can guarantee data privacy. Data desensitization technology mainly uses encryption algorithms such as hash processing to effectively protect personal privacy and prevent leakage of core data. In addition, the distributed database of the blockchain uniformly stores data on the decentralized blockchain, and can perform data analysis without accessing the original data, thereby protecting the privacy of the data and safely providing to relevant institutions and personnel to study and use, to give play to the value of the data itself.

(4) The chain structure of the blockchain has traceability and effectively solves the problem of data ownership

Let big data connections circulate to generate value, and realizing assetization is the goal of big data development in the future. Data as an asset is essentially different from other assets. The potential threat of data replication makes data ownership unclear and becomes a major obstacle in the flow of big data. Based on the decentralized blockchain, it can break the threat of mediation to copy data. Once the data is on the chain, it will always bear the imprint of the producer. Even after multiple copies and reprints, the data receiver traces the data itself or the transaction through the record. Protecting the legitimate rights and interests of data producers or owners is conducive to building a trustworthy data asset trading environment. The blockchain is used for registration and authentication, so that transaction records are recognized, transparent and traceable throughout the network, thus clarifying the source, ownership, use rights and circulation path of big data assets, and providing guarantee for data circulation.

(5) The traceability and irreversible modification of blockchains
   contribute to the accurate measurement of data values

The blockchain data pricing model requires a comprehensive consideration of multiple elements of the data, such as the underlying value, the time of the data, the history of the use of the data, the frequency of use of the data, and the value of the particular use. The traceability and irreversible modification of the blockchain can clearly record the entire historical process of the generation, circulation, transaction and use of each piece of data. The size and use of the contributions of all parties are clearly visible. Recording multi-dimensional labels of data through blockchains helps to design a more flexible data pricing model. What's more, if there are more data sources, weighted distributed pricing can be based on the activity and the total value of each data in the trading market.

(6) Application scenario

The blockchain traceability platform can solve the problems of low information transparency, data forgery or tampering and illegal resale of data transactions in the data transaction process. Jingdong Vientiane, a data transaction traceability platform based on blockchain technology, is shown in Figure 6.1.

   In the process of data transaction, many legal disputes are often caused, such as illegal reselling of data and intellectual property disputes of data. In the process of solving problems, because the data transaction information is opaque and even has false information, it is often difficult for the participating entities to accurately understand the status of related matters, which makes it difficult to prove and blame. The function of the blockchain cannot be falsified, due to the existence of the timestamp and other traits, which are in place just to solve such problems.

   The application of blockchain technology can make the data transparent among the parties to the transaction. Any personal or institutional valuable data assets can be registered by the blockchain, and the

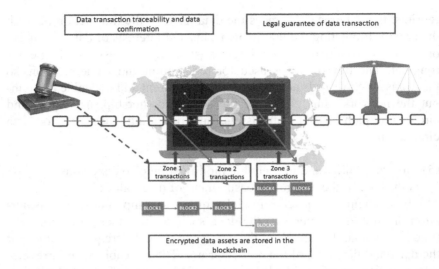

Figure 6.1. Jingdong Vientiane — Data transaction traceability platform based on blockchain technology

Source: Jingdong Cloud official website.

transaction records are recognized, transparent and traceable throughout the network. Using blockchain technology, every data released by Jingdong Vientiane merchants can be published on the blockchain and become virtual currency for trading. In the event the data is lost, it can be found on the blockchain. The issuance and circulation of data assets in the blockchain is shown in Figure 6.2.

The data transaction traceability platform developed based on block-chain technology will help users solve the problem of data traceability and confirmation. Users can use this platform to clarify the source, ownership, use rights and circulation path of data assets, and achieve easy proof and accountability, thereby maintaining their legitimate rights and interests.

1.3. *The development of the integration of blockchain and big data*

(1) Big data is the transformation of production materials, and
blockchain is the transformation of production relations

Big data and blockchains, as well as emerging technologies such as cloud computing and artificial intelligence, are interrelated, mutually

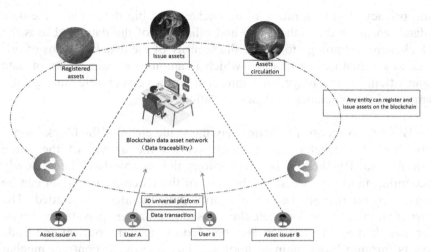

Figure 6.2. Jingdong Vientiane — Distribution and circulation of data assets in the blockchain

Source: Jingdong Cloud official website.

reinforcing. Big data is the basic resource. Cloud computing is the infrastructure. Artificial intelligence relies on cloud computing and big data, and promotes the industry to gradually move toward an intelligent era. The blockchain creates conditions for the transformation of the infrastructure and trading mechanisms of various businesses, and its implementation is inseparable from the support of data resources and computational analysis capabilities. From the perspective of future development trends, big data and blockchains are becoming more and more compact in practical application processes. And the technical boundaries of each are steadily weakening. Future technological innovations will increasingly focus on technology intersections and integration areas. Especially in the specific application of the industry, blockchain and big data will realize new social integration and promote the development of science and technology in the industry to a new stage.

(2) Blockchain as a technology has improved the question of the development of big data to some extent

As a kind of distributed database technology, blockchain solves many problems encountered in the development of big data by using its characteristics such as decentralization, tamper-resistance, traceability, security and privacy. The integration of blockchain and big data breaks the data island, ensuring the authenticity and reliability of the data, and uses the blockchain technology to ensure the security of the data by means of private key signature verification, which is among the pain points of data circulation. It has played a significant improvement role and greatly improved the efficiency of data circulation.

(3) Big data as an asset to better play the value chain of the blockchain
The use of blockchain technology heralds the arrival of the value Internet era. Blockchain is a technology that people have been slowly becoming familiar with since the start of the Bitcoin. Any asset can be registered on the blockchain platform, authenticated and traded. The owner and the buyer complete the transaction through private key transfer. Big data as an asset can also be used to register, confirm and trade assets through blockchain technology. The intelligent contract mechanism of the blockchain can handle the processing of data transaction-related services.

(4) The integration of blockchain and big data drives the development
    of digital sharing economy
The digital sharing economy relies on emerging technologies such as big data, cloud computing, Internet of Things and blockchain to recombine and efficiently use social resources and elements, breaking the time and space constraints, and fully utilizing its economic construction and production, thus maximizing social benefits. The integration of blockchain and big data technologies solves the bottleneck of the current development of big data technology, while making the distribution of social resources more reasonable, the credit system is more perfect and the information is more accurate. And it has played a great promotional role in the rapid development of the shared economy.

2. Blockchain + Internet of Things

The Internet of Things, based on the Internet, realizes the interconnection of objects. It is the third wave of information industry development after computers and the Internet. The Internet of Things is a multi-disciplinary field that spans cloud computing, machine learning, artificial intelligence, security and privacy. From smart homes to smart manufacturing to smart Internet and public utilities, the Internet of Things will bring huge social benefits.

Billions of sensors and intelligent controllers have been used worldwide, and this number will increase exponentially in the next few years. While the Internet of Things is booming, it also faces many problems and challenges, and blockchain technology offers the possibility to solve these problems. At the same time, with the broad application space provided by the Internet of Things, the blockchain will be used more and more in mature applications, and promote the ecological improvement of the industry.

2.1. *The blockchain escorts the Internet of Things*

The various industrial machinery and equipment, sensors, controllers, infrastructure, automobiles, household appliances and personnel in the Internet of Things are connected to each other through the network, generating a large amount of data. Combined with powerful data analysis capabilities, it has the ability to connect the machines and personnel in the network with better management and control, improving the efficiency and level of resource use, and bringing great commercial value to human society. However, while the Internet of Things brings development opportunities, it also brings enormous challenges. How to ensure the security of data has become a weak link in the development of the Internet of Things. And how to use the Internet of Things industry to strengthen business innovation and accelerate the construction of an ecological system is also an important problem.

Blockchain technology adopts distributed storage, point-to-point transmission, consensus mechanism and asymmetric encryption technology, which can make up for the lack of security performance in the Internet of Things. At the same time, it can reduce the operation and credit cost of centralized network, improve operational efficiency and industry asset utilization, thereby enhancing the value of the IoT system. Combined with blockchain technology, the Internet of Things will generate more commercial application scenarios and accelerate the construction of the ecosystem of the Internet of Things.

(1) Decentralization and rational allocation of resources for the Internet of Things

With the rapid development of Internet of Things technology, the number of devices in the Internet of Things has grown geometrically. And the management and maintenance of these devices will bring huge cost pressures. The computational, storage and bandwidth costs of a centralized service can also increase to an unaffordable level. Blockchain technology provides point-to-point direct interconnection for data transmission for the Internet of Things. The entire IoT solution does not require the introduction of large data centers for data synchronization and management control, including data acquisition, command delivery, and software updates. The network of blockchains is transmitted, which greatly reduces the operating costs of the Internet of Things and rationally allocates IoT resources.

(2) Making data such as user privacy in the Internet of Things more
    secure
In the field of Internet of Things, the centralized service system, all monitoring data and control signals are stored and forwarded by the central server. And the central server has the risk of security breaches and privacy leaks. The blockchain technology adopts the method of asymmetric encryption, and the data is irreversible, effectively solving the possibility of centralized privacy leakage in the Internet of Things, and the user's data and privacy will be more secure.

(3) The equipment is more intelligent, and new business scenarios
    will follow
Blockchain technology can provide direct transactions to trusted intermediaries, rather than simple interconnection of devices in the Internet of Things. The application of blockchain smart contracts enables direct transactions between devices. Autonomous Decentralized Peer-to-Peer Telemetry (ADEPT), a proof-of-concept system jointly developed by IBM and Samsung, uses blockchain technology to build a distributed network of intelligent devices, verifying the decentralization feasibility of the IoT architecture. ADEPT enables devices connected to it to communicate directly, securely and efficiently with complex business logic.

2.2. *The* status quo *of development and application*

Some enterprises at home and abroad have laid out blockchains. At present, there are some cases in the application of blockchains in the Internet of Things. However, in general, the development of this industry is still in the early stage, and it is likely to enter a critical development period in the next few years.

The application of blockchain in the Internet of Things is mainly focused on the Internet of Things platform, equipment management and security, including intelligent manufacturing, vehicle networking, agriculture, supply chain management, energy management and other fields. At present, there are some mature projects in the fields of intelligent manufacturing and supply chain management at home and abroad. And most of the projects in other fields are in the research and development stage.

IBM, Microsoft, Amazon and SAP all offer Blockchain-as-a-Service on their respective cloud platforms, providing an elastic resource pool for future IoT device access and advanced layout. In October 2016, the blockchain project of the Bluemix platform launched by IBM added blockchain services based on the IoT cloud platform, thus different functions can be implemented according to user requirements.

Start-up companies cut into the blockchain field from different perspectives such as distributed energy systems, new trading models, certification and trading markets, and initially involved related IoT hardware manufacturing. For example, Sweden's state-owned power company VattenFall (Water Falls) invested in PowerPeers in Amsterdam, the Netherlands, to build an energy-sharing platform that allows consumers to freely choose power channels; Germany's RWE and the startup Slock.it collaborated, and the BlockCharge electric vehicle charging project was launched; RWE's subsidiary, Innogy SE, launched a blockchain trading platform Share&Charge that connects electric vehicle owners, public and private charging stations.

In September 2016, Wanxiang Holdings' "Wanxiang Innovation Energy City" project realized the new decentralized energy transaction and management system by using the technology represented by blockchain, Internet of Things, artificial intelligence and microgrid. In March 2017, Alibaba, ZTE and China Unicom announced the joint creation of the IoT blockchain framework. In May 2017, Jingdong and Horqin Agriculture conducted a retrospective case of whole-course beef based on blockchain technology. In June 2017, Zhongan Technology launched the step-by-step chicken project, and consumers can use the product traceability APP to conduct anti-counterfeiting traceability information.

The six-domain chain SDA provides a trusted infrastructure for the Internet of Things. SixDomainChain (SDChain) is the world's first decentralized public blockchain ecosystem that integrates the Internet of Things' "six-domain model" with international, national standards and distributed blockchain reference architecture standards. It is led by China and is based on the six-domain model of the socialization of the Internet of Things. It has been voted by 33 member states and has become the world's first international standard project for the top-level architecture of the Internet of Things (ISO/IEC 30141:2018). In December 2017, the material chain (CPChain) was officially released, and a basic data platform for the IoT system was constructed to maximize the data value of the Internet of Things. Other blockchain applications in the Internet of Things include IOTA, WTC (Walton Chain), ITC (Wan Chain), RUFF, UCT (Excellent Chain), DATA, INT, etc.

2.3. *The technical principle*

The blockchain provides a complete technical solution for the application practice of the Internet of Things, and provides an important support for the establishment and improvement of the Internet of Things. Through the concept of device identity rights management, intelligent contract mechanism, data security and privacy protection, data resource transaction trust mechanism, etc., the concept and technology of blockchain are applied, and the entities of the Internet of Things and the resources of finance and insurance are integrated with each other, increasing trust, protecting privacy and reconstructing online and offline open value credit systems, greatly expanding the value-added services and industrial incremental space of the Internet of Things, which will affect industries, agriculture, health care, health, environmental protection, transportation, security, finance, insurance, item traceability, supply chain, integrated management of smart cities and many other fields, leading to huge transformation from information interconnection to value interconnection.

The converged application framework of the blockchain and the Internet of Things is divided into three layers, from bottom to top: communication and infrastructure, blockchain, and Internet of Things. Communications and infrastructure provide the infrastructure hardware and communications-related equipment for the blockchain and the Internet of Things. As an intermediate layer, the blockchain uses the hardware resources of communication and infrastructure to provide trust or consensus support mechanisms or services for the Internet of Things layer. The Internet of Things layer leverages the services provided by the blockchain layer to enhance its security and privacy capabilities.

2.4. *The application scenario*

Both the blockchain and the Internet of Things are technologies that are widely used, and the integration of the two can promote innovation in many fields. Figure 6.3 shows a panoramic view of the blockchain and IoT convergence applications.

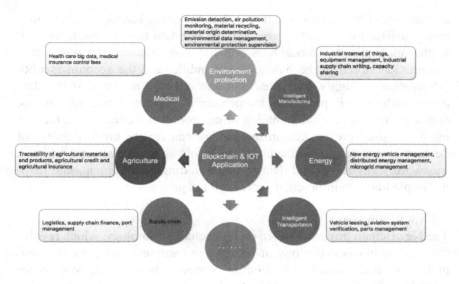

Figure 6.3. Blockchain and IoT integration application Panorama, other areas of application are described in other chapters.

The following is the application of blockchain in the field of environment protection.

(1) Problems from the environmental protection field
In the construction of systems such as automatic monitoring of key pollution sources and online monitoring of environmental quality, sensors, RFID and other related equipment and technologies are commonly used. These devices and data are stored in enterprises, and there are real problems. Enterprises may directly change device status and tamper with relevant data. Moreover, the open sharing of environmental data is also a problem. On the one hand, some localities and enterprises do not publish or disclose pollution data in order to avoid exposure to pollution, making it difficult for regulators and the public to supervise; on the other hand, due to lack of reasonable solutions, environmental, meteorological and other related departments cannot be realized. Data sharing has increased the cost of environmental management.

(2) Solution ideas provided by blockchain
The integration of blockchain and Internet of Things can solve the problem of environmental protection business supervision. First, the

application of blockchain technology can make the identity of each environment-friendly IoT device trustworthy and data tamper-proof. Second, in the application of blockchain and IoT convergence, the transaction information stored in the blockchain is public, and the account identity information is highly encrypted and can only be accessed if the data owner authorizes it, protecting the privacy of businesses and institutions, and enabling the necessary sharing of environmental data. Third, the IoT platform based on blockchain technology can realize unified access of devices of different manufacturers, protocols and models, establishing a trustworthy environmental data resource trading environment, and helping implement environmental protection tax policies.

(3) Application case
The NewBchain project is based on blockchain technology, which revolutionizes the business ecology of wastewater treatment and environmental protection, and creates a distributed economic business ecosystem for innovative blockchain wastewater treatment.

The NewBchain project will document the entire life cycle of water pollution treatment. Project creators, participants and consumers can participate in NewBchain to invest in environmental protection and wastewater management, and receive for consumption, trade, and manage their various interests through NewBchain. In this way, the participants in each ring of NewBchain are motivated to promote the development of NewBchain and water pollution environmental protection.

2.5. *Future prospects*

Blockchain technology provides new ideas for solving the development problems of the Internet of Things industry and expanding the industrial development space of the Internet of Things. The speed of the transformation of the Internet of Things to the blockchain network may far exceed the current general expectations. When the Internet of Things truly realizes the interconnection of all things, the value of the blockchain will be more exerted.

3. Relationship between Big Data, Artificial Intelligence and Blockchain

In 2014, Yan Yang, the author of the book, presided over the National Development and Reform Commission's "Informatization (Big Data)

Enhancement of Government Governance Capability Research" project, focusing on "Strategic Needs for Big Data Technology and Application Development". During the project's advancement, the research work of the subject that was active in the field of big data transactions was organized. In the research report submitted to the National Development and Reform Commission, the research team proposed that the application level of the big data strategy, especially the big data transaction market, includes four aspects: interaction, integration, exchange and transaction.

Interaction is the first level of big data, such as the user's Web access, which interacts with the Web site to generate data; when the operator initially integrates the data formed in production, it can process and service the data. This is the second level of data application; different data producers or suppliers, according to mutually agreed rules, exchange data and obtain their own data, which is the third level of application; when participants are not necessarily taking the use of data as a single principle, entering the data market for transactions, the pricing of the data market has played a role in price discovery, which is the fourth level. Today, in dozens of big data transaction centers (station) in various places, the status of the transaction is dazed. Why is this happening?

When we enter the era of big data, we will consciously or unconsciously shuttle through the atomic world (real world) and the bit world (virtual world). When the subject matter of the transaction in the trading market of the atomic world can be perceived, its copying is also costly. We can call it a competitive resource. But the subject matter of trading in the bit world is virtual, in some cases it can be costly copying, almost infinitely costly, so such resources may become non-competitive resources.

Fortunately, the application of blockchain technology can identify and add timestamp resources in the bit world, using blockchain encryption technology to protect property rights, and trade through smart contracts. It's a better solution for the above problems.

At the same time, the breakthroughs in artificial intelligence (including computing power, algorithms, etc.) make the various steps in the application process of big data, especially in the breakthrough of artificial intelligence modeling capabilities, solve the bottleneck for many years.

Chapter 7

Application Cases of Blockchain Combined with Real Industry

1. Blockchain + Finance

1.1. *The new power of financial technology — blockchain*

Blockchain technology is considered to be the core technology that has the potential to trigger the fifth wave of disruptive revolutions, following steam engine, power, information and Internet technologies. "Blockchain technology" has become the most fashionable term in the scientific and financial world. Looking at home and abroad, experts in various fields, especially financial people, are all interested in it. As the underlying technology of Bitcoin, the blockchain is not only as controversial as Bitcoin, but is also being accepted and expanded to a greater extent. In the future, the blockchain will surely bring new developments in financial technology.

(1) Blockchain + finance
"Blockchain + finance" is an unprecedented subversion and innovation in the financial sector. The blockchain can bring great value to the financial industry, mainly in the following two aspects:

(a) Reduce costs and improve efficiency
    (i) Reduce communication costs: Taking securities trading as an example, the securities trading market often requires the participation and coordination of the central clearing system,

securities companies, exchanges and banks, which will result in excessive costs. However, the blockchain can realize one-stop service through technologies such as multi-signature, and the information can be shared, thereby effectively improving the cooperation efficiency of the entire business.

   (ii) Reduce manual labor and increase automation.

  (iii) Shorten the settlement period: The process of confirming blockchain transactions is actually the process of clearing, settlement and auditing.

  (iv) Preserving regulatory records and audit trails to facilitate supervision and auditing.

(b) Reduce risk

   (i) As the transaction confirmation completes the settlement, the risk of the counterparty is greatly reduced.

  (ii) The blockchain digitizes the transaction process and performs a complete record, which can effectively control the operational risks caused by human factors such as fraud and manual input.

  (iii) Due to the existence of distributed networks and consensus mechanisms of blockchains, system risks such as hacker attacks by financial enterprises are also reduced.

(2) Driving the birth of a new business model

The feature of blockchain technology is the ability to implement business models that are difficult to implement in a centralized mode. At present, in the Internet of Things industry, relevant organizations have proposed to use blockchain technology to manage the identity, payment and maintenance tasks of hundreds of IoT devices.

(3) Promoting decentralization

The driving force of financial decentralization lies in the transformation of technology. Decentralization may directly affect the rules of financial activities. Such rules include various aspects such as legal level, business culture and financial culture. It should be noted that the emergence of financial intermediaries has been decentralized, and decentralization has effectively solved the asymmetry of financial information, as well as search costs, matching efficiency, transaction costs and other issues. The blockchain promotes the centralization of the financial district, making the new information matching of the financial industry possible.

The decentralization of blockchain finance will have three effects on the financial industry:

(i) The decentralization technology of the blockchain is applied to the financial field, which can improve the efficiency of resource allocation.
(ii) The decentralization technology of blockchain has a certain impact on the real economy, and it will also affect the development direction of finance, which leads to the emergence of "small and beautiful" industries and enterprises, which makes decentralization timely and intelligent. The implementation of new financial services with cooperation and a win–win mindset has become more necessary.
(iii) Implemented at the institutional level, based on program algorithms, etc. Create a set of open and transparent public "rules of the game".

1.2. *Blockchain + financial scenarios*

According to McKinsey & Company, the impact of blockchain technology on finance is most likely to occur in payment and the main application scenarios for transaction banking, capital markets and investment banking, namely, digital currency, cross-border payment and settlement, bills and supply chain finance, securities issuance and trading and customer credit and anti-fraud.

Blockchain technology itself is a low-level technology of Bitcoin, and it is also a technology for all people to participate in bookkeeping, which can be regarded as a database sharing large ledger. From a technical perspective, the blockchain is bound to have a fairly close relationship with finance. Based on the characteristics of decentralization, that is, non-tamperable, consensus mechanism, and anonymity, the application of blockchain in the financial field will also become an important starting point for promoting the transformation of finance to a higher stage.

(1) Digital currency
As a digital currency, Bitcoin has completely subverted the concept of money in human minds. From the past human use of physical goods transactions to the current physical currency transactions to the future credit currency, this development process has evolved with the commercial activities of human beings and the continuous development of society.

With the rise of e-finance and e-commerce, digital currency has become more and more secure, convenient and low in transaction cost, has been applied in network-based business practices, and will gradually replace the current physical currency to become a mainstream circulation approach.

Specifically, digital currency based on blockchain technology includes the following three types:

(a) Community figures "coins"

The community number "coin" is endorsed by the community's recognition. As a representative of digital currency, Bitcoin can be said to be the first decentralized community digital "coin".

(b) The internal virtual "coin"

At present, the use of virtual "coins" within the enterprise is lagging behind the currency "coin". The main forms of virtual "coins" that exist within the enterprise are game virtual currency, points, Q coins, stored value cards, etc. But these digital currencies often do not form a real ecosystem with blockchain technology. In the future, if the issuance of digital currency can have certain rules to follow, I believe that more companies will step into the digital virtual "coin" field. At that time, global enterprises will form multinational production and financial activities under the connection of digital virtual "coin" to achieve interconnection and interoperability between global enterprises.

(c) National Digital Currency

In April 2018, Venezuelan President Nicolás Maduro Moros said that in the face of a deteriorating liquidity crisis, the government authorities would receive $1 billion in revenue through the sale of oil, the new cryptocurrency. The purpose of this move is to increase the country's international reserves and foreign exchange reserves, and to prevent the appreciation of the black market dollar.

After Venezuela issued the national digital currency "Petro", Sweden also decided to launch its own cryptocurrency E-Krona in order to compete with private cryptocurrencies in the global market. As Sweden is gradually becoming a cashless society, the Bank of Sweden — Sveriges Riksbank — believes that there should be an alternative for those eager to use digital currency. The Swedish Central Bank has planned to launch E-Krona as the equivalent currency of the country's regular currency, which can be used for small transactions between consumers, businesses and government agencies.

In fact, many countries are exploring the potential of national crypto-currencies. In 2016, China's central bank also held a digital currency seminar to conduct an in-depth discussion on the early implementation of digital currency.

At present, global central banks generally believe that digital currency can replace physical cash, which can reduce the cost of issuance and circulation of traditional banknotes, and greatly help to improve the convenience of payment settlement. At the same time, the use of digital currency can increase the transparency of transactions, which plays an important role in the following three aspects:

(i)   anti-counterfeiting;
(ii) reducing criminal acts such as money laundering and tax evasion;
(iii) automating financial services.

(2) Bank credit

Credit has always been an important factor affecting the efficiency of social and economic resource allocation. As a financial intermediary with a more important position in the economic society, the core role played by the bank in the current social credit system is mainly reflected in two aspects: on the one hand, it solves the problem of information asymmetry between the two sides of the fund supply; on the other hand, it effectively controls and prices the credit risk issues that arise during financial transactions.

Based on this, it can be said that the bank credit information system based on blockchain technology has great advantages compared with the credit information systems of other institutions in the financial industry. Specifically, we start with the following three aspects:

(a) Forming traditional resources for credit customers

Based on the social division of labor, the bank has a very large financial customer base, and the customer attributes contained in this customer group cover almost the entire economic and social individual. For banks, individual bank account data is important for the construction of bank credit information system, which contains data information that judges customer credit risk. Therefore, bank account data is an indispensable advantage in the construction of bank credit information system.

In addition, bank customer data has a certain historical significance, and it is difficult to find alternative resources to a large extent, even for those technology companies or emerging "Internet + " companies which do not engage in data traceability.

(b) Raise regulatory thresholds and legal compliance costs

At present, the state's supervision of social credit is very strict, which raises the threshold for entry in this field and raises the cost of legal compliance. However, as a traditional operating institution in the financial field, banks are actually in a uniquely advantageous position compared to technology companies and Internet platforms that attempt to enter the credit evaluation field.

(c) Anti-fraud behavior to prevent financial crimes

In the past few years, in order to meet the increasingly stringent regulatory needs, commercial banks around the world have chosen to increase investment credit review and customer credit, so as to effectively promote the occurrence of anti-fraud behavior, thereby reducing the occurrence of financial crimes. The data recorded on the blockchain, including customer data information and customer transaction records, are of great help to banks in effectively identifying anomalies and preventing fraud. Based on the credit characteristics of the blockchain technology, a bank can store the bad customer information data in the blockchain when distinguishing the customer credit, so that the stored customer data information and transaction records can not only be updated in real time, but also be better protected. The bank judges and eliminates fraud in a timely manner by analyzing and monitoring the abnormalities of the customer's trading behavior in the shared distributed ledger.

Chainalysis, a Swiss startup designed to combat money laundering and fraud with digital currencies, designed an anti-fraud monitoring system for banks. The system is designed to help banks monitor and analyze abnormal trading behaviors in their blockchains, thereby effectively controlling illegal activities in the transaction process, and ultimately helping banks achieve anti-money laundering and anti-fraud purposes.

(3) Digital notes

The bill itself is a tool that integrates payment and financing functions, and has been greatly favored by banks and enterprises in recent years. The current bill market has become an important part of the money market and has received great attention from financial institutions. The bill business provided an important supporting role for the development of the real economy, promoted the further expansion of the money market and enriched the product categories in the financial market.

Since May 2015, there have been many credit storms in China's domestic bill business. While the bill business created a large amount of liquidity, the related market also breeds illegal operations, and there have been a number of commercial bank bill business incidents.

The so-called digital bill is actually not a kind of physical bill, but it is also not simply a kind of virtual bill. It is a new kind of presentation form of bill born on the basis of existing bill attributes, laws and market by means of blockchain technology. Based on the combination of blockchain technology, it has formed a more secure, intelligent, convenient and more promising form of bill. The emergence of digital bills has brought another new look to the development of the money market and the entire financial sector.

Specifically, digital tickets built on blockchain technology have the following three advantages:

(a) System setup and data storage cross the central server, and no central level application is required. This will bring the following four advantages:

  (i) Eliminates the development costs of central applications and intervention systems.

  (ii) Reduces the maintenance and optimization costs of the system in the traditional mode, including equipment input costs, data backup costs and emergency management costs.

  (iii) Reduces the risk of system centralization, so that there is no server crash or hacker control caused by too much centralization, as distributed database has strong fault tolerance.

  (iv) Reduces the waste of cost duplication caused by repeated recording and storage of data in centralized mode. The data book recorded by each participant can be regarded as a sub-ledger and is actually a part of the general ledger.

(b) Because the data of the digital ticket has completeness, transparency and verifiability through timestamp, any transaction can be tracked and queried. The data is not only saved in one server or one participant. In the machine, the content related to trade secrets can also be shielded by the corresponding technology, thereby achieving the purpose of protecting privacy.

(c) The form of smart contract makes the whole life cycle of digital bills have certain programmability, that is, it is restrictive and controllable.

Based on these advantages, the application scenarios of the three links in the scene of the digital ticket are as follows:

(i)   acceptance link;
(ii) the circulation link;
(iii) collection link.

(4) Cross-border payment and settlement

At present, cross-border e-commerce is in the initial period, and the demand for imported food, daily necessities, beverages, infant milk powder, etc. has promoted the development of cross-border e-commerce. But while providing more business opportunities for countries, cross-border payments have also shown many pain points.

Specifically, these pain points are manifested in the following three aspects:

(i)   The handling fee is extremely high and the turnover period is long.
(ii) Cross-border payment fraud is becoming more and more serious, which has led to cross-border capital risks and other legal business risks.
(iii) There are many intermediate links.

However, the blockchain has emerged and been applied to cross-border payment and settlement scenarios. It has done away with the role of the intermediary bank and achieved point-to-point fast and low-cost cross-border payments. Specifically, the application advantages of blockchain in cross-border payment and settlement scenarios are mainly reflected in the following three aspects:

(i) Reduce operating costs and other costs

First, the blockchain eliminates the transfer bank, which means that the intermediate fee is removed.

Second, because there is no need for banking relationships with transit banks, competition will intensify, putting pressure on fees and foreign exchange business profits, and leading to lower overall costs.

Finally, the process is more transparent.

(ii) More security

The distributed ledger technology of the blockchain enables the security of cross-border payment and settlement to be better protected.

(iii) The overall speed of the transaction is accelerated.

In the future, banks will no longer need to use a third-party, but the point-to-point payment method created by blockchain technology, so that the traditional intermediate links can be saved, real-time payment and accountability can be realized all the time, and cash withdrawal is convenient and fast. It meets the timeliness and convenience requirements of cross-border e-commerce payment and settlement, and improves the transaction speed as a whole.

Ripple is an emerging financial company in San Francisco, US, that aims to develop cross-border payments and settlements using blockchain-like technology concepts. Ripple has built a distributed digital payment network without a central node, using distributed authentication technology, thus helping small and medium-sized banks around the world to complete the instant cross-border transfer business at a low cost.

Ripple is just a typical example of using blockchain technology to provide solutions for financial institutions such as banks. Currently, well-known companies such as Chain, Ethereum, IBM and Microsoft are also beginning to use blockchain technology to develop cross-border payment and settlement services. It can be predicted that in the near future, the existing traditional trading model of the financial system will be replaced by high-performance, high-security and low-cost blockchain technology.

(5) Securities trading

The process of issuing and trading securities is very complicated in the normal course of operations, and its efficiency is relatively low. Under normal circumstances, before issuing securities, the company will find a brokerage company to sign the entrustment and collection agreement with the securities issue intermediary, and then carry out a series of application procedures before finally seeking investors to subscribe. This cumbersome process takes a long time to complete and usually takes three days.

Based on this situation, it is necessary to seek an effective technology that can simplify the fundamentals of securities' issuance and transaction efficiency. Using blockchain technology is a good solution. Based on the characteristics of the blockchain itself, blockchain technology enables all participants in the financial transaction market to share and use data information equally, making the transaction process more open and transparent, thus greatly improving the timeliness of the transaction. The parties use the shared network to participate in the securities trading activities, which makes the traditional transaction mode that relies heavily on the intermediary to complete the operation process, and further transform into a decentralized flat network transaction mode. The application of this blockchain-based trading model in financial markets presents some distinct advantages.

(a) Reduce the cost of securities transactions
It has the ability to reduce the transaction cost of securities to a large extent. And the application of blockchain technology can make the process of securities trading more simple, transparent, fast and efficient.

(b) Improve the efficiency of making business decisions and reduce the possibility of black-box operations. Blockchain technology can record real-time and accurate information about the identity and transaction volume of two or more parties, which is more conducive to securities issuers. There is quick and clear understanding of the ownership structure, thereby improving the efficiency of making business decisions. The open transparency and traceability of the blockchain make electronic records in the securities trading process reduce the possibility of black-box operations and insider trading. It is beneficial to the security issuers and regulatory authorities in maintaining the stability and security of the securities market.

(c) Shorten delivery time and reduce trading risk
The use of blockchain technology in the securities trading process has shortened the previous trading time from 1 to 3 days to 10 minutes. It takes only 10 minutes to complete the entire delivery process, reducing the risk of trading and improving the efficiency and controlability of the transaction.

The use of blockchain technology in securities trading scenarios has greatly improved efficiency. As a result, more and more securities companies have begun to pay attention and have tried it, such as the National Association of Securities Dealers Automated Quotation (NASDAQ), Chicago Mercantile Exchange, Dubai Multi-Commodity Center, etc. In China, this is spearheaded by the Shanghai Stock Exchange. The organized ChinaLedger Alliance has also tried in this regard. As it turns out, most have achieved good results.

The Australian Stock Exchange (ASX) would like to implement blockchain technology by 2020.

On December 13, 2017, BTCManager reported on ASX's use of blockchain technology to improve its equity trading platform. Previously, the exchange conducted a two-year test of DLT, including building proof of concept, allowing potential users to test the platform and conducting a basic version of the finished product in a real-time trading environment. The exchange has become the first major stock exchange in history to begin implementing the blockchain trade matching system. At the press conference, ASX Managing Director and CEO Dominic Stevens said: "We believe that using DLT to replace CHESS will enable our customers to develop new services and reduce costs, and will put Australia at the forefront of financial market innovation. Although we still have a lot of work to do, the news announced today is a milestone in this journey".

1.3. *Blockchain + financial application in the banking sector*

(1) Blockchain + credit lending

In the financial system, the most important thing for lending is to investigate and evaluate the credit of the borrower, thereby ensuring the security of the credit business, and that the credit enterprise can make a profit. Therefore, the word credit is crucial for lending.

At present, in addition to bank lending, such as P2P lending, microfinance companies, guarantee companies providing loan business, finance companies, financial leasing companies, pawn companies, insurance companies with lending business, and specialized loan companies are springing up. In particular, P2P lending, as an important part of Internet finance, has shown a barbaric growth in recent years. However, due to technical factors, management capabilities, the legal environment and the credit environment, the credit risk of P2P lending has become more and more prominent.

Obviously, the issue of credit reporting has become the focus of many credit institutions' current business. Usually, before the loan, the relevant lending company will predict the risk that the loan may be exposed to, evaluating the borrower's willingness and ability to repay, and take effective precautions to reduce or avoid credit risk. The credit evaluation of the borrower often passes its personal morality (whether it is honest and reliable), capital (own property status), ability (the ability to repay the loan in time) and collateral (reviewing the value of the collateral and the difficulty of realizing it). Comprehensive assessment of the business environment (whether it is adaptable to a changing environment, the stability and sustainability of the business) is also assessed as is the continuity (predicting the life cycle and market share of the company's products, and the market prospects of the company). However, at present, the development of the credit loan business mainly considers the borrower's own debt repayment ability.

The credit investigation and analysis of the lender is completed through a series of processes. This process not only has a large workload, but also has many problems such as incomplete information, inaccurate data, low efficiency and ease of tampering.

However, the application of blockchain technology in the credit loan business makes this information more transparent by automatically recording the massive information in its program algorithm and storing the massive information on each computer in the blockchain network. Openness, which increases the difficulty of tampering with information, still greatly reduces the cost of use. Each lending institution stores and shares the credit status of the customer in the form of encryption. At this time, the customer can apply for the loan instead of going to the central bank to apply for credit inquiry, which means decentralization. Taking the corresponding data information of the blockchain can quickly complete all the credit investigation and analysis work.

In addition, blockchain-based smart assets can build credit-free lending relationships, and data assets already registered on the blockchain can be used at any time through private keys. When lending institutions lend money to borrowers, they can use smart assets as collateral, and then use smart contract constraints to automatically execute smart assets that can be positioned as collateral. When all the payment processes are completed, that is, after the loans are fully repaid, they can be automatically unlocked through the conditions of the smart contract, which can well resolve the problems and disputes that may exist between the borrowers.

In January 2017, China Postal Savings Bank and International Business Machines (China) Co. Ltd. (IBM) launched a blockchain-based asset management system.

In January 2017, Zheshang Bank also released a mobile digital money order platform based on blockchain, which provides enterprises and individuals with the function of issuing, signing, transferring, trading and redeeming mobile digital money orders for mobile clients.

On February 4, 2017, the blockchain-based digital bill trading platform promoted by the People's Bank of China was successfully tested.

In May 2017, China UnionPay and JD Finance jointly announced that the two parties had cooperated to open up the bottom of the blockchain technology and tested it successfully. As part of the strategic cooperation agreement between the two parties, the landing of this blockchain platform means that both parties will have the conditions to implement more commercial applications on the basis of the underlying platform.

In June 2017, the Agricultural Bank of China tendered the blockchain platform project and planned to base many of the banking core system applications and other innovative businesses on the underlying platform of the blockchain and landing digital bills.

In July 2017, CITIC Bank and China Minsheng Bank jointly launched the banking domestic letter of credit blockchain application.

Further, in July 2017, 22 international banks including China Construction Bank joined the SWIFT blockchain pilot program PoC.

At present, many banks in China are exploring the application of blockchain, and have recognized that within a certain scope it improves the efficiency of certain aspects. The change due to blockchain technology to the banking industry is moving from concept to widespread application. Such uses of blockchains will be able to replace inefficient banking systems.

Of course, the blockchain technology can also be applied to the loans between enterprises and enterprises as well as between individuals and individuals, especially in the case of borrowing between strangers, which can solve the problem of trust well, so that the loan business can create a more friendly lending environment for both borrowers and lenders, and can effectively reduce the risk of default on lending.

In addition to the above lending scenarios, blockchain technology can also be applied to digital corporate bonds. The issuer is registered on the blockchain autonomously. If the mortgage is carried out or the third party is used for guarantee, the relevant assets or guarantees also need to be locked by the registration method. The bond investors access the automatic issuance system through their respective ports. Subscription, when the issuer repays the principal and interest, can automatically unlock through the conditions in the smart contract, and the relationship between the bond debts is automatically lifted.

(2) Blockchain + trusted electronic voucher application
The current electronic voucher relies on the storage platform provided by the third-party organization. It is based on the centralized architecture and uses the credit/credit of the organization to provide services such as storage, security, traceability and verification of electronic vouchers. It is easy for electronic vouchers to be tampered with, deleted, or lost, resulting in the effectiveness of electronic vouchers not being strong, thus restricting the promotion and development of the paperless record.

Based on the above questions, UnionPay proposes a trusted electronic voucher solution. Taking an electronic purchase order as an example, UnionPay, merchants, institutions and regulators constitute the underlying blockchain platform, and the characteristics of electronic purchase orders obtained by users on the merchant side. The value (hash value) is automatically stored in the blockchain platform. The feature of the blockchain that cannot be tampered with ensures the authenticity and credibility of the data, and the subsequent participants can verify the authenticity of the voucher, effectively promoting the paperless development of the voucher, as shown in Figure 7.1.

(3) Blockchain + digital integration application
At present, there are three aspects to bank points. The sense of points is weak, the acceptance of points is limited, and the points are too fragmented.

Based on the above issues, in September 2016, UnionPay and IBM jointly issued a prototype of the quotation and exchange PoC, that is, the inter-bank points can be exchanged, even across industries, such as exchange of aviation points, supermarket points and so on. However, because each bank's points have different values, each bank's views on point redemption are not consistent.

At this stage, in the process of re-combing the points scene with Wanda Group, a new scene was discovered — the point collection, that is, the scene of consumption directly through points. Subsequently, UnionPay, UnionPay Business and Wanda Group plan to build a blockchain underlying platform for digital integration application practice. UnionPay is responsible for the design and operation of the integration

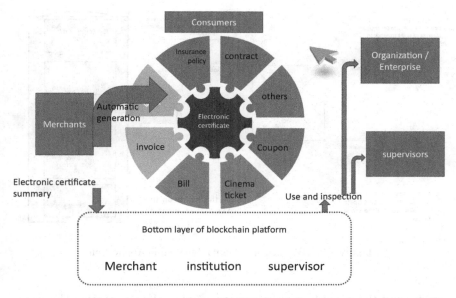

Figure 7.1. Blockchain + Trusted Electronic Voucher Application

platform business plan (point clearing). In the early stage, it will seek a bank access network as a point. The issuer, Wanda Group provides resources, and the UnionPay, business transformation POS machine to collect points. It is hoped that from the point of receipt of the points, the business of gradually expanding points, such as point marketing, point redemption, electronic voucher, etc., as shown in Figure 7.2.

1.4. *Blockchain + application in asset custody*

Currently, especially since 2016, the blockchain has relied on its distributed decentralization.

The characteristics of non-tampering and encryption security have attracted more and more attention, and 2016 is called the first year of blockchain technology. People from all walks of life place great expectations on the tremendous changes that can be made by the application of blockchains in the industry.

The asset custody industry is actually the principal's acceptance of the trustee's asset entrustment, including the tangible assets and intangible

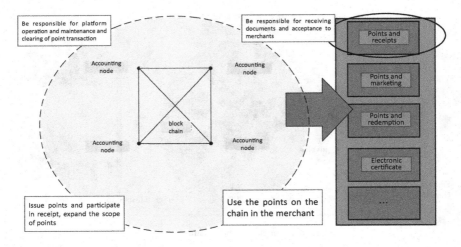

Figure 7.2.　Blockchain + Digital Integration Application

assets, and the custody and protection of the relevant assets. The main steps of the asset custody business include signing custody contracts, opening accounts, valuation accounting, fund clearing, investment supervision, information disclosure, reconciliation, etc. The process is rather cumbersome and the participation in the custody business is considered to be extremely high. The main risk points facing the asset custody business include legal risks, operational risks and reputation risks. Faced with many risk issues, it must be said that the application of blockchain technology has provided an innovative technical support for the organization, transaction methods and business process changes in the asset custody industry chain.

Although there is no explicit stipulation that blockchain technology cannot be used to solve many risk problems in asset custody business, from the perspective of asset custody business itself, blockchain technology is adopted to achieve the cap on asset custody contract and in accordance with investment supervision indicators. It is possible to run, control and track managed assets for smart contracting, and to structure and automate the storage and updating of valuation data and voucher data. From this perspective, the application of blockchain technology in the asset custody business will certainly improve asset custody greatly in terms of simplifying security and efficiency processes.

The specific implementation steps of the blockchain in the asset custody application are as follows:

(1) Building a chain of alliances

Because the customer type is relatively fixed, combined with the characteristics of organizational collaboration and business process interaction, the cooperation model between the asset escrow client and the asset custodian should be the best in the business operation process. Based on the alliance chain, the hosting industry or the manager needs to build a blockchain by working together.

For a simple example, take asset securitization as an example. The Nasdaq exchange realizes the digitization of assets. In the functional division of labor, the issuer node for asset digitization is specially designed to be responsible for the issuance of assets under custody. At the same time, the asset-managed business blockchain in the alliance chain also introduces encrypted digital currency, which can realize the whole process of implementing blockchains, from asset issuance, transaction, custody, circulation to supervision, and finally realize assets and funds' traceability.

(2) Both sides set the key

In the asset custody business, there are three types of people involved, including asset managers, asset custodians, exchanges or registration and settlement companies. Based on the custody business, it also includes the supervision information reporting and the supervision information query. Therefore, the blockchain node type can be divided into the asset manager node, the asset custody node, the exchange and the registration and settlement company node, and the supervision node, all of which can be thought of as parties on the blockchain. On the data security issue, each type of node needs to be encrypted with the public key of the receiver node (i.e., the asset custodian) during the transaction sending process, and the private key of the sender node (i.e., the asset escrow client) needs to be signed.

(3) Process transformation

In the process of business process transformation, the most complicated part of the asset custody business is the valuation of the custody products, and the managed product accounts and subject accounts are updated in real time.

(4) Building a consensus mechanism

When the asset custody business is bookkeeping, considering the continuity of the business, the block generation of the asset custody business blockchain is still the node of the asset custodian, but in which asset custodian node generates the block, it still needs to be based on the current business situations to develop and select algorithms and consensus mechanisms.

(5) Smart contract constraints

When using smart contracts, it is necessary to consider the current development status of the blockchain technology, and also consider the real-time efficiency of the asset custody business blockchain, and carry out the technical transformation of the blockchain according to business needs. The use of smart contracts can help automate the execution of contracts or agreements between principals, managers and custodians, while also enabling online and automated transactions and disclosures.

1.5. *Blockchain + insurance*

The transformation of blockchain in digital assets: In the field of financial services, the real revolution in bitcoin blockchain technology is the digitization of assets. The blockchain is to realize the digitization of assets and how these digital assets are traded, processed and flowed in the entire economic environment, and this will really change the way financial services operate.

No matter which industry, the strategic goal is always of maintaining the customer and maximizing the interests of the enterprise, and the insurance industry is also the same. From the beginning of the Internet in the financial sector, the insurance industry has always been a slow-paced industry. In the current situation, the traditional insurance industry is driven by a series of human operations from quotation to insurance application. From underwriting to compliance review, or from billing to first-time loss notification, every link involved is inseparable from the participation of "people". This situation makes inefficiency flood all parts of the insurance company's value chain, and at the same time brings certain risk issues. It is also true that the use of blockchain technology is in place.

The blockchain is essentially composed of a series of distributed ledgers, and its existence makes it possible to have both trusted interactions and immutable audit trails simultaneously. In this way, the application of the blockchain in the insurance industry can have the following three effects:

(1) Decentralization

Throughout history, human development and the formation of industry have always been achieved through gradual centralization. The same is true for the insurance industry. Insurance companies are actually risk transferring and distribution centers authorized by the government and regulatory authorities. It is these centers that seriously control and influence the future operation and future development of the insurance industry. For a long time, people have been accustomed to completing insurance related business through these centers.

Blockchain has the characteristics of decentralization. The application of blockchain technology in the insurance industry can help decentralize it. Therefore, it is no longer necessary for banks to be considered as unshakable third-party intermediary structures. The use of blockchains in the insurance business is completed, and it is more efficient and safer than the traditional insurance business.

(2) Go to trust

Currently, when the regulatory authorities approve the establishment of an insurance company, they have actually posted a basic trust label for all of the insurance company's business. In addition, insurance companies improve their capital and solvency, and their purpose is to raise the level of self-trust tags. In addition, the ultimate goal of all the advertising and brand promotion is to promote the trust of the people through communication. This shows that for the insurance industry, trust can be said to be the core of its development.

Blockchain technology can ensure the execution of financial transactions through algorithms, passwords and data validation. And as blockchain technology is used in the insurance industry, both the buyer and the seller can safely insure and complete the transaction without the endorsement and guarantee based on the integrity system. Moreover, based on the use of blockchain technology, the maintenance of all orders in the insurance industry is carried out by means of algorithms, passwords and codes.

(3) Dehumanization

As mentioned earlier, the role and influence of people in the traditional insurance industry is very prominent. Almost every link is inseparable from human operations, but the application of blockchain technology will safely achieve unmanned operation. This is because the blockchain-based smart contract technology enables the operation of the insurance business, even if there is no policyholder to apply for claims, or even if the insurance company approves claims, as long as the relevant claim conditions are triggered, then the policy automatically claims for the user and completes the payment of the claim amount in a short period of time. This will greatly reduce the underwriting period, and the related underwriting products can also be customized. No human manipulation is involved in the whole process, and fraud is avoided. The end result is reduced costs and risks, as well as lower premiums and a more innovative experience for insurers.

Here is a simple example. When there is a delay in the flight of the passenger, it will trigger a smart flight delay insurance contract originally stored through the blockchain technology, and then with the connectivity of the Internet, the flight delay becomes an open record, through the relevant disclosure of the data, the system will determine the event as the time to claim, so the passenger claims will be paid automatically and in a timely manner. Based on this smart contract technology, no public data can be arbitrarily falsified, and efficient claims can be achieved, reducing the cost of claims processing, improving the satisfaction of both customers and insurance companies.

In terms of auto insurance, it is mainly to help policyholders cover the cost of repairs due to accidents. Through the storage conditions of the blockchain technology, the vehicle is connected to the Internet, and so when a traffic accident occurs, and after the cause of the accident is determined according to the stored conditions, the smart car insurance contract is triggered, and then enters the claim phase. In the smart contract, the repair location of the claim is also pre-designated, which can well avoid the possibility that the insured chooses an expensive repair shop and can effectively control the expenses of the claim.

Of course, in addition to aviation accident insurance and auto insurance, the blockchain smart contract technology can also be used in many insurance scenarios such as car rental insurance, travel insurance, smart family property insurance, crop insurance claims and medical insurance claims.

In short, blockchain technology has become a turning point in the development of the traditional insurance industry. In the future, it is hoped that through the use of blockchain technology, the insurance industry will be able to release more industry potential, and the development of the insurance industry will be able to go further".

1.6. *Blockchain + promote a new era of financial technology*

(1) Blockchain helps the realization of financial technology

On April 8–11, 2018, the annual meeting of Boao Forum for Asia was held in Hainan, and the blockchain became one of the topics set in the 2018 Boao Forum for Asia. In response to media oversight of the block-chain, Yi Gang, governor of the People's Bank of China, said that he is studying how to use the positive energy of digital currency to better serve the real economy. "For the study of digital currency worldwide, China's research is ahead.... We are also studying how digital money can serve the real economy in the best form, developing safely in the best form, avoid-ing some possible negative effects, thus making digital currency better serve the economy. The researches include blockchain technology as well as financial technology. Overall, our regulation of virtual currency is very strict, and we are also studying how to play the positive energy of digital currency and better serve the real economy". Yi Gang said.

On April 19, 2018, Financial Technology Shanghai Summit and Blockchain World Forum was held. At the closing ceremony, 500 people from the blockchain sector and industry investors attended the conference.

The blockchain professional media Golden Finance and many compa-nies won the 2018 Financial Technology and Blockchain Innovation Award, which was unanimously affirmed by the jury and the industry.

Whether it is the Boao Forum for Asia or the Shanghai Summit on Financial Technology, it actually shows that the current blockchain finance has become an important driving force for the development of the financial industry.

Before discussing shared finance, the first thing to talk about is the sharing economy. In the past, solving the problem of fairness was often achieved by means of average distribution. However, with the changes of the times, the average distribution has not been convincing, so more work has become another way to solve the problem of fairness. However, this solution is achieved in a positive economic situation. How can we achieve fairness and justice in a negative economy? With the constant change and development of the economic system, the original "average distribution" and "more and more work" have been unable to adapt to new problems.

Therefore, the old routine theory cannot solve new problems, and innovation is inevitable. Sharing the economy is a good way. Because the sharing economy is fundamental and from the access level, it solves the mechanism for everyone to participate and enjoy the fruits of economic development. As the counterpart of the economy, finance must have its deep roots in the economic system. Since the entire economy has a demand for development in the direction of sharing, there is a need to develop shared finance.

(a) What is shared finance?

Yao Yudong mentioned in the book *Sharing Finance*, the so-called shared finance is to build a financial development model characterized by resources, elements, functions and benefits through financial technology and institutional innovation in the information and network era, and strive to achieve financial development. The resources are more effectively and equitably allocated, so as to promote the balanced development of modern finance and highlight the sovereignty of financial consumers. Also it can better serve the innovation, coordination, green, open and shared development of the economy and society. The focus is on emphasizing and embodying the personality and democracy of finance and the new requirements of small and beautiful finance in the post-industrial era and consumer sovereign society, focusing on inclusive finance, user experience, win–win for all parties, sharing of interests and sharing of mechanisms.

(b) Blockchain lays the foundation for the realization of financial resources for everyone

(i) The foundation of shared finance is blockchain technology

The combination of blockchain and the Internet is an effective supply for the transition of Internet finance to shared finance. Blockchain, as an emerging technology combining Internet distribution technology and financial manufacturing, goes further than the development of financial models. Under the existing systems and rules, more discourse power in financial activities is in the hands of intermediaries, such as banks, third-party payment agencies, etc. The core of finance is to realize the rational distribution of capital resources and effectively control financial risks. Therefore, this puts higher demands on financial intermediaries, that is, it must be specialized. The Internet is a tool that can electronically finance financial intermediaries. Blockchain technology can help the financial industry effectively control the risks that may arise in the process of electronic transformation. The realization of the financial model makes it necessary to achieve equal supply and demand in the business operation mode, so that the trust, information, rating and financial technology related to the financial industry can be in a symmetrical stage. The blockchain is characterized by its decentralization. Sharing finance has laid a solid foundation for everyone's sharing of finance.

(ii) Blockchain is a tool for sharing financial realization

To a certain extent, the blockchain can be seen as a tool for achieving shared finance. With the blockchain, it is possible to fully reveal the essence of finance as an information industry. So far, especially in China, finance has not effectively and fully demonstrated its characteristics in the information industry. In fact, finance is essentially an information industry. The reason for this is that some people have studied the source of financial profits and found that 90% of the profits are obtained from the process of information collection, analysis and processing. In the past, even with a large amount of data generated, due to the lack of innovative technology, these data information were unavailable. However, based on the blockchain technology, more information has now become available, and a user's credit can be judged by collecting data information in the financial transaction process. The user can provide tailor-made financial products and services. In addition, the application of blockchain and the Internet in the financial sector has greatly reduced the cost of sharing finance, and everyone can share financial resources. Thus, financial activities such as crowdfunding, online lending, insurance and supply chain finance have emerged. Let more people get benefits from the process of enjoying shared financial services.

(iii) Blockchain makes shared financial costs tend to zero

Sharing finance can allow more people to enjoy financial services, not only because of the convenience brought by the Internet, but also because the blockchain itself has the characteristics of reducing transaction costs, improving transaction efficiency and even reducing costs to zero.

Financial services are about nothing more than satisfying the needs of the majority of users for investment, financing and payment.

For traditional finance, there is often a higher threshold for these three businesses, because if there is no threshold or a low threshold, financial institutions will lose money. But if you use blockchain technology to develop shared finance, then the problem is solved. The blockchain enables participants with permissions on each node to share related financial information through multiple signatures, reducing additional labor costs and effectively improving the collaboration efficiency of the entire business.

Although sharing finance based on blockchain technology is currently in the initial stage of development in the areas of investment, financing and payment, it is worthy of recognition that shared finance has become a trend in the development of the financial sector and has exceeded the expected fall out. For this, it is predicted that by 2020, shared finance will develop a richer ecosystem, and then a large number of businesses will be subdivided, with a total scale of several trillion yuan; more people boldly predict that in the future, perhaps a large part of banks will disappear from the financial sector, as will a number of professional financial institutions. Most of the remaining financial institutions will be attached to various commercial activities to solve problems encountered in the transaction process. In short, blockchain technology has profoundly affected and transformed people's lives, especially in the financial sector, and has promoted financial resources to move forward in a more fair, equitable and universal direction.

(2) Blockchain starts financial 3.0 era

According to the latest data from IBM, in 2017, 14% of the financial market institutions in the world entered the blockchain; in 2018, 91% of banks were expected to invest in blockchain solutions, 80%–90% of which are adopting the blockchain to save costs.

Looking at the world, major banks are accelerating the layout of the blockchain.

The US banking industry is currently actively deploying blockchain technology. For example, according to the "2017 Global Blockchain Enterprise Patent Rankings", Bank of America's patent applications ranked second in the world. In addition, banks including JPMorgan Chase, Citigroup and Goldman Sachs have been involved, and these banks have joined the R3 Blockchain Alliance (now Morgan and Goldman Sachs have withdrawn). It is understood that the alliance is mainly dedicated to providing banks with channels to explore blockchain technology and to build blockchain conceptual products.

More and more authoritative financial institutions have found that with the emergence of blockchain technology in people's lives, its influence on traditional financial institutions cannot be underestimated. It can even be said that blockchain will open for traditional finance. Going to the door of the financial 3.0 era, especially the disruptive results of the re-engineering and restructuring of the banking industry, has surpassed the role of Internet technology.

(a) Reduce financial transaction costs

As a financial institution in the financial field, banks usually need to invest a lot of manpower, material resources, funds, etc. to build a customer database. At the same time, they need to spend a lot of money to maintain and update the data system frequently. However, as the system scales up, maintenance costs are overwhelming and beyond imagination. The emergence of blockchain technology can help banks achieve decentralization. Through distributed accounting and collective data maintenance, the cost of the banking industry will drop significantly. Santander, the largest bank in Spain, has published a report saying: "If blockchain technology is used internally in banks around the world around 2020, it will save about $20 billion a year". The blockchain will bring tremendous changes and breakthroughs to the traditional financial sector.

(b) Improve the efficiency of financial transactions

In many financial transactions, banks can conduct electronic transactions, asset custody and other third-party service functions, but under blockchain technology, wealth owners have full control over their accounts, and they often choose to bypass banks. This intermediary directly implements peer-to-peer transfer transactions, which is sufficient to show that the intermediary value of the bank has ceased to exist in the process of blockchain technology applied to transfer transactions. In addition, Hyundai Bank also has very complicated regulatory functions such as loan review, and the procedures that need to be passed during the lending process are very complex. The delivery time is very long, and it also involves multiple parties. However, on the basis of blockchain technology, banks can not only better and accurately identify the qualifications and creditworthiness of borrowers and repayment ability, but also obtain all the information of the guarantors related to the borrowers in time, which is very beneficial.

Banks have made lending plans and arrangements, which has made the loan business more efficient than the traditional model.

(c) Improve the security of financial transactions

In the traditional mode, bank data management is often a centralized management method that is managed internally by banks. This often results in data islands, so that each bank's internal data can only be enjoyed and used by itself, with the result that ultimately it cannot expand its own data volume as quickly as possible. The application of blockchain technology has changed the bank's centralized management of data to a more distributed management, and has the characteristics of being non-tamperable, making the bank's data system more secure and reliable than the traditional model. Not only that, the data under the blockchain technology can be distributed and automatically generated, which not only saves the bank data collection cost, but also reduces or completely avoids the error caused by subjective factors or carelessness during data collection, which in turn effectively reduces the moral hazard of the bank. In addition, the blockchain itself is a distributed, generalized, traceable and non-tamperable distributed general ledger system. Banks can use blockchain technology to monitor and query the status of capital flows in real time, which can effectively prevent and eliminate illegal activities such as illegal fund transfer, money laundering and fund fraud.

Banks are just one of the application scenarios in the financial sector blockchain. In addition to banks, there are financial transactions such as securities trading, P2P online lending and insurance. Goldman Sachs has made an estimation: "Blockchain technology can save $2 billion annually in US securities trading, so globally, assuming annual costs are proportional to stock market capitalization, the annual cost savings may exceed $6 billion. Similarly, in the insurance industry, traceability can be achieved for every transaction, and blockchain technology can help the insurance industry effectively solve insurance fraud problems. It can also activate many traditional insurance models such as mutual insurance. In the field of P2P online lending, the application of the blockchain makes it unnecessary for the two parties to complete the supply and demand configuration of the funds directly through the peer-to-peer method. This avoids the risk of platform reversal and running.

The application of blockchain in the financial field has many advantages. It can be said that the blockchain is about to open the financial 3.0 era, which makes many financial institutions at home and abroad regard the blockchain as a market competition tool for themselves. In the process of development, the international giants are also rushing to take the lead and begin to lay out in advance in the blockchain field.

2. Blockchain + Cultural and Creative Industry: Creating Infinite Space

Blockchain + cultural and creative industries will become the new engine for the development of the digital economy. The application of blockchain technology in culture, entertainment, games, film and television, media, content, intellectual property, etc. will create unlimited space for the development of Wenchuang and the digital economy.

According to the 2018 government work report, the average annual growth rate of Chinese cultural industry has exceeded 13% in the past five years. In the statistics released by the National Bureau of Statistics in 2017, the added value of the cultural industry in 2016 exceeded 3 trillion yuan for the first time, accounting for 4.07% of GDP. According to the "Outline of the National Cultural Reform Plan for the 13th Five-Year Plan", the cultural industry at the end of the "13th Five-Year Plan" will become a pillar industry of the national economy.

The blockchain has the characteristics of decentralization, peer-to-peer transmission, transparency, traceability, non-tamperability, and data security. It can be used to solve some pain points of existing businesses and innovate business models. The wide application of blockchain technology is changing the format of the cultural and creative industries. The blockchain + cultural and creative industries will bring about new changes in business models, business processes, organizational forms, ecosystems and so on.

Blockchain technology integrates and accelerates the circulation of all links in the cultural industry chain, effectively shortening the value creation cycle. Through the blockchain technology, the works such as text, video and audio are authenticated to prove the existence of works, their uniqueness and consistency of the ownership, and to protect intellectual property rights. The works are confirmed on the blockchain, and subsequent transactions are recorded in real time to achieve full lifecycle management of the cultural industry.

As early as in the 2016 Ministry of Industry and Information Technology's blockchain technology and application development white paper (2016), the application scenarios of six industries in China, such as financial services, supply chain management, culture and entertainment, intelligent manufacturing, social welfare and education and employment, were covered. These are typical application scenarios, which is sufficient to illustrate the feasibility, maturity and importance of the application of blockchain in the cultural industry.

Blockchain in the cultural industry can involve cultural entertainment, news media, games, film and television, culture and art, digital media, digital content, live broadcast, IP (intellectual property), etc. It can be used in content creation, source certification, news review, copyright protection, paid subscriptions, social communication, privacy protection, digital assets and more.

2.1. *Blockchain + cultural entertainment*

Cultural entertainment is an important part of the cultural industry, including digital music, digital books, digital video, digital games and so on. Cultural entertainment products involve production, reproduction, circulation and dissemination. With the arrival of the "blockchain +" era, culture and entertainment will usher in new development opportunities.

(1) Pain points in the cultural and entertainment industry
With the rise of the knowledge economy, intellectual property has become a core element of market competitiveness. The Internet should be the frontier of intellectual property protection, but the phenomenon of intellectual property infringement in the current Internet ecology continues to occur. Disputes over network copyright lawsuits are frequent, the erosion of originality, weak administrative protection, difficulty of proof, and high cost of safeguarding rights are sharp pain points in the content industry.

(2) Blockchain + solutions for the cultural and entertainment industry
Using blockchain technology, the work can be confirmed by timestamp and hash algorithm to prove the existence, authenticity and uniqueness of a piece of text, video and audio. Once confirmed in the blockchain, subsequent transactions of the work will be recorded in real time. The entire life cycle of the cultural and entertainment industry can be traced and traceable, which provides a strong technical guarantee and conclusive evidence for judicial forensics.

In addition, the starting point of culture and entertainment is creativity, the core is content, and blockchain technology can effectively integrate all aspects of the cultural and entertainment value chain, accelerating circulation and shortening the value creation cycle. Second, the use of blockchain technology can realize the value transfer of digital content and ensure that the transfer process is credible, auditable and transparent.

Finally, based on the blockchain policy supervision, industry self-discipline and individual multi-level trust consensus and incentive mechanism, and through the security verification nodes, parallel communication nodes, trading market nodes, consumer terminal manufacturing and other infrastructure construction, and constantly enhancing cultural entertainment, the storage and computing power of the industry helps the cultural and entertainment industry enter the digital age.

(3) Blockchain + cultural and entertainment industry application scenarios

(a) Blockchain changes the music market

The music market is huge. But in the traditional mode, it is difficult for musicians to obtain reasonable royalties. The use of blockchain technology, to make the fees and uses throughout the production and dissemination of music transparent and authentic, can effectively ensure that musicians directly benefit from the sale of their works. In addition, musicians bypass publishers to publish and promote their own work through the blockchain platform, without worrying about infringement issues and better managing their work.

(b) Build culture IP

Using blockchain technology to create cultural IP, based on blockchain characteristics and virtual market rules, enables users to participate in the entire process of cultural IP creation, production, investment, dissemination and consumption without relying on a third-party platform. At the same time, the use of blockchain technology, the addition of trust confirmation nodes, IP and related rights transactions, and equity distribution and other functions, can solve the problem of transaction opacity and content openness, and can also achieve cross-regional interactions through blockchain, establishing a trust relationship between people.

(4) Application case

(a) Blockchain + music

In the field of music, blockchain technology is seen as "once it is widely used, it will become a powerful force to subvert the existing music industry structure". It can maximize the "fans" economy and solve digital music copyright management problems. Also it will help musicians to achieve full income generation.

Ali Music: In March 2018, Ali Music officially announced a strategic cooperation agreement with Merlin, an independent music digital copyright agency. Ali Music said that it will adhere to the Internet open spirit of being "open-minded and cooperative", researching AI and blockchain technology, providing comprehensive protection for the legitimate rights and interests of independent music companies, musicians and music works, further regulating the industry and market, and promoting the healthy growth of the music industry.

Spotify, the world's largest music streaming platform, acquired the blockchain startup Mediachain last year. By providing open source peer-to-peer databases and protocols, the company allows creators to associate their identities with their work, ensuring that all songs are tracked to creators and copyright holders. Spotify uses reasonable way to pay for copyright fees, easing the conflict between the streaming media platform and the copyright owner.

(b) Blockchain + game

CryptoKitties, which first tried to combine game elements, took advantage of some of the characteristics of blockchain technology. For example, through the encryption advantages of blockchain technology, CryptoKitties allows users to safely hold the "cat pet" asset. At the same time, pairing and breeding can produce new cats. Based on the blockchain's operating mechanism, individual cats have unique and non-replicable attributes that make such assets form high rarity outcomes under certain combinations and thus sell for high prices.

This is also the basic form of such blockchain games.

The first three monthly sales of "CryptoKitties" on line amounted to nearly 40,000 Ether (equivalent to more than RMB 100 million). Once the product was in high demand, domestic companies followed suit. NetEase launched "Netease Lucky Cat". Baidu Company launched "Leetz Dog". And Blueport announced the joint development of "Dog" with US companies. In addition to not involving direct legal currency transactions, the above products are similar to CryptoKitties. The pets are unique and the value is related to the rarity. New individuals can be produced through pairing.

According to statistics, at least 100 blockchain games have appeared in the world at present. These games are mainly divided into pet development, real estate, business, purchase and gaming.

2.2. *Blockchain + media*

The widespread use of blockchain technology is changing the traditional media format and triggering a new round of changes in business processes, organizations, governance systems and business models. The blockchain will produce specific applications in the media IP, blockchain ecosystem, smart community, social credit system, etc., and explore a new path for media integration.

(1) Pain points in the media industry

Since 2016, the "black swan" incident in the Western political circles has been frequent, and social consensus and cultural identity have suffered, leading to severe tears, which has confirmed the amazing destructive power generated by the proliferation of fake news.

On March 12, 2017, inventor Tim Berners-Lee published an open letter, smashing fake news and personal information raging like a wildfire, and spreading it to the Internet. The "spray" manipulation is listed as the three major challenges that the Internet brings to human society.

How to reduce online rumors and purify the news communication environment has become a difficult problem for Chinese and foreign media supervision.

(2) Blockchain + media solution ideas

The technology application innovation of "blockchain + media" is expected to build an efficient value transmission system, with credit information recording, sharing and application as the main line, promoting media to become the cornerstone of social credit system construction, expanding new industries and public services. The model further enhances the efficiency of news dissemination, reducing the cost of trust, and enhancing real-time supervision. The application of media blockchain in intellectual property, blockchain ecosystem, smart community, social credit system will open up a new path for media integration.

(3) Blockchain + media application scenario

(a) News source certification and news review

Blockchain technology can provide a complete set of solutions to track news sources for media source authentication. At the same time, blockchain technology can construct an open distributed news database, establishing a citizen news review mechanism, solving the problems of subjectiveness and abuse of editorial authority in the process of traditional media review. Also it can improve the quality of the review. During the review process, the author's original manuscript, revision history, reviewer's comments and reader comments can be traced back.

(b) Blockchain + new media

At present, new forms of online media, video media, social media, live broadcast, community and self-media continue to increase. As new media flourishes, it also brings a series of management problems.

The regulatory department can use the blockchain technology to register each legal media with a unique digital identity, recording all the information of the digital identity through a jointly maintained account book, and achieving the verification of press release qualification. It automatically follows the smart contract and artificial intelligence technology, reviewing the scores of groups and individuals reporting from the media platforms, and verifying their trust points. All users on the blockchain network participate in the scoring, and dynamically manage the trust scores of various media through certain algorithms. The whole network was announced, making the trust points an important evaluation standard for measuring the new media public trust index, and raising the cost of violations; through intelligent contracts, the self-media accounts with trust credits below the threshold are directly shut down.

Blockchain technology will promote the new media governance system for establishing a central trust mechanism or a bilateral mutual trust mechanism for establishing a social consensus mechanism.

(c) Blockchain + content subscription

In the era of mass media, writers can only get the manuscript fee from the media platform. With blockchain technology, contributors and self-media can price content independently through smart contracts, without the need for a media platform, and can directly interact with "fans" to obtain rewards and subscription fees. For example, the US DECENT platform builds a secure and trustworthy digital content sharing platform for creatives, authors, bloggers and publishers and their "fans". Users can pay with a timestamp and get the content they need the first time.

(d) Media communication effect statistics

Blockchain technology can solve the problem of opaque and biased advertising marketing effects in the media industry, such as cheating on clicks.

For example, Xiaomi Company has proposed the Ad Tech Consortium Blockchain with data collaboration, anti-fraud and effect monitoring as the main scenarios. The US advertising technology company MetaX launched the first protocol for tracking the digital advertising supply chain adChain, helping advertisers and media improve operational efficiency and accuracy.

(4) Application case

(a) The European Commission will use blockchain to combat fake news
The European Commission announced that it will use blockchain to combat fake news. The European Commission said that technologies such as blockchain can help maintain content integrity, verify the reliability of information and its sources, enhance transparency and traceability, and promote trust in Internet news. This can also be combined with the use of reliable electronic identification, authentication and verification pseudonyms.

(b) The new generation of Wikipedia will introduce blockchain technology
Larry Sanger, the founder of Wikipedia, said that the new generation of Wikipedia will apply blockchain technology to make the world's knowledge belong to people all over the world, and the knowledge can be more fully shared. The new blockchain + encyclopedia is called Everipedia, and the intelligence and efficiency brought by blockchain technology is why Larry added this innovation.

(c) Facebook plans to use blockchain to prevent over-centering
One of Facebook's founders, Mark Zuckerberg, is considering using blockchain technology to prevent Facebook from becoming over-centered, and decentralizing Facebook was its 2018 goal.

2.3. *Blockchain + digital copyright protection*

(1) Industry pain points
With the rise of the Internet and the digital economy, intellectual property has become a core element of market competitiveness. Users hope that their digital content can be protected. However, in the current Internet ecological environment, digital copyright is infringed and copyright protection is difficult. Many issues such as the pursuit of blame involve

production, reproduction, circulation and dissemination of multiple links, involving many relevant stakeholders, thus copyright maintenance is more difficult.

The current social network is a centralized structure, users create content, social platforms make rules, and store and distribute content. The interaction between the users is realized through a centralized network. The service party can benefit from collecting user data for analysis to achieve accurate advertisement recommendations. Users who are sensitive to privacy and security have evinced great dissatisfaction with this mode.

(2) Solutions and application scenarios

The blockchain technology can accurately track the copyright of digital works, and completely record the copyright circulation process of new works from the three aspects of confirmation, using rights and doing rights protection. The records, transmission and storage results of value exchange activities are all credible.

Through the blockchain technology, peer-to-peer information interaction can be realized. Nodes can be interconnected in real time. When there is a need to store information, user information can be stored in encrypted form on the node. And the person who stores and contributes the computing power and creates Users who maintain content can receive rewards. Users' own data can be accessed through their own private key. When there is no need to store information, the information generated by the user will be encrypted and transmitted, but will not be recorded in the blockchain. It may be stored in the user's mobile phone cache, which enables private peer-to-peer information transmission.

For the registration of works, the blockchain technology can conveniently store the timestamps together with metadata such as author information and original content into the blockchain.

After using the blockchain technology in the content field, the creation information of the content and the information used can be recorded by the timestamp with the non-tamperable feature. After the smart contract is added, the creator can be rewarded every time the content is used. This protects the rights of content creators on the one hand, and reduces or even eliminates the service fees of middlemen on the other hand, which can better motivate content producers to produce better quality content.

Blockchain technology can break the current mode of registering from a single point into the data center, enabling multi-node access that is convenient and fast. In the transaction process, all the copyright-related use and transaction links in the blockchain can be recorded, and traced through the whole process, but cannot be tampered with.

(3) Application case

Fengyu Technology is a blockchain application company with LawTech as the entry point. It has launched a number of products, and built a legal digital infrastructure system, providing basic services such as evidence, certificates and electronic signatures for enterprises, institutions and individuals.

The information on the works registered in the billion-book block-chain has reached tens of thousands. The main users are some professional writers, self-media people, and some tryters who are curious about new things. In addition to protecting copyright, the basic functions of the Yishu blockchain are also the combination and distribution of knowledge. On the one hand, the blockchain uses encryption technology and electronic signature technology for the original information to further verify the copyright information technically, which provides a more effective techni-cal means for evidence collection. On the other hand, with deep coopera-tion between users of Yishu, the author can set the price of the sale of the work, and share profits with collaborators, forwarders, and even editors and publishers. That is to say, the content creator can directly reach the user. Each time the author's content is shared, they can directly obtain the proceeds. Each payment transaction occurring on the blockchain is com-pleted through the smart contract. At the same time, each reload is an authorization, which will be written to the blockchain. Even if it is reprinted many times, it will faithfully record the original contribution. This open and transparent trading process, recording the contribution of each link, and distributing the benefits through the blockchain, allows the original author to focus more on creation and creating greater value.

A series of applications around digital copyright protection have been launched. The "Family Whole Family" application platform launched in March 2018 uses artificial intelligence and blockchain reinforcement tech-nology to provide a series of services such as copyright registration, trans-fer authorization registration, copyright search, copyright transaction, royalty settlement, infringement reporting and rights protection appeal.

"Fairy Shopping Street" shares the "Fairy Wardrobe" with million users and tens of thousands of artist resources. The direction of integration with the blockchain is to crowdsource the design review process to the player, which greatly realizes the efficiency of anti-plagiarism and scoring; by taking the business flow information of the design chart to the chain, it has a reference effect on the secondary transaction of the pattern: carrying out the overall settlement system of the project, increasing the share ratio, increasing the motivation of designers and operators, and solving cross-border settlement problems.

Intel Corporation applied for digital copyright patents based on blockchain technology. According to a patent application filed by the US Patent and Trademark Office on March 8, 2018, Intel said they found a way to download, edit and store digital images using blockchains. Intel Corporation claims that the attributes of the blockchain can be used to assist in the recording and verification of digital content related to copyright protection, such as when to indicate when content is created and to detect duplication and modification of content.

2.4. *Blockchain + development and recommendations of cultural and creative industries*

The wide application of blockchain technology will change the traditional format of the cultural and creative industries, and trigger a new round of changes in business processes, organizations, governance systems and business models.

(1) Blockchain + developmental format of cultural and creative industries

Blockchain Cultural and Creative Industry Development Format: In the business process, blockchain technology can provide cross-platform transactions and data value-added services for cultural works through digital signatures and trusted timestamps that cannot be tampered wit, construct a network-wide infringement monitoring system and an electronic evidence preservation system to build a mass-market, shared and credible cultural industry blockchain business system.

In terms of organizational structure, the "de-intermediation" blockchain technology will effectively promote the transformation of corporate roles and functions, and promote the flattening of organizational structure, thus creating a "de-intermediation" platform. In the business model, it is represented by a new model of shared economy and digital economy.

(2) Blockchain + development ideas of cultural and creative industries
There is an imperative need which promotes government departments, industry associations, industry alliances, research institutes, and entrepreneurs to form a cooperative and sharing mechanism, to realize the linkage of government and enterprise and collaborative innovation, and to create a cultural chain blockchain ecosystem. The joint development of cultural industry blockchain application service nodes can be jointly developed to form a complete and smooth information flow based on the creative copyright protection model, ensuring that all parties can discover problems in the operation of the copyright supply chain system in a timely manner and improve overall efficiency. The cultural industry blockchain community, with entrepreneurs as the center, promotes the cultural industry blockchain guidance fund; builds a blockchain cultural and creative product system to provide services to the government, industry, enterprises and society.

(3) Blockchain + problems in the existence of cultural and creative industries

(a) Technology maturity is not enough
At present, the blockchain technology needs to be improved in many aspects such as performance, scalability, ease of use, functional completeness, operation and maintenance cost, etc. It should be actively guided by the application layer business system, supplemented by the underlying improvement and optimization, to develop the blockchain technology applications.

(b) Shortage of professional talent in the industry
The blockchain is a multi-disciplinary integrated technology solution, including distributed storage, cryptography, network communication, chip technology, economics, law, etc., with high technical expertise, long history of technical learning, personnel training and practical experience accumulation. Particularly, the professional talent for the blockchain technology and the cultural industry are in short supply, and it is necessary to increase the training of professional talent.

(4) Blockchain + development suggestions for cultural and creative industries

(a) Establish a good policy environment and industrial environment
The scale application of the blockchain + ChuangChuang industry requires a good policy and industrial environment. The cultural industry is an important industry supported by the state. The relevant national departments and local governments can actively introduce supportive policies to accelerate the development of cultural industries by using blockchain technology. Focusing on the key links of blockchain + cultural and creative industry development, we will vigorously support core key technology research, industry application solution research and development, major application demonstration projects, and public service platform construction, etc., and research and formulate cultural industry blockchain technology and application standard system.

(b) Accelerate the application of blockchain technology in key areas
There is a need to actively support the typical application needs of culture and entertainment, digital media, games, content copyright, film and other industries, establish industry alliances, research and propose application solutions for blockchain industry, and promote the integration and development of blockchain technology and cultural industry applications.

(c) Strengthen professional talent training
In the long run, institutions of higher learning should speed up the development of blockchain-related courses and majors. In the near future, universities and social forces should be encouraged to actively carry out education in the form of training, lectures in the application of blockchain technology. At the same time, the use of the Internet new media platform for the popularization of blockchain applications is recommended.

(d) Strengthen exchanges and cooperation
It is crucial to encourage and support blockchains and cultural enterprises to actively participate in domestic and international relevant blockchain communities, forums, events, etc., learn from the international blockchain + cultural industry innovation model, focus on core key technology research, industry application solution research and development, major application demonstrations, standards development, etc., to carry out exchanges and cooperation.

3. Blockchain + Health and Medical Industry

The global healthcare industry is undergoing major digital changes. Most countries have policies and strategies that target digital health. As an emerging computer technology, blockchain has gradually penetrated into the development and application of the medical industry. With its features of distribution, decentralization, information security and traceability, it can break many shortcomings of traditional medical care. For example, in the past, the organization model was centralized. Information asymmetry, low transparency and intra-network transaction integrity were centrally maintained. Therefore, there was the possibility of negligence and loopholes in security. The emergence of blockchain can just make up for the previous deficiencies and improve the vulnerabilities and other issues of the traditional model, which is also the most attractive part of the blockchain.

It can be said that blockchain technology provides a new solution for the potential application of medical treatment. In 2017, IBM released a report on healthcare and blockchain, saying that foreign healthcare organizations have adopted blockchain technology and are even more advanced than the financial industry. The report shows that blockchain technology will deliver significant value in clinical trial records, regulatory compliance and medical/health monitoring records, as well as in health management, medical device data logging, medication, billing and claims, adverse event safety, medical asset management and medical contract management.

Looking at the international market, many foreign companies have begun to lay out the technical application of the blockchain, such as issuing the exclusive tokens for the medical industry for payments. During the transaction process, the patient's data can be safely recorded for future inquiries; the blockchain correlation is introduced. The APP also expands the application scenario, including streamlining the medical process, calculating and controlling medical expenses, providing insurance and claims for health insurance companies; blockchain technology can also be integrated with wearable devices or other healthy digital platforms to reach patients. The purpose of real-time data collection, accurate monitoring and timely feedback of its own data has even spawned a "robot doctor" to replace the physical doctor for medical services such as initial medical treatment. Because there are three types of blockchain technology, namely, open blockchain, cooperative blockchain and private blockchain, it can adapt to different scopes and levels of needs to derive different types of applications, including enterprise-level blockchains and government jurisdictions, blockchain applications, etc. All in all, the application of the blockchain in the medical field is still in its infancy. I believe that the future will be promising.

3.1. *The background of digital medical*

Traditional medicine has been criticized. We deeply feel that the hospitals' medical treatment process is cumbersome and inefficient, which is a great waste of time and economic costs. The lack of in-depth communication and mutual trust between doctors and patients has led to poor doctor–patient relationships and escalating conflicts, and the quality of medical services is worrying. Increasingly expanding medical data is stranded in different hospitals, most of which are not fully exploited and utilized due to idle storage. The data between hospitals are also isolated and not shared with each other, resulting in incomplete information dissemination. In the field of drug circulation, information is still not smooth, posing great challenges to research and development, supply and regulation.

Under the impact of the Internet and information technology, medical care has entered the digital age. Digital medical technology includes the use of modern technology to complete a comprehensive system of telemedicine, AI medical, personalized medicine, customized medical treatment, body sign sensing and tracking technology, etc., greatly extending the doctor's ability in providing treatment that is on a quantitative or refined numerical basis.

The blockchain is seen as an innovative technology in the digital economy era, and digital healthcare will naturally not let go of this hot new technology. With the world's growing population, especially in populous countries such as India and China, the shortage of medical resources will be the norm for a long time. Therefore, innovative technologies such as digital medical care are needed to change the *status quo*, and the inclusion of blockchain can bring in a new dimension in digital medical care.

With the rise of the concept of precision medicine in recent years, medical care has higher requirements for accurate acquisition, real-time transmission and safe storage of individual data. The doctor's diagnosis and treatment behavior is also more dependent on high-end medical equipment and intelligent data analysis, and the hospital's comprehensive management is also inseparable from medical informatization. Medical care nowadays has already been integrated with computer science such as information technology and automation. As a frontier branch of computers, blockchain has become an inevitable trend in participating in and transforming traditional medical care and practical application.

Medical care is a global pillar industry. So far, Britain, the United States, Japan, Germany, Canada, Australia and other countries have recognized the huge prospects of blockchain technology. They have begun to increase their layout and explore many industries, expanding and deepening application scenarios in areas such as healthcare.

3.2. *The blockchain application scenario overview*

According to the White Paper on China's Blockchain Technology and Application Development (2016), the general concept of blockchain is to use blockchain data structures to validate and store data, distributed node consensus algorithms to generate and update data, passwords to ensure the security of data transfer and access, and smart contract consisting of automated script code to program and manipulate data in a new distributed infrastructure and computing paradigm.

It is simple to understand that the blockchain is a decentralized distributed ledger database that connects data blocks into a ordered chain structure, and uses cryptography to ensure high security of data tampering and forgery. Therefore, the blockchain can solve the problems of monopoly, information asymmetry, low transparency and central integrity of intra-network transactions, which are brought about by a centralized network and organization. It has wide distribution, decentralization, information security and traceability. Such subversive features make blockchains very attractive.

As far as the medical industry is concerned, the blockchain can build a more reliable Internet system and solve the fraud phenomenon in value transactions, making the economic behavior in medical care more transparent and fair. At the same time, it can simplify the process and reduce the cost, and have practical significance for improving the industry environment.

In the EHR (Electronic Health Record), the individual's complete health history including every vital sign, efficient and accurate recording of medication, doctor diagnosis, patient disease, surgery-related information, medical staff, location, event-related historical data are valuable for precise treatment and disease prevention, and the blockchain can store and share data from individuals and communities in real time.

In the blockchain, each event and transaction has a timestamp that becomes part of a long-chain of permanent records which cannot be tampered with afterward. On a blockchain without permission restrictions, all parties can view all records. On a blockchain with restricted permissions, parties can determine which parties can view transactions by agreement, thereby maintaining privacy and allowing parties to hide their identity when needed. In this way, the blockchain achieves a complete record of the entire lifecycle of the asset. All records are clearly visible as the asset flows through the supply chain, whether it is a patient health record or a bottle of pills.

IBM surveyed the value of the blockchain among medical executives. Executives generally believe that blockchain can most effectively eliminate medical information friction, including imperfect information, information risks and inaccessible information. For example, computer records can ensure the accuracy of information input, and the attributes of the blockchain itself, such as selecting the fastest and best information into the database and the security of high confidentiality, will break through the barriers of medical informatization in the past and maximize all that was best.

The standardization of smart contracts in blockchain applications is a key link and has great value in the regulation of medical behavior. When a non-compliance event occurs, the smart contract will automatically track compliance and send notifications to relevant parties in real time, effectively removing inspection links, simplifying the execution process and reducing regulatory costs. If the patient signs a "smart contract" when he seeks medical treatment, the tedious information can be eliminated and the medical process can be optimized through the automatic verification and authorization function of the blockchain.

On the basis of data confidentiality and reliable quality, organizations, institutions and enterprises can join the system and use data to cooperate. Using personal health data, medical device data, and data collected by healthcare professionals, blockchains can be used for developing new medical applications or providing services, implementing health management and creating new data sources, thus creating a larger blockchain ecosystem and creating a virtuous circle.

In terms of billing and claims, the blockchain can also effectively prevent misconduct such as fraudulent protection and reduce the waste of medical resources. PokitDok, Capital One and Gem propose a blockchain-based platform designed to help patients determine the amount of out-of-pocket payments in advance of treatment, as well as provide prepaid services to avoid unanticipated costs for patients. Medical institutions can also reduce uncollected payments.

The traceability of the blockchain also includes the traceability of medical incidents and backtracking and supervision of drugs. Thus it can implement drug tracking, and streamline drug development, testing and distribution processes, playing a role in supply chain management. Various types of counterfeit drugs are known to cause up to $200 billion in damage worldwide each year. However, if a drug-consistent logistics distribution and management system is established, including a blockchain-based chain of custody log system, allowing relevant personnel to track every step of the drug or product supply chain, it can be a fatal blow to counterfeit drugs.

The complex and outdated central system operations employed by large pharmaceutical companies currently hinder the supply chain from achieving optimal efficiency. Because blockchain data is instantly updated and widely shared, pharmacies, vendors, buyers, regulators, and more can view data flows in real time, including drug manufacturing and distribution information, making supply chain management more flexible, transparent and safe, which strengthens drug regulation and prevents counterfeit drugs from entering the market. It is reported that Blockverify in the United Kingdom is one of the organizations that carries out drug source pilot projects to help medical personnel verify the authenticity by scanning drugs.

Blockchains can eliminate undesirable security incidents, such as addressing the security of medical devices, especially connected health devices. In 2016, Johnson & Johnson warned patients that their "OneTouch Ping" insulin pump was vulnerable to hacking; not only that, the FDA reported a network security vulnerability in St. Jude's medical heart device. Therefore, the normal operation of medical devices connected to the network is very important. Maintaining network security is also an important application of the blockchain in medical scenarios.

3.3. *The global blockchain medical case*

Because blockchain technology has the advantages of decentralization, transparency and security, many companies in the world have joined the army of blockchain medical applications in 2017.

(1) Case 1: Token trading

In April 2017, Patientory announced the launch of the PTY token sales program, which officially opened the token sales business one month later. This is the first encryption token in the medical and health field. The principle is similar to Bitcoin, which helps medical institutions enjoy the information storage space of health data for smart contracts and transactions, and also to receive corresponding token rewards when improving high-quality medical services. This is the PTY token.

Patientory's network is a secure, closed-loop distributed ledger system that connects all parties in the healthcare ecosystem to seamlessly exchange health data in a highly secure Health Information Exchange (HIE) platform. The PTY token is like "fuel" and provides power to the network. Using blockchain technology, Patientory can encrypt patient information from hospitals and insurance companies, coordinating patient care through HIE, radically reducing unnecessary services and duplicate inspections, as well as reducing costs and making medical care continuous. This is the value of promoting bitcoin in the medical field.

(2) Case 2: Highly secure medical data

An application example in medical operations management is PokitDok, which is a development medical Application Programming Interface (API).

The company first launched a blockchain called DokChain in October 2016, a distributed network that spans the medical industry and runs on financial and clinical data transactions.

PokitDok also partnered with Intel Corporation in 2017 to develop the Dokchain Medical Blockchain Solution. With Intel's open source blockchain platforms, Sawtooth and Intel Chip together with SGX technical support, PokitDok can significantly improve DokChain's scalability, privacy and security. Especially, security will reach unprecedented heights to meet the privacy and confidentiality needs of the medical field.

In addition, a number of companies including the US insurance company The Guardian Life Insurance Company of America have made strategic investments in PokitDok to expand the scope of PokitDok API solutions, such as simplifying patient registration, automating health insurance management and calculating beyond estimated budget expenditure. Also it can simplify various medical redundancy processes (such as medical payments and reimbursement) and ultimately help patients save time and effort for a better medical experience.

(3) Case 3: Government digital reform

In government affairs, adoption of blockchain has been similar to medical care. In August 2017, the Illinois government of the United States partnered with Hashed Healthcare to develop a medical pilot program based on distributed ledger and blockchain technologies. The project will optimize the sharing of medical certificate data and smart contracts to help automate Illinois and interstate related licensing workflows.

The blockchain framework used by the project identifies health care providers in a secure, verifiable and scalable manner. Qualification agencies can view and certify, medical service providers can verify and maintain a single record, and all participants can trust that the center's records are valid, certified and unique.

The local government believes that blockchain technology can strengthen trust relationships with citizens from the perspective of data transparency and contribute to the digital reform and transformation of the state.

(4) Case 4: natural language processing (NLP) platform based on blockchain

Today, digital medical technology is popular, monitoring human health data through wearable devices. And linking AI deep learning platform to achieve accurate care has become a reality.

In August 2017, Digital Health Startup doc.ai Incorporated ("doc.ai") announced the introduction of a blockchain-based NLP quantitative biology platform. The datasets on the blockchain are timestamped, and a large amount of medical data is processed through AI analysis to personally provide health feedback to users. The patient can talk to the AI robot doctor at any time to get his or her health information.

Subsequently, the company also plans to introduce three artificial intelligence-based NLP modules for medical services and payment, including a robotic genomics platform that understands genetic data and provides decision support for users. The robotic hematology platform can answer more than 400 blood biomarker questions based on the user's age, gender and medical history, using face predictions including height, weight and various anatomical features, including gender.

Based on these platforms, patients needn't go to the hospital to ask the doctor, but just ask the AI doctor about their health problems, which largely solves the current shortage of doctor resources and brings more convenience to patients.

(5) Case 5: Enterprise-level medical blockchain

In September 2017, ChangeHealthcare, one of the largest independent medical IT companies in the United States, announced the launch of its first blockchain solution for enterprise healthcare. The company uses the open source blockchain architecture HyperledgerFabric 1.0, initiated by the Linux Foundation, to create distributed ledgers that make payers and suppliers' claims processing and secure payment transactions more efficient.

ChangeHealthcare first introduced blockchain technology to create distributed ledgers. All healthcare stakeholders are able to process claims and conduct secure payment transactions more efficiently. This technology will enable many enterprise-level healthcare organizations to avoid numerous claims and payment issues, improving medical services and revenue cycle efficiency.

(6) Case 6: Medical blockchain application

In September 2017, Florence, a company that promotes clinical research using software, and Verady, a blockchain asset guarantee company, announced the joint development of a medical blockchain application APP to advance medical and clinical research. Verady's Application Programming Interface (API) will provide an easy-to-use, standardized Representational State Transfer (ReST) interface that reduces the complexity of the blockchain for customers of Florence. Florence and Verady will work with several pharmaceutical companies to develop an open source blockchain APP for managing patient and clinical trial data.

It is reported that Florence is the fastest growing workflow tool in clinical research, managing patient and trial data for thousands of clinical researchers and research sponsors, and Verady can develop technologies that ensure asset security through blockchain.

(7) Case 7: Intelligent monitoring equipment

In October 2017, communications giant Nokia and OPFinancialGroup, one of Finland's largest financial services groups, teamed up to launch a new medical blockchain pilot project. The medical blockchain pilot project will focus on enabling consumers to securely control their personal health data, including sharing, accessing and using consumers' personal health data through blockchain technology.

The pilot project will select 100 participants to share their daily steps and sleep time with the wearable smart monitoring watch NokiaSteelHR and save relevant data on the blockchain. The blockchain encrypts the shared data that passes through the application, and this data can only be read by OPFinancialGroup. In addition, the company will compare the user's performance with their fitness goals and reward points for the users who reach the goal. The project hopes to create an incentive model in health insurance and medical programs that will enable customers to pursue a healthy lifestyle, which is the goal of Nokia's global digital health ecosystem.

(8) Case 8: Electronic medical record
Around the world, electronic medical records are faced with data leakage and other issues. As patients' awareness of consumption increases, they hope to have their own health data available anytime, anywhere. In November 2017, HealthWizz announced a mobile platform that leverages blockchain, mobile and data management technologies to help patients organize their medical records, giving patients secure access to their databases anytime, anywhere. HealthWizz also released the encrypted digital Ethernet Coin OmCoin, which allows users to exchange their health information through the blockchain securely.

The HealthWizz mobile platform leverages blockchain technology to provide consumers with the tools they need to bring together, manage and share medical data with stakeholders, including research organizations and pharmaceutical companies, while ensuring data integrity and protecting patient privacy, really returning the ownership of patient health care information to the patient himself.

(9) Case 9: Encrypted wallet
BurstIQ is a HIPAA-compliant medical blockchain data logging integration and security company. It entered into a strategic partnership with UnifiedSignal in November 2017, and the two companies jointly launched the world's first blockchain encryption wallet bundled with mobile phone services.

This encrypted wallet is used as an automatically updated e-wallet for UnitedSignal's mobile network. With this e-wallet, people can use their mobile phones to spend on any retail store that supports Android and iPhone mobile payments. Currently, it can support some payment scenarios for hospitals, care providers, insurance companies, biotech companies, digital healthcare companies, value-added service providers and government agencies.

(10) Case 10: Medical union plus blockchain

In China, the "Medical Link + Blockchain" pilot project of Ali Health and Changzhou is the most eye-catching. In August 2017, Ali Health teamed up with the Changzhou Medical Association to help connect the medical business data. It is reported that the technology will first land in Changzhou Wujin Hospital and Zhenglu Town Health Center, and will be gradually be promoted to the medical association of Changzhou Tianning District. All tertiary hospitals and primary hospitals will form a rapidly deployed information network.

3.4. *Blockchain medical industry trends*

According to IBM, 56% of healthcare organizations worldwide would have invested in blockchain technology by 2020. But experts also reminded that the hidden risks behind the blockchain madness are worthy of vigilance. Some companies' blockchain business is not mature, and may only be covered by the concept though there is no substantive application. This may be related to the overall development level of the technology, because the blockchain technology is still in the exploration and research stage.

In addition, the blockchain industry has not yet formed a unified standard. The standard gap makes it impossible to spread globally and can only be self-contained within countries. In 2016, as mentioned earlier, China's Ministry of Industry and Information Technology released the White Paper on China's Blockchain Technology and Application Development (2016), which clearly defines the roadmap for China's blockchain standardization and also has important guiding significance for the development of the industry.

Secondly, although the blockchain is not a new thing, it has never been more popular in recent years. Therefore, policy supervision is relatively lagging behind, it will take time to gradually achieve regulatory compliance, and recognition and support of large financial institutions for blockchain.

Finally, the characteristics of blockchain technology, such as decentralization and complete transparency, not only break the past centralized binding, form new production relations and social habits, but also have a huge impact on traditional businesses, and will inevitably encounter old forces and old ideas. However, there are still some doubts about whether new technologies can pass unimpeded.

4. Blockchain + Real Estate

In February 2018, the blockchain rental in Xiong'an District became a hot spot in the media. This is most likely the first practice in China to apply blockchain technology to the rental sector. On the housing lease management platform based on blockchain technology, listing house information, the identity information of the landlord's tenant and the information on the lease contract of the house will be verified by many parties and cannot be tampered with. This is expected to solve the most important problem of "real people, real rooms, real living" in the renting scene.

According to Alibaba, one of the builders involved in the blockchain rental platform, the house is the foundation of the citizens in Xiong'an New District. The credit system is the foundation of the Xiong'an New District. The innovation of science and technology based on the "blockchain +" will protect the "truth, goodness and beauty" of the housing rental market.

The blockchain reshapes the social credit system, which will save huge social costs caused by credit problems. The real estate future may be the largest application scenario of the blockchain. The "Blockchain and Commercial Real Estate" report released by Deloitte has pointed out that blockchain technology has great potential to improve the transparency and efficiency of commercial real estate, as well as cost savings, by eliminating many of the shortcomings in existing key processes.

4.1. *Blockchain + real estate application scenario*

(1) Speed up the improvement of reliable real estate information
Real estate buyers and sellers or intermediaries are mostly matched on the trading platform by location, rent, house price or some characteristics. The platform charges the user a part of the fee. However, because there is no unified process and data standard, the platform is subjective, which leads to outdated, incomplete, inaccurate information, etc. The two parties will pay a lot of money to verify the data and the specific situation. These search processes are inherently inefficient, as they become fragmented on different platforms, resulting in less efficient decision-making by landlords and renters, so people don't trust this approach.

Blockchain technology can increase efficiency and credit in this process. The blockchain can detail the location, address and even the occupancy rate, house price, previous landlords and tenants, allowing market participants to obtain more reliable data at a lower cost.

According to Deloitte's report, 36% of the 308 respondents believe that improving efficiency and reducing costs is one of the core strengths of blockchain technology.

(2) Improve the efficiency of house due diligence
In the process of buying and selling a house, it usually consumes a lot of time and energy to conduct financial, environmental, legal and other investigations to assess rent and price. A large part of it is the verification of the authenticity and compliance of physical documents. This verification has increased the administrative work of the government, and it is also easy to make mistakes and losses in the verification process. At the same time, third-party service providers will charge a lot of commissions during the lengthy investigation process.

Blockchain can increase the efficiency and accuracy of this process. Commercial real estate participants can develop digital identities for real estate and add market participants' information and features to digital identities. With the features of blockchain technology, these records will not be tampered with, which simplifies financial and legal information and shortens the due diligence process.

(3) Optimizing asset management after renting and selling
Managing the property of real estate developers is a fairly complex job due to the dependencies between homeowners, tenants, properties and suppliers. Since the signing of the contract, there have been payments and service transactions, which need to be executed, tracked and recorded. Therefore, real estate companies need to pay the cost in the financial, legal and other management links.

Blockchains can make property and cash management easier, more transparent and more effective in the form of "smart contracts". Smart contracts are a series of digital commitments. If smart lease contracts are used on the blockchain platform, the lease term and transaction transparency can be achieved, and the contract can automatically pay rent to homeowners, properties and other stakeholders.

(4) Helping developers make accurate decisions
At present, the "information asymmetry" of the real estate industry is not only reflected among the individual traders, but also in commercial real estate institutions. The valuable information is mostly scattered in

different nodes. This model leads to data that is redundant, repetitive, opaque. Managers' decisions are based on such relatively one-sided, static data, rather than more accurate dynamic data.

Blockchain technology allows these data to be linked, which in turn improves the quality of decision-making and analysis. Connecting the real estate company to other participants in the lease transaction provides a shared database for all interested parties, which improves the quality of data and makes the data easier to record and retrieve.

(5) Achieve more effective financing and payment processing
Slow, expensive, opaque financing and exits have plagued property developers for a long time. This phenomenon is particularly evident in cross-border transactions, where foreign exchange charges and the participation of multiple intermediaries often increase payment delivery time and transaction costs. If a US buyer wants to buy a UK property, the funds need to pass through four banks in the United States and the United Kingdom before they can eventually be transferred to the seller. The entire payment and transfer model is usually opaque.

The blockchain can include the details of buyers and sellers, transaction costs, exchange rates, trading hours, etc. in the smart contract. The transaction between the two parties is done through the network, so the settlement process can be more seamless. Improving the availability of funds by verifying their availability and facilitating the simultaneous transfer of funds can minimize settlement risks and payment delays.

4.2. *New opportunities in blockchain + real estate*

In the report "Blockchain — New Opportunities for Commercial Real Estate", DTZ has listed three advantages for commercial real estate using blockchain:

(1) Commercial properties will be able to have electronic signatures containing details of building information, enforcement information (such as rent and vacant information) and legal information. Authorized parties will be able to access this information quickly over the network.
(2) Commercial real estate transactions will be able to be completed in a matter of seconds rather than days, weeks or even months.

(3) Commercial properties' sales or leasing, payment methods, etc. will benefit from this.

In the report of DTZ, in the case of office lease management, it is mainly divided into the following steps:

The office owner starts the smart office lease contract by entering all relevant lease conditions. These leases are property details and rental details including rent, property fees, frequency of payment and details of repairs. When this step is completed, the leasing party is notified and reviews the contents of the lease contract.

If the management does not have a public entity to operate and manage these types of accounts, the triggering of these smart office lease contracts will require the leaser to deposit the specified amount of money into the designated security account.

In each specified payment cycle, the Smart Office Leasing Contract will withdraw funds from the designated account. At that time, the money will be deposited into the account of the office owner immediately.

When the smart office lease contract expires, the remaining money in the designated account will be allocated to the owner and tenant's account. The amount allocated to the respective accounts will be determined by the terms of the lease, including reasonable depreciation, negotiated between the parties in the Smart Office Leasing Contract.

Today, blockchain technology is in the early stages of development, especially in the commercial real estate sector. Many applications are still in the experimental phase. Blockchain technology does not solve all the problems of inefficiencies. Industry professionals in the real estate sector should understand that it is impossible to achieve fully automated transactions because some intermediaries must intervene, such as to evaluate a building to understand its innovation requirements.

In fact, if the blockchain technology is not well-designed, this will increase costs. Considering this, Deloitte believes, blockchain technology is used in the leasing sector. Short-term leasing is more popular than long-term leasing, because short-term leasing has more tenants and more contracts and costs. We can see the application of blockchain technology in different real estate sectors. The blockchain seems to be the most widely used in short-term rent or shared space, because there are more flexible leases compared to traditional models such as offices and warehouses. For example, tenents and shorter lease terms.

4.3. *Application case in blockchain + real estate*

(1) Xiong'an New District blockchain rental platform

Xiong'an New District has built a blockchain rental application platform. Ant Financial is the provider of the core blockchain technology of this platform. China Construction Bank and Chain Company provide services such as rental information and listings through this platform. Source information, identity information of landlord tenants, and rental contract information will be verified by multiple parties. This information has characteristics that cannot be tampered with. This way, the tenant does not have to worry about encountering a fake landlord and renting a fake house.

It is reported that the "1+1+1" housing rental management platform model of Xiong'an New District is mainly composed of three sub-platforms, including rental management platform, credit integration system and blockchain unified platform. Among them, the blockchain rental application platform is not a public platform that everyone can log in, but an internal management platform. Ensuring the authenticity, credibility and transparency of housing rental data is the key and core of digital governance, as well as how to build a fair, just, transparent and friendly rental service platform.

Alibaba hopes that the platform will provide convenient, credible and comfortable housing rental services for Xiong'an citizens with innovative technology. It will promote the population to settle down in Xiong'an New District, improving social stability, and enhancing the credibility and improvement of the government of Xiong'an New District's administrative efficiency and service level, and ultimately back to the digital governance of Xiong'an New District City.

(2) American Rentberry

The United States has a decentralized leasing platform Rentberry, which recently raised more than $25 million in just one month. Rentberry is actually the first company in the world to apply blockchain technology to the rental market. The Rentberry platform uses smart contracts between owners and tenants, eliminating any need for expensive brokers.

Rentberry also came up with a clever solution to solve the problem of excessive margin fees that tenants must pay when signing a new lease. Individual tenants can choose to crowd out their deposits with the Rentberry community instead of reluctantly delivering large deposits.

With this solution, tenants only need to pay a 10% deposit in advance. Then they can pay back to the community every month until they are fully paid off.

It is essentially a decentralized microfinance system in which every participant can make a profit. And since all fees are paid using BERRY tokens (Rentberry's native virtual currency), the risk of fraud is greatly reduced because everything is recorded on the blockchain ledger.

(3) Sweden ChromaWay

Sweden began exploring the use of blockchain and smart contract technology for real estate transactions last year. The Swedish Land Registry Lantmäteriet worked with a blockchain company called ChromaWay to test how progress of real estate transactions can be tracked on the blockchain.

Accounting in this database is not controlled by someone or a centralized subject, but all nodes maintain and co-book together, and no single node can tamper with it. That is to say, a single node cannot be modified, but when all nodes reach a consensus, the information of the blockchain may still be modified.

The head of development at Lantmäteriet stated that Sweden has always been a pioneer in legislation and processing of property data. The registry was first created on paper, and in the 1970s it was moved to the digital arena along with EDP (Electronic Data Processing). I believe that the blockchain is a new era technology in the field of work, and this project reinforces this philosophy.

(4) The "house chain" of Yiju (China) Co. Ltd.

On March 9, 2018, Yiju (China) Co. Ltd. announced that it has established a "house chain". According to the idea of Yiju (China) Co., the people who have a demand for buying and selling houses have time-stamps, property rights, management rights, effective contract terms and transactions. The key necessary information such as price is entered into the "house chain" and shared in the inventory of the 5,000 + intermediary stores that will be owned by E-House. Any actions taken by all users on the "house chain" will be recorded by timestamp, lease, property transaction, default, etc.

Chairman and President of E-House (China) Co. Ltd. Zhou Wei said: As China's first "open source" real estate blockchain scene application research center, I hope to use "blockchain thinking" to create technology for China's real estate that Serves as Intermediary empowerment in the system model of the chain, where everything can be based on time-stamped chain block structure, distributed node consensus mechanism, consensus-based economic incentives and flexible programmable smart contract records and delivery. This is the most representative innovation point of blockchain technology and thinking.

By digitizing the assets of the housing chain, in the future, the investment income of the real estate can support "one room and two rights", which is the property rights income of the real estate and the reasonable distribution of the operating rights income. The investor who conducts the property rights transaction gains the value-added of the property market, and the property management right will realize the digitization of the assets through the blockchain technology, which can be subdivided and tradable, with the price being determined by the market supply and demand.

4.4. *Application value in blockchain + real estate*

(1) Reduce and eliminate fraud
With a completely transparent real estate ownership system and the ability to trace historical data on every real estate transaction in the market, the risk of fraud is reduced. There is currently a huge sum of money invested in real estate transactions to check ownership, ownership transfers and other rights. If the blockchain makes an accurate record, determines the current owner and gives evidence that he is indeed the owner, it will make buying and selling the property safer and more reliable.

(2) Improve the efficiency of real estate development
Accelerating the process of real estate development, the non-tamperable nature of blockchain technology can guarantee the execution of smart contracts, and can provide a platform for running smart contracts. Using blockchain-based smart contracts, asset exchanges are coded as part of real estate transactions, executed immediately upon completion of agreed standards, and all participants' computers in this network can verify each transaction. This avoids the complicated procedures and problems in the development process and can greatly accelerate the progress of project development.

(3) Transparency in real estate transactions
Blockchain can make this process transparent, increasing the trust of all parties, and reducing bureaucracy. Automated execution of a contract (or "smart contract") ensures that after all necessary steps have been completed, the funds are transferred, released from the escrow or repaid to the bank, and any ownership is transferred. The distribution of blockchains will no longer rely on any single source (usually a lawyer) of truth in the transaction. At the same time, it will increase the trust of all parties, also reduce costs, and accelerate transactions. It is not difficult to imagine that if the buyer and the seller can see and approve the other party's actions more clearly, the middleman is no longer the only person who has the key information and so their numbers will reduce or even disappear.

(4) Increase the ownership of tenants
The UK government's "stepped shareholding" program is designed to help first-time buyers purchase a portion of the property with the remainder paid for in the form of rent, so that the public can afford it. Renters can purchase additional properties if they can afford the property. This process is called "staircasing".

Blockchains can open the door to this ownership model. At present, "stepped shareholding" is only applicable to a small number of properties. Only buyers who meet the strict standards can obtain it. The application of the blockchain may open such a property rights model to all buyers, smashing the traditional property rights model of "either own, or leased". It is not difficult to understand that both sides of the transaction will be attracted: the original owner enjoys stable rental income without having to worry about renting an "empty window", rent problem or property management fee; the tenant can have his own home and be able to renovate the property, having improvement right, making adjustments they feel are appropriate. Smart contracts can do this: each payment is automatically adjusted based on the level of ownership recorded in the blockchain ledger, and the additional benefits can be automatically and continuously valued.

(5) Clarifying property rights and liberalizing capital
Having unquestionable, unchanging ownership of property is crucial. This makes mortgages viable, which can free up large amounts of capital into the economic ecosystem. The characteristics of the blockchain itself contain powerful checks and balances. Due to its decentralized nature, the blockchain becomes an ideal choice in the absence of trust in market institutions.

(6) Smart contracts make transactions more convenient and efficient

Smart contracts can function as efficiently as multi-signature accounts, where funds can only be issued a specific percentage if the person agrees to the terms. This also means that the agreement between users can be effectively managed, increasing the possibility of people buying insurance and other user-specific insurance premiums. Ethereum smart contracts have the potential to change specific contracts for real estate. For example, a typical lease contract can become a smart lease contract that makes the lease terms and subsequent transactions transparent.

5. Blockchain + Agriculture

At present, the new round of scientific and technological revolution represented by information technology is in the ascendant. The Internet has increasingly become the leading force for innovation-driven development, representing new productivity and new development direction. The Party Central Committee of China and the State attach great importance to the deep integration of the Internet, big data, artificial intelligence and the real economy. In accordance with the strategic plan of "four synchronizations", they have successively implemented a series of major strategies such as "Internet" actions, network powers and national big data. They have made corresponding arrangements for agricultural and rural informatization, promoting the deep integration of modern information technology and various fields of agriculture, and improving farmers' ability to understand the world and transform the world. Now they are profoundly changing the production and life style of farmers and bringing leaping change in terms of productivity, and triggering a major change in production relations. Blockchain technology is a major innovation in the history of Internet development and has very important strategic significance. The development of China's blockchain is basically synchronized with the international, technological innovation and application explorations are increasingly active. There are huge opportunities for innovation.

5.1. *Grasping the opportunities and challenges of the blockchain + agriculture*

Informatization and agricultural modernization have formed a historic intersection. The integration of informatization, agricultural production, management and service is expanding in breadth and depth, providing a rare historical opportunity for transforming and upgrading traditional agriculture, realizing agricultural modernization. Since the 18th National Congress of the Communist Party of China, agricultural and rural informatization has made great progress. Information technology such as Internet of Things, big data, spatial information and mobile Internet has been applied to different degrees in agriculture. Production informatization has taken solid steps and business informatization has been rapid. Development of management informatization has been further promoted. Service informatization has been comprehensively improved. Basic support capabilities have been significantly enhanced. And informatization has become a leading force driving modernization, laying a solid foundation for the wide application of blockchain in agriculture. However, the technology of agricultural blockchain is still far from being fully realized, and the inherent shortage of agriculture and rural areas lags far behind the chemical, water and mechanization issues of agriculture. Therefore, there are still many problems and difficulties in promoting the development of "blockchain agriculture".

First, there is insufficient thinking and understanding. Because the application of modern information technology such as big data, Internet of Things and artificial intelligence in agriculture is not significant enough, and the current blockchain technology is still in its infancy in agriculture, it is difficult for everyone to understand blockchain technology. The changes that can be brought about by it in agriculture are difficult to understand and value.

Second, the application of blockchain in agricultural and rural areas is unique. Agriculture is different from industry, and objects are all living things. Rural areas are different from cities. In practice, the development model and practice of industrial and urban blockchains will be used. There will definitely be problems with soil and water, affecting the application of blockchain in agriculture promotion.

Third, the blockchain technology itself needs to be optimized. Many people think that blockchains are tall, ubiquitous and highly interconnected. However, from the current application point of view, at the beginning of the blockchain, its underlying technology still has certain constraints. Currently, the biggest technical challenges of blockchain are throughput, latency, capacity and bandwidth, and security. Agriculture is a living industry that needs to further break through the technical constraints of blockchain and the integration of agriculture.

Fourth, blockchain technology has a high barrier to entry. Blockchain technology is very complex, involving cryptography, computational mathematics, artificial intelligence and many other interdisciplinary and cross-disciplinary technologies. It may be difficult for general engineers to master in the short term. In the construction of national informatization, the development of agricultural and rural informatization is weak. At present, the most lacking is the agricultural informatization talents. Those who understand agriculture do not understand informatization. Those who understand information do not understand agriculture. As a new type of technology, the application of the blockchain in the agricultural field is already a few times slower than in industry. Therefore, the barriers to blockchain technology entering agriculture are extremely high. At present, there are few articles on the Internet that involve the application of blockchains in agriculture.

Fifth, the blockchain application scenario needs to continue to expand. At present, most of the blockchain application scenarios can be divided into virtual currency classes, record notarization, smart contracts, securities, social affairs, etc. These scenarios are currently not very close to agriculture, lacking the application of agricultural and rural characteristics and grounding as the blockchain is based on the Internet. In the process of opening up the rural Internet market, enterprises must constantly expand the application of blockchain. Only when you have a large user base to participate in the blockchain can its value be reflected.

5.2. *The implementation of blockchain agricultural application scenarios*

(1) Blockchain agricultural Internet of Things
At present, the main factors restricting the large-scale promotion of agricultural Internet of Things are high application cost, high maintenance cost and poor performance. Moreover, the Internet of Things is a centralized management. With the proliferation of IoT devices, the infrastructure investment and maintenance costs of data centers are difficult to estimate. The combination of the Internet of Things and the blockchain will enable these devices to be suitable for self-management and

maintenance, thus eliminating the high maintenance costs centered on cloud control, reducing the maintenance costs of Internet devices and helping to improve the agricultural Internet of Things in terms of level of intelligence and scale.

(2) Blockchain agricultural and rural big data
The three major achievements of traditional database are relational model, transaction processing and query optimization. Until the rise of the NoSQL database after the Internet prevailed, database technology has been constantly developing and changing. With the advent of the 5G era, the Internet of Things will be as developed as today's Internet in the next 10 to 20 years. Sensors and the Internet of Things will become important channels for agricultural and rural digital resource systems. How to solve the authenticity and effectiveness of data in a scaled manner?. It will be an urgent problem faced by the whole society. The technology represented by the blockchain has the requirements that the data be real and effective, also the data cannot be forged and cannot be falsified. Compared to the current database, it is definitely a new starting point with new requirements.

(3) Blockchain traceability of agricultural product quality and safety
In 2018, the No. 1 Document of the Central Committee clearly stated that it is necessary to implement the strategy of promoting agriculture through agriculture, promoting the shift of agricultural production from quantity-oriented to quality-oriented, strengthening the research and application of agricultural green ecology, quality improvement and efficiency improve-ment technology, and strengthening the construction of agricultural input products, their quality and safe traceability system.

In the process of agricultural industrialization, the distance between the place of production and the place of consumption is huge. Consumers have no way of understanding the information on pesticides, fertilizers and additives used in transportation and processing, and consumers' trust in producers is reduced. Based on the blockchain technology of the agri-cultural product traceability system, the data cannot be changed once recorded in the blockchain account. The advanced technology relying on asymmetric encryption and mathematical algorithms fundamentally eliminates the influence of human factors and makes the information more transparent.

(4) Blockchain + rural finance

For rural revitalization, where does the money come from? This is a key issue that needs to be addressed urgently. At present, farmers' loans are still relatively difficult to come by overall. The main reason is the lack of effective collateral. In the final analysis, there is a lack of credit mortgage mechanism. Since the blockchain is based on decentralized P2P credits, it breaks the national and regional restrictions. And in the global Internet market, it can play the role of high-efficiency and low-cost value transfer that traditional financial institutions cannot replace. When a new agricultural business entity applies for a loan, it needs to provide corresponding credit information, which requires relying on the corresponding information data recorded by the bank, insurance or credit reporting agency. However, there are problems such as incomplete information, inaccurate data and high cost of use. The use of blockchain involves relying on program algorithms to automatically record massive information and store it on every computer in the blockchain network. Information is transparent and falsified with great difficulty and low cost of use. Therefore, when applying for a loan, the farmer no longer needs to rely on banks, credit reporting companies and other intermediaries to provide credit certificates, as the lending institution can retrieve the corresponding information data from the blockchain.

(5) Blockchain + agricultural insurance

For a long time, China's agricultural insurance products have been mostly at the stage of materialization cost. The varieties of agricultural insurance are small and coverage is low. And fraudulent insurance incidents may occur. Using blockchain technology for agricultural insurance will greatly improve agricultural intellectual property protection and agricultural property rights trading, and will further simplify the agricultural insurance process. In addition, because smart contracts are an important concept in the blockchain, applying the smart contract concept to the agricultural insurance sector will make agricultural insurance claims more intelligent. In the past, if a large agricultural natural disaster occurred, the corresponding claims cycle would be longer. After applying the smart contract to the blockchain, once an agricultural disaster is detected, the payout process is automatically initiated, which makes the payout more efficient. Through the blockchain technology, the problem of "quasi-, fine, fast and good" in agricultural insurance services can be solved, that is, accurate indemnity to the household, fine management of the whole process, quick and efficient compensation operation and good user experience.

(6) Blockchain + agricultural product supply chain
The supply chain is based on customer demand, with the goal of improving quality and efficiency, and integrating resources as a means to achieve efficient and coordinated organization of product design, procurement, production, sales and service. With the development of information technology, the supply chain has developed into a new stage of intelligent supply chain that is deeply integrated with the Internet and the Internet of Things. At present, the supply chain may involve hundreds of processing links and dozens of different locations, which brings great difficulties to the tracking management of the supply chain. Blockchain technology can record all the information involved in the supply chain process on different ledgers, including the name of the responsible company, price, date, address, quality, product status, etc. And the transaction will be permanently recorded in a decentralized way, which reduces time delays, costs and manual errors.

5.3. *Promote blockchain agricultural policy recommendations*

(1) Improve policies and regulations and strengthen market supervision
Blockchain is a "double-edged sword". If used well, it can greatly promote the development of modern agriculture. If it is not used well, it may blow through the "blockchain agriculture" bubble and seriously damage the informatization of agriculture and rural areas. With the arrival of the blockchain, adhering to the principle of prudential supervision, it is necessary to improve the relevant laws and regulations as soon as possible to prevent the digital currency that uses the blockchain as the gimmick to enter the countryside to carry out illegal fund-raising and damage the interests of farmers. The agricultural sector must strengthen post-event supervision and ensure that blockchain technology is being integrated with relevant agricultural links and fields to enhance the digitalization, networking and intelligence of modern agriculture.

(2) Innovating institutional mechanisms and improving the standard system
With blockchain, it becomes possible to establish a pre-entry credit commitment system for market entities in the "blockchain agriculture" field,

promote the formulation of industry regulatory standards, establish an industry supervision model that is conducive to the development of innovative businesses, implement corporate public information disclosure, social supervision and joint disciplinary action, accelerate the establishment and improvement of the "blockchain agriculture" standard system, optimize the standard layout, enhance the right to seek international standards, strengthen the use and protection of intellectual property rights and encourage enterprises to carry out intellectual property strategic reserves and layout.

(3) Focus on team building and strengthen talent support
To adopt blockchains, there must be efforts to actively introduce cutting-edge technical talents from foreign "blockchain agriculture" programs, and actively participate in and understand the latest industry trends. Joint research institutes and related companies have set up R&D laboratories to carry out the core technology research of "blockchain agriculture" and develop relevant application procedures. It is also important to establish and improve scientific research results, intellectual property rights and interest distribution mechanisms, and increase the proportion of scientific research personnel, especially the main contributors, in the transformation of "blockchain agriculture" scientific and technological achievements. An industrial technology innovation alliance needs to be established to carry out research on forward-looking and overall issues of "blockchain agriculture".

(4) Adhere to the main body of the market and carry out pilot demonstrations
Blockchain technology originated in the open source community and has market-oriented genes from the start. In the development process of "blockchain agriculture", it is necessary to give full play to the enthusiasm of market players, actively guide and support agricultural and rural information enterprises to increase R&D investment in the blockchain field, and carry out software innovation, technological breakthroughs and product development. It is also imperative for the government to accelerate the pilot demonstration work of "blockchain agriculture", build a number of demonstration projects with good foundation, high effectiveness, drive and promotion. And increase publicity and demonstration efforts to accelerate the blockchain with point and face development applications in agriculture.

5.4. *Blockchain + agricultural traceability*

Today, food safety is attracting attention. How to use new technologies to ensure food safety has become a concern of enterprises in the agricultural sector. In today's hot blockchain technology, the application of blockchain principles and technologies in agriculture has made the security of agricultural products as a new trend.

As we all know, there are two most important issues in food safety: the first is the use of agricultural inputs (pesticide); the second is the problem of production and distribution to the circulation process. In the existing traceability system, the data has centralized storage and can be unilaterally modified by the authorized party or modified afterwards. The "trust" issue of information can be resolved.

The source of traceability may be a source of forgery. Although the data modification problem can be solved by means of authorization, etc., the untrustworthiness of the information still exists, so the decentralization principle of the blockchain is naturally generated for the trustworthiness of the data. Solving traceability and anti-counterfeiting are the first steps in our application of blockchain technology in the field of agriculture.

The traditional agricultural traceability platform is often a centralized data management platform. In order to realize the traceability of the agricultural industry chain, it is necessary to produce the enterprise, the circulation enterprise, the sales enterprise supply chain and upload the data to the centralized data center. Centralization brings ease of use and high performance, but it also creates a series of problems such as complexity, business data monopoly, data ownership and data security. The blockchain system is a point-to-point network composed of a large number of nodes. There is no centralized hardware or management organization. The rights and obligations of the nodes are equal. The data blocks in the system are all nodes with maintenance functions in the whole system. Common maintenance, damage or loss of any node will not affect the operation of the entire system. Therefore, blockchain technology can effectively solve the monopoly of third-party institutions on regulatory data.

(1) Blockchain + agricultural traceability application
Due to the special attributes of agricultural production, whether it is from the aspects of enterprise data business security, social public safety, personal privacy and security, the public chain is not suitable for agricultural

field trace application or supply chain application. At this stage, in order to realize the agricultural production process and the production of anti-counterfeiting applications, the "private chain" is mainly used for the technology application based on the blockchain principle.

The decentralized and distributed feature requirement for the blockchain is that each access node is a book with responsibility, and we require the enterprise to be the most basic participant and provide a unique identification. From the perspective of the participants, first of all, all participants will create a corresponding information file when registering, and the files should contain the necessary information such as information, functions, addresses and qualifications of the company. After successful registration, participants will receive a public key and a private key. The public key is exposed to all members of the blockchain, and the private key is the key to verifying identity and information during the transaction. Each participant can enter the specified blockchain network using the unique identification ID. Based on the requirement of traceability, it is no longer necessary for PoW and PoS to reduce the degree of decentralization. Maintaining the traceability system is the responsibility of each participating node in the blockchain. Therefore, the operation of the blockchain system does not require an incentive mechanism. It can simplify the recording of books and reduce the cost of running the system without relying on digital currency.

(2) Blockchain + agricultural traceability application case
The Yimin Chain is a private chain defined by Yimin Hongyuan Company and is used by nodes authorized by the company, as shown in Figure 7.3.

(a) Scope of use
The enterprises, institutions and regulatory units that are authorized to join are called organizations.

Figure 7.3.   Blockchain trusted storage node

(b) Organization node

This allows the organization server to join the private chain node, implements the blockchain source of the sub-creative block that is uniquely identified by the organization, and creates a book to receive or publish the transaction broadcast. If there is no hardware access, in the server cluster of the private chain, the node is created on the nearest server by the location of the transaction, and the account is created, the user is authenticated through the browser or the APP, and then the book records in organization node are read on the server.

(c) Trading operations

The transaction defines the operational record at the time of the user transfer of the block. When a transaction occurs, the counterparty and the party being traded automatically generate a smart contract, and the contract is broadcast to all nodes. Whether the broadcasted node can view the contract content or the contract part content by the authority, both parties to the transaction have all the information of the contract, and lock the number of items traded by the trader, also pass all the block information of the traded item to the counterparty, and include the assets of the trader.

(3) Blockchain + agricultural traceability application scenario

There are several characteristics based on agriculture (planting):

(a) Agricultural inputs (pesticide, fertilizer), etc., the use of agricultural inputs (regulatory requirements, the amount of drugs allowed, the different processes for growing different fertilizer requirements, the corresponding drug demand for pests and diseases in different regions).
(b) Recording requirements for the regularity and irregularity of frequent farming operations in the production process.
(c) For the fairness of the test results of the enterprise or organization.
(d) Based on brand protection (origin, production quantity, etc.).

5.4.1. *Input production enterprise use scenario*

(1) Add pesticide two-dimensional code management system, which assigns unique user identification sequence number.

(2) The production company creates a production batch. The production lot creates an asset block based on (user identification serial number, creation block information, location information, responsible person, timestamp, commodity attribute, quantity). The asset block contains the smallest item unit and packaging unit. The production completed asset block divides the asset according to the defined minimum asset unit, and the divided asset is coded by the two-dimensional code, with the coded information containing the block index information of the current asset.

(3) The input product manufacturing enterprise and the circulation enterprise generate the smart contract according to the order quantity. Once the contract is generated, it will be broadcast to all nodes inside the private chain, and the transaction will take effect after being approved by the consensus mechanism.

(4) When the transaction of the smart contract takes effect, the two-dimensional code on the package is scanned for asset division. The divided assets belong to the circulation enterprise, and the circulation enterprise adds the identity of the user to the owned assets to start the transportation, warehousing, and sales of the asset as per block data created.

5.4.2. *Input product circulation enterprise scene*

(1) This involves first, joining the agricultural input supervision platform to obtain a unique user identification serial number.

(2) Initiating an order application to the input product manufacturer. After the input product manufacturer determines the order application, the system generates a smart contract, and the contract is broadcast to all nodes of the private chain.

(3) Receiving the assets of the input manufacturer through the QR code assigned by the manufacturer, and adding the timestamp, user serial number and other information in the block where the asset is located.

(4) Further, the circulation enterprise adds information such as time and geographical location in transportation, warehousing and other environments to create block data after acquiring the assets.

(5) The circulation company creates a smart contract and broadcasts to the private chain when it deals with the input user.

(6) The circulation enterprise identifies the assets to be transferred to the users of the input products through the QR code identification, and adds the users of both parties to the transaction and the timestamp in the asset block.

5.4.3. *Agricultural production enterprise scene*

(1) The user joins the traceability monitoring system of the agricultural product's production process and creates a serial number uniquely identified by the user.

(2) The user creates a parcel, and the system assigns a unique identification number to the parcel.

(3) Information is stored on the block based on the serial number of the user and the parcel, and the production plan (including the production variety and production quantity) of the sub-creation level.

(4) Based on the production planning block and the production plan created as per the standardized production modeling during the agricultural operation, the smart reminder operation content is operated by the responsible person and confirms whether the operation is performed. If there is no confirmation within the time range of the reminding operation, the default is no operation.

(5) When the block information is created, IOT data (such as atmosphere, soil, temperature and humidity, moisture, etc.) with the same geographical, plot, and time attributes are automatically added.

(6) When the agricultural input is used in the block creation, the assets of the corresponding QR code are automatically added to the block information.

(7) When the block is created, the relevant operations of the detection organization and the enterprise detection are automatically added to detect the result based on the plot and time.

(8) When the agricultural production ends, the creation of harvesting block data (including time, quantity, and test results) ends.

(9) The packaging process determines the minimum packaging unit and pastes the QR code.

Appendix A: CIFC Blockchain + Hundred People Summit

Blockchain + Hundred People Summit is based on CIFC think tank, Puzhong Research Institute, Zhongguancun Digital Media Industry Alliance blockchain laboratory, by CIFC think tank member, Zhongguancun Big Data Industry Alliance Deputy Secretary Yan Yang, CIFC think tank founder, general Chairman of Zhong Capital, Executive Director of Zhongguancun Digital Media Industry Alliance Wang Bin, author of Blockchain Technology Guide, well-known expert in blockchain technology Zou Jun, founder of Fengyu Technology, executive director of CIFC Financial Alliance Law Center, well-known lawyer Wang Yunjia. The Deputy Secretary-General of China National Center for Smart City Development of the National Information Center and the Deputy Secretary-General of the Secretariat of the Inter-Ministerial Coordination Working Group of the National New Smart City Construction Co. Ltd. jointly initiated the joint construction and sharing of blockchain exchange learning and research cooperation platform.

A.1. Initiative

On January 27, 2018, the "CIFC Blockchain Technology and Application Practice Closed Meeting and CIFC Blockchain + 100 People Summit Initiative" hosted by CIFC Think Tank was held in Beijing. The blockchain + empowerment figures were released at the conference, as also the Economics Publishing Program and the CIFC Blockchain + Hundred

People Summit Program, and the "CIFC Blockchain + Hundred People Summit and CIFC Blockchain Alliance" was launched.

The conference revolves around blockchain technology and application trends, the application areas and application values in the blockchain, policy regulation and healthy development, artificial intelligence, cloud computing, big data and digital economy. The regional economy and the blockchain industry have conducted in-depth exchanges and discussions.

A.2. Core Positioning: Blockchain +

Blockchain, artificial intelligence and virtual reality have been hailed as the next generation of disruptive core technologies after the Internet, and a new impetus for the transformation of the industrial economy era into the digital economy era.

2018 is considered the first year of blockchain +, and CIFC blockchain + 100 people summit explored blockchain technology and industry applications, such as finance, energy, culture, media, entertainment, industry, agriculture, intellectual property, tourism, and real estate. In-depth research, discussion and exchanges and cooperation in industries and fields such as forensics and traceability were also included.

A.3. Core Values

1. Study the blockchain technology and application, establish a blockchain + system, and empower the digital economy.
2. Establish blockchain + industrial systems to help upgrade traditional industries and empower the real economy.
3. Establish a blockchain + community to guide the healthy development of the blockchain industry.
4. Carry out blockchain + project research, publish monographs related to blockchain and digital economy.
5. Carry out blockchain + closed-door exchange meetings, forums, conferences, international inspections and other activities to promote blockchain exchange and cooperation.
6. Develop blockchain technology application training and train blockchain technology application professionals.

7. Provide blockchain + related research and consulting services for government and industrial parks.
8. Provide enterprises with value-added services such as technology, talents, projects, investment, market and brand.

A.4. Business

CIFC blockchain + co-founder of the 100 people summit (founder)

Yan Yang, CIFC Think Tank Member, Deputy Secretary General of Zhongguancun Big Data Industry Alliance.
Wang Bin, Founder of CIFC, Chairman of Puzhong Capital, Executive Chairman of Zhongguancun Digital Media Industry Alliance.
Zou Jun, Author of *Blockchain Technology Guide*, well-known expert in blockchain technology, Deputy Secretary-General of the China Smart City Development Research Center of the China National Information Center and Deputy Secretary-General of the Secretariat of the Inter-Ministerial Coordination Working Group of the National New Smart City Construction.
Wang Yunjia, Founder of Fengyu Technology, Executive Director of CIFC Financial Alliance Law Center, well-known lawyer.

First group of founding members (in no particular order)
Zhang Jun, Planning Research Department General Manager, HUIHUA Fund Management Co. Ltd.
Chen Xiaohua, Executive Director of Beiyou Online Education Investment Group and Dean of Beiyou Online Finance Technology Research Institute.
Pan Gaofeng, Tai Kang Online Assistant President and Chief Technology Officer.
Han Han, Senior Engineer, China Information and Communication Research Institute, Director of the Office of Big Data Development Promotion Committee.
Yang Xuecheng, Associate Dean, Professor, Doctoral Supervisor, School of Economics and Management, Beijing University of Posts and Telecommunications.
Ge Zhenbin, Director of Internet of Things, xinhuanet Co. Ltd.

Ma Zhaolin, Author of *The Age of Artificial Intelligence: A Book on Blockchain Finance.*

Wang Jianyu, Founder of Blue Shield Trust Sun Dong Hammer Technology, Product Director.

Zhang Xiaochen, Founder of FinTech4Good, USA.

Li Sheng, Chairman of Shanghai Netcom Communication Technology Development Co. Ltd.

Li Jianjun, Director, Rural Business Development Center, Ministry of Agriculture.

Lu Lihong Guangzhou, Zhongguancun General Manager of E-Valley Big Data (Block Chain) Industrial Park.

CIFC blockchain + 100 people summit self-discipline convention

On March 31, 2018, the "First Blockchain + Hundred People Summit and CIFC Blockchain and Digital Economy Forum" hosted by the CIFC Blockchain + Hundred People Summit was successfully held at the Zhongguancun Innovation Center in Beijing to promote the blockchain. For the healthy development of the industry, the CIFC Blockchain + 100 People Summit Self-discipline Convention was issued at the meeting. The full text is as follows:

General: Blockchain + Hundred People Summit will consciously abide by the national laws, regulations and policies on blockchain application, and promote the development of blockchain + industry application health norms.

The principle of 30 words: Adhere to compliance orientation, implement national strategy, practice normative application, open and transparent information, and build a healthy ecology.

1. Adhere to compliance orientation: Summit members should thoroughly study national policies, strengthen risk awareness and compliance assessment, and strictly abide by the policies and regulations of the regulatory authorities.
2. Implement the national strategy: Play the role of think tanks, provide suggestions for regional economic and industrial upgrading; be development-oriented, be credible, objective and controllable.

3. Practice the application of norms: Aim at the development of the real economy, and make the application credible, objective and controllable.
4. Information disclosure and transparency: The summit will realize the sharing of technology, management and business exploration under the premise of protecting intellectual property rights in line with the principle of openness and transparency.
5. Building a healthy ecology: Strengthening risk education, not inducing, not initiating, not participating in ICO.

Such fundraising activities promote the industrial ecology of healthy and coordinated development.

Blockchain + co-founder of the 100th Summit and the first founding members
Beijing Zhongguancun Innovation Center
March 31, 2018

Appendix B: Blockchain Events

In 1991, S. Haber and W.S. Stornetta published a paper entitled *How to Time-Stamp a Digital Document*.

In 1998, Wei Dai (Dai Wei) published a book called *A Scheme for a Group of Untraceable Digital Pseudonyms to Pay Each Other with Money and to Enforce Contracts among Themselves Without Help* (a kind of ability to use electronic pseudonyms within the group), which included papers on mutual payment and forcing individuals to follow the rules without outside assistance for an electronic cash mechanism.

In 1999, H. Massias *et al.* published a paper titled *Design of a Secure Timestamping Service with Minimal Trust Requirements* (designing a timestamp server based on minimal trust).

In 2002, A. Back published a paper titled *Hashcash-a Denial of Service Counter-Measure*.

On November 1, 2008, Nakamoto published a paper entitled *Bitcoin: A Peer-to-Peer Electronic Cash System*.

In 2009, Nakamoto released the first bitcoin software and officially launched the Bitcoin financial system.

On January 3, 2009, Satoshi Nakamoto dug up the first 50 bitcoins on a small server in Helsinki, Finland, called the "God Block".

On May 22, 2010, Laszlo Hanyecz bought two pieces with 10,000 bitcoins.

As for pizza, if you calculate it for $400 per bitcoin, each pizza is worth two million dollars.

On July 17, 2010, the first bitcoin trading platform MT.GOX was established.

On February 9, 2011, Bitcoin was equivalent to the US dollar for the first time, and each bitcoin price reached $1. After the media reported this news, people's attention was aroused, and new users of Bitcoin surged. In the next two months, Bitcoin and the British pound, Brazilian currency, Polish currency exchange trading platform opened.

On March 6, 2011, Bitcoin's entire network was calculated at 900G Hash/s, but it quickly fell by 40%. The graphics card "mining" became popular.

In August 2011, MyBitcoin, one of the commonly used Bitcoin transaction processing centers, was hacked and caused a shutdown. 49% of customer deposits, more than 78,000 bitcoins (about $800,000 at the time) were unaccounted for.

On August 20, 2011, the first Bitcoin conference and the World Expo were held in New York. Bitcoin has a new level of attention in Google Trends. At the time, the price of each bitcoin was $11.

On November 25, 2012, the first bitcoin conference in Europe was held in Prague, Czech Republic.

On December 6, 2012, the world's first officially recognized bitcoin exchange, the French Bitcoin Central Exchange, was born, the first bitcoin exchange to operate under the EU legal framework, at this time bitcoin price for each was $13.69.

On May 14, 2013, the US Department of Homeland Security obtained a court license to freeze two accounts of MT.GOX, the world's largest bitcoin exchange, at which point the price of each bitcoin was $119.4.

On May 28, 2013, the virtual currency service of Liberty Reserve, a currency exchange company based in Costa Rica, was banned by the US Department of Homeland Security on the grounds of suspected money laundering and unlicensed operating fund transfer operations. US prosecutors said it would be the largest in history. In the international money laundering lawsuit, the scale of money laundering reached US$6 billion, and a large number of users, including China, lost their money. At this point, the price of each bitcoin was $128.

On July 30, 2013, Thailand opened the world's first place and blocked Bitcoin. The Bank of Thailand banned the purchase and sale of Bitcoin and any goods and services that were subject to bitcoin transactions. It was forbidden to accept or transfer bitcoin to people outside Thailand.

On August 19, 2013, Germany officially became the first country in the world to recognize Bitcoin. The German government officially recognized the legal currency status of bitcoin. The currency owner will be able to use bitcoin to pay taxes or for other purposes.

In October 2013, GBL Bitcoin trading platform was registered in Hong Kong, China, taking away the bitcoin that was held by the user at the time worth $4.1 million.

In October 2013, the world's first Bitcoin ATM was launched in Canada, and the Canadian dollar and Bitcoin exchange was available through the cash machine.

On October 2, 2013, the famous drug trading website Silk Road was officially banned by the US FBI (FBI), and 29-year-old founder Ross Willian Ulbricht was arrested. In this investigation, a total of 26,000 bitcoins were confiscated, with a total value of about $3.2 million.

On November 29, 2013, each bitcoin price reached $1,242, a record new high, and the price of gold for the day was $1240 per ounce.

On December 5, 2013, the five ministries and commissions of the People's Bank of China issued the Notice of the Ministry of Industry and Information Technology of the People's Bank of China, China Banking Regulatory Commission, China Securities Regulatory Commission, China Insurance Regulatory Commission, on the Prevention of Bitcoin Risks (Yinfa [2013] No. 289, hereinafter referred to as "Notice"). In this Notice, the central bank clearly stated that Bitcoin is a "network virtual commodity", not a currency. At the same time, the "Notice" stipulates that financial institutions and payment institutions may not conduct business related to Bitcoin.

In December 2013, Taobao announced that its payment platform Alipay stopped accepting bitcoin payments.

On February 25, 2014, due to website security vulnerabilities, MT.GOX, the world's largest bitcoin platform based in Tokyo, Japan, closed the site and stopped trading.

On March 15, 2014, the first Bitcoin ATM in Hong Kong, China, was licensed to a coffee shop.

On March 21, 2014, Bitcoin investors called it the "321 Incident" A gossip about China's central bank's ban on bitcoin transactions was quickly spread on Weibo, triggering panic in the market.

In May 2014, Dish Network Inc. of the United States announced support for Bitcoin payments.

In July 2014, Dell Inc. of the United States announced support for Bitcoin payment methods.

In September 2014, the US ebay company announced its payment subsidiary Braintree where Bitcoin transactions can be accepted.

In December 2014, Microsoft Corporation of the United States announced support for Bitcoin payment methods.

In 2015, Bitcoin broke through the full network of 1P Hash/s.

In 2015, IBM announced its participation in the Open Ledger Project. In 2015, Microsoft announced support for blockchain services (Blockchain as a Service).

In January 2015, Bitcoin received the largest financing at the time, and the Bitcoin Coinbase C round raised $75 million. BBVA (Spain Bank) participated in the financing through equity ventures through its subsidiaries to help them become familiar with blockchain technology and understand how it works.

In March 2015, JP Morgan Chase executive Blythe Masters resigned and moved to blockchain company Digital Assets Holdings (Digital Asset Holdings) as CEO.

In May 2015, Goldman Sachs said in its report that digital currency is the "big trend" of the market and will participate. At the same time, Goldman

Sachs carried out the technical reserve and exploration of blockchain technology, and joined other investment companies to inject $50 million into the Bitcoin Circle.

In June 2015, Santander announced the blockchain test through the financial technology investment fund InnoVentures.

In June 2015, Barclays Bank, the UK's second-largest bank, reached an agreement with the bitcoin exchange Safello to explore how blockchain technology can be applied to the financial services industry.

In June 2015, Overstock Corporation of the United States announced the issuance of an encrypted digital bond using blockchain technology.

In July 2015, Deloitte launched Rubix, a software platform that allows customers to create applications based on blockchain-based infrastructure, the most important of which is financial auditing (Deloitte's main business).

In August 2015, a new version of the Ethereum platform was released and announced that any blockchain-based application could be implemented.

In August 2015, the Bitfinex exchange, headquartered in Hong Kong, China, suddenly closed some accounts, causing Bitcoin prices to fall from $250 to $211 in 24 hours, while Bitcoin's lowest price on Bitfinex was $162 each.

In September 2015, distributed ledger startup R3CEV, LLC announced and the top nine banks, including Jen, JPMorgan Chase and UBS, form an alliance to find blockchain-based solutions for the financial industry, sharing data, research, ideas and technology.

On September 30, 2015, R3CEV announced that it has added 13 new bank partners. The number of banks involved in its blockchain projects reached 22.

On January 5, 2016, the Global Shared Finance 100 People Forum (GSF100) announced the establishment of the "China Blockchain Research Alliance".

On January 20, 2016, the People's Bank of China held a digital currency seminar. Once the news was released, Bitcoin rose. Within 24 hours, the price of Bitcoin rose from 2,539 yuan to 2,810 yuan, an increase of nearly

10%. This meeting is considered to be China's recognition of the value of blockchain and digital currency.

In January 2016, the total market value of Ethereum was only US$70 million in just 2 months.

After that, the market value of Ethereum rose to a maximum of 1.15 billion US dollars, an increase of 1600%.

On April 30, 2016, "The DAO" project started crowdfunding in just 28 days.

In the meantime, more than $150 million worth of Ether had been raised, making it the largest in history.

Crowdfunding project. On June 18, hackers stole 3.6 million Ether, worth more than 50 million US dollars.

On May 14, 2016, Gatecoin, the Hong Kong digital currency exchange, was hacked.

The Ethereum-related assets worth more than $2 million were stolen.

On June 24, 2016, the biggest decline in the pound on the day of Brexit was 11.11%. The global currency of Bitcoin surged within 24 hours of the Brexit referendum, and the price rose by 8%.

On July 9, 2016, Bitcoin experienced history at a blockchain height of 420000.

The second production was halved. The coin-reward bonus for each block was reduced from 25 to 12.5.

On July 20, 2016, the second largest market capitalization in the blockchain world was completed by Ethereum. On July 25, Poloniex (P network), the world's largest ETH exchange, announced the launch of the ETC transaction.

On August 4, 2016, Bitfinex, the world's largest Bitcoin-dollar trading platform, was hacked and 120,000 bitcoins were stolen, worth more than $72 million. After the biggest dollar market was stolen, the market value of Bitcoin reacted violently, falling 25% in 6 hours.

On September 19, 2016, the blockchain summit hosted by Wanxiang Blockchain Lab was held in Shanghai, and the second Ethereum Developers Conference was held.

On October 29, 2016, the first anonymous cryptographic currency developed using Zero Knowledge Proof technology — Zcash — released the Genesis Block. A Zcash can be priced at up to 3,000 bitcoins.

In February 2017, the Digital Money Research Institute under the People's Bank of China was formally established.

In March 2017, Bitcoin trading volume continued to increase. Related to Bitcoin on Github, the number of projects has exceeded 10,000.

In April 2017, Tencent released a white paper on blockchain solutions aimed at creating a blockchain ecosystem.

On April 25, 2017, the first "blockchain ranch" promotion conference was held in Shanghai. This is the world's first blockchain farm, mainly used in agricultural Internet of Things, agricultural big data and blockchain technology, and proposed the management model of "platform + base + farmer".

On August 1, 2017, Bitcoin generated a hard fork and a new electronic cryptocurrency Bitcoin Cash appeared.

On September 4, 2017, a number of ministries and commissions jointly issued the "Announcement on Preventing Financing Risks of Tokens Issuance", which initiated the reorganization of ICO activities and suspended ICO.

At the end of October 2017, the three major digital currency trading platforms, such as Bitcoin China, Firecoin.com and OKcoin, announced that they would stop trading in the RMB and move overseas.

On November 28, 2017, CryptoKitties was launched based on the Ethereum cat game, and it became popular all over the world in less than a week.

On December 22, 2017, Bitcoin rose from RMB 6,949.07 to RMB 10,016.25 at the beginning of the year, and reached RMB 130,581.23 at the highest. In less than a year, it has risen from less than 10,000 yuan to over 100,000 yuan.

On December 18, 2017, the Chicago Mercantile Exchange (CME), the world's largest futures exchange, launched its own bitcoin futures contract and traded under the code "BTC".

On December 19, 2017, Youbit, a famous digital currency exchange in South Korea, was attacked by hackers and eventually declared bankrupt.

On January 1, 2018, the European Union Securities and Markets Authority (ESMA) announced that it would have the right to ban the use of blockchain or Distributed Ledger Technology (DLT).

On January 27, 2018, the "CIFC Blockchain Technology and Application Practice Closed Meeting and the CIFC Blockchain Alliance Inauguration Ceremony" hosted by CIFC Think Tank was held in Beijing.

On March 11, 2018, the "Second CIFC Blockchain Technology and Application Practices Closed Meeting" was held with the theme "Blockchain + and Digital Economy".

On March 31, 2018, the "2018 First "Blockchain +" Hundred People Summit and CIFC Blockchain and Digital Economy Forum" was held.

On May 12, 2018, the "Blockchain +" Hundred People Summit Wuzhen Forum and 2018 CIFC were jointly organized by CIFC Blockchain + Bairen Summit, Puzhong Research Institute, Zhongguancun Digital Media Industry Alliance Blockchain Committee. The launching ceremony of the Puzhong (Wuzhen) Global Blockchain Competition was successfully held in Wuzhen. Wuzhen Puzhong District Block Chain Institute was formally inaugurated at the meeting.

On May 27, 2018, Blockchain Empowering Digital Economy (Chinese version) was officially released for the first time at the China International Big Data Industry Expo in Guiyang.

Appendix C: Design of Digital Economy Industrial Park

In recent years, China has vigorously developed strategic emerging industries. Cluster-based development has become an important task for local governments, and the park is main carrier for this task. After nearly 30 years of rapid development, China's park economy has become an indispensable part of the national economy, promoting reform and technological innovation across the country. The technological innovations of the Internet, the Internet of Things, cloud computing and big data are seen everywhere, and competition has intensified. The homogenization between parks has become more and more obvious. The effects of the parks in different regions are also very different. The gap between government policies, land assets, tax reductions and other investment methods is getting smaller and smaller. At the same time, the new national economic development strategy of "regulating structure and promoting growth" also requires all levels of parks to adapt to the situation and promote industrial ecological transformation. The key is "the transformation from an industrial cluster of exogenous industries to an industrial format of an endogenous innovation economy engine".

In this development process, the structure of various industrial parks is becoming more and more complex, and business is growing up more and more. The speed of the rapid advancement of technology is really overwhelming and has greatly increased.

It is difficult to add investment and operation management in the park.

Explore Eco-operating platform (EOP) in the park according to the WSS big data feedback economic model proposed in the main text.

217

EOP in the new industrial ecology, accelerates scientific and technological innovation, promotes industrial transformation and upgrading, improves the security system, proposes a new economic construction and operation model based on digital economic industrial park, and creates a new innovation park through digital reorganization and establishment of a new incentive mechanism. The unique brand has practical significance.

C.1. The Design of Digital Economy Industrial Park

"Trust is the biggest value behind blockchain technology", said Don Tapscott, an economist known as the "father of the digital economy", at the 2017 IEBE (International E-Commerce Expo). Blockchain technology will bring a far-reaching second round of revolution to the Internet world. The first round of revolution in the past was the information revolution, the information age of the Internet, and now it is entering the age of the Internet. In Don's view, Uber and Airbnb are just a kind of aggregated service, and the blockchain brings the real sharing economy. For example, suppose there is no such company as Airbnb, but there is a distributed application based on blockchain, which is essentially owned by anyone who wants to rent a room. When someone wants to rent a room, he can log in to the blockchain database and filter to find the right room. After that, the blockchain will help them sign a smart contract. The smart contract will determine the identity of both parties and be in the transaction. Payments are processed through the system's own digital currency. After the transaction is over, the occupant can give the room a score, and the score is not changeable. No one can tamper with it, so that the transaction is completed using the blockchain. Don believes that the owner of the room and the renter participate in a blockchain, just like a cooperative, the owners really share their stuff into the corresponding field, and their profit is only for the owner, there is no such thing as a centralized organization, it is called the real sharing economy.

Therefore, in the design of the digital economy industrial park, we must first embed the idea of sharing the economy from the top-level design, and create a new industrial ecological model through the "blockchain +" architecture system.

The WSS model proposed in the text, combined with the industrial Internet panorama, designed a digital economic innovation industrial park model based on blockchain to promote the steady, accurate and rapid development of the local digital economy.

C.2. Digital Economy Industrial Park and EOP

Industrial parks are an important form of space for implementing urban industrial functions. The park has played an active role in improving the regional investment environment, attracting foreign investment, promoting industrial restructuring and developing the economy, and has become a booster for the cities' economic take-off. As the leading industries of industrial parks continue to transform from traditional industries to high-tech industries, this is also the content that needs attention in the planning and development of industrial parks in the future.

Park planning is at the forefront of the park construction, and the plan determines the scale, direction and taste of the park. Therefore, the new model is breaking the traditional pattern.

The design path of the digital economy industrial park includes several stages: project master plan, park industry plan, capital plan, construction plan and operation plan.

Overall plan of the project: The local construction digital economy industrial park will generally set a target of 3–5 years. The ultimate goal and status in the region and even the whole country should be demonstrated in the natural ecology, industrial ecology and park ecology. This goal is in line with the local production development, and gradually achieves the ultimate goal from the industrial aggregation stage (1–2 years), the industrial maturity stage (3–4 years), and 5 years later.

In a park's industrial planning (see Figure C.1), there are four major steps:

(1) Create an industry base. We will choose the direction of related core industries such as big data, integrate the introduction of high-quality

Figure C.1. Industrial planning of the park

industries in the country, and carry out the integration of "block-chain +" in a targeted manner to form a core "industry population" like Silicon Valley. For example, the same is the choice of smart manufacturing, some regions choose to use the family car in the car as the core industry, and then assist the future car market; while other regions choose heavy-duty vehicles to assist the logistics service industry.

(2) Build an industrial system. The industrial system includes the clustering of industrial design, research and development, production, manufacturing and sales integration. In order to achieve this goal, it is necessary to establish a closed loop of "production, research, investment and government use" to realize "base of first-class talents" and "innovation". The goal of the research highland is that "cooperative center for industrial incubation and sublimation" has been created.

(3) Typical application of digitization. This stage is an important node in the process of promoting the digital economy industrial park, and it is also a symbolic stage that reflects the characteristics of regional industries. At this stage, industrial clustering and digital industrialization will be realized through industrial clustering. That is to say, with certain data resources, it is possible to carry out services of a certain size of the data-driven industry.

(4) Create an industrial ecology. At this stage, in order to establish the digital ecology of EOP, it is necessary to have a digital reorganization ecological design. Each industry aggregate becomes a "block" of WikIT's sharing economy, and the way to link these "blocks" needs to rely on "financial ecologicalization" to fulfill. The realization of financial ecologicalization has laid a solid foundation for data assetization.

For example, according to the WSS model proposed in the text, the big data of "operation, perception, and wisdom" is opened, and the non-standardized production (operation) process is standardized (segmented) to achieve the ecological link target of enterprises inside and outside the park. Factor markets (such as trading centers) enable the periodicity of production to effectively interface with the periodicity of consumption, avoiding time risks, and at the same time minimizing the path of realization from production to consumption, and accelerating financial liquidity (such as the aforementioned "pig networking").

In order to realize the sustainable development of the digital economy industry ecology, it is necessary to effectively integrate the development of the "blockchain +" industry in the park and gradually improve the "production relationship" of the ecology.

The specific approach is to establish a "chain of alliances" to allow enterprises in the park to gradually carry out the incubation and upgrading of the "blockchain +" industry. With regards to financial innovation, it is possible to establish a financial supervision sandbox, which will be promoted after maturity.

Starting from the top-level design of the entire park, it is necessary to change the G2B (first design, post-investment operation) into an efficient model of B2G (design is investment, construction or operation), and reduce the cycle of digital economy industrial park input to output.

For example, the nine major industries in the digital economic industrial park in a certain region are imported:

A sandbox (also known as a "sandbox") is primarily used to provide a test environment for programs that are untrustworthy, destructive or incapable of determining the intent of the program. The "regulatory sandbox" mainly refers to a set of regulatory mechanisms established by the regulatory authorities in some areas to provide a safe space for financial institutions (or pan-financial institutions) to innovate.

(1) Establish the full amount of basic data of "sky and sea", realize the safe and orderly open application by means of blockchain technology, effectively solve the pain points such as data islands and data segregation and information traceability in the process of big data application, and choose government affairs. Pilot of big data + blockchain applications.

(2) Promote local financial sandbox innovation pilot (cross-border payment, blockchain + supply chain finance, etc.).

(3) Reshape the supply chain system with the energy blockchain to realize the data circulation and realization of the industry.

(4) Promote AI with points and face, and form breakthrough innovations in basic areas (such as identification).

(5) Promote the post-automotive market, including auto insurance innovation, with the help of a strong industry in a certain place.

(6) Re-engineering supply chain systems such as manufacturing through blockchain technology.

(7) On this basis, with the help of high-end corporate resources with excellent social organizations (such as alliances, associations,

chambers of commerce, etc.), promote local industry (industrial, agricultural and consumer) upgrades and comprehensive data realization.

(8) Cooperate with relevant institutions to promote digital economic training and certification.

(9) Establish a digital economy innovation open laboratory and industrial innovation research institute, build a public chain environment, incubate digital economy innovation industries and enterprises, and promote the establishment of digital economy industry application standards.

The business models of the above nine industry import routes include:

(1) Industry introduction leverages the potential of the big data industry to achieve blockchain + big data + Industry integration (the enterprise ecology of social organizations can achieve the introduction of initial traffic).

(2) With the advantage of "core enterprise", form industrial cohesion — warming up.

(3) Promote innovation research institute, case by case blockchain + industry upgrade (Introduction of cash flow from high-end manufacturing);

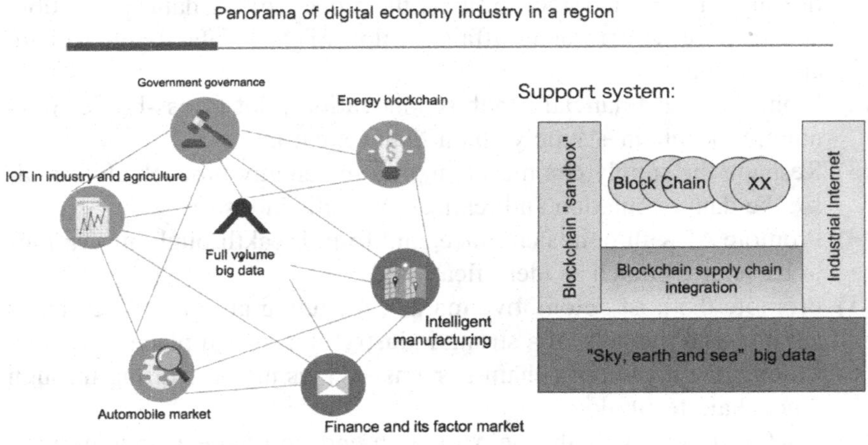

Figure C.2.   Panorama of the industrial ecology of EOP in a certain area

(4) To achieve breakthroughs in financial monitoring and leapfrogging, and to seize the commanding heights.

The panoramic view of the industrial ecology of EOP in a certain area is shown in Figure C.2.

C.3. Industry Synergy Initiatives

To improve the EOP ecology of the park, it is necessary to have strong operational guarantees. The parks in different regions need to adopt

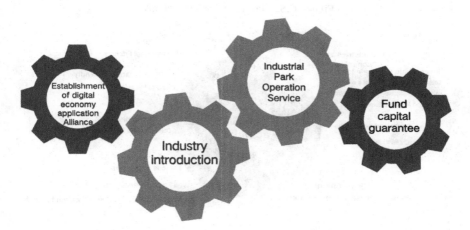

Figure C.3. Operational support

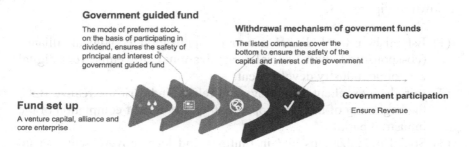

Figure C.4. Participation model of the park fund

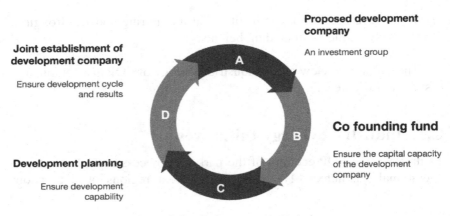

Figure C.5.   Project company's choice

Figure C.6.   Specific practices

different measures according to the specific economic development, as shown in Figure C.3.

(1) Establish a local digital economy application ecological alliance (co-sponsored with social organizations) to empower digital economic industry development.

(2) Introduce excellent technology and related industries to realize B2G, the beginning of industrial operation on the date of completion of the industrial park.

(3) Social organizations and institutions and local governments set up operating companies to make industrial innovation the norm.

(4) Central and local government guidance funds + social capital leads the industrial ecological clustering and expansion of the park.

The participation model of the park fund is shown in Figure C.4. The size of the fund is determined by the overall project design volume of the park. It is initiated by a venture capital fund and the project development work begins after the fund is completed. The choice of the project company can be carried out according to Figure C.5.

In order to improve the influence of the park, it is necessary to strengthen the ability of public relations communication (Figure C.6).

The Digital Economy Industrial Park has followed the orderly promotion mode of "industrial digitalization", "digital industrialization" and "financial ecologicalization", which is the closed-loop model of "production, circulation and trading" mentioned in the book.

Index

A

access control, 17
Ad Tech Consortium Blockchain, 167
agricultural modernization, 40
agricultural sector, blockchain
  application in
    agricultural modernization,
      191–193
    formulation of industry
      regulatory standards, 197
    identifying technical talents, 197
    insurance, 195–196
    policy recommendations,
      196–197
    product supply chain, 196
    rural finance, 195
    traceability platform, 98–202,
      194
    trading operations, 200
Ali Health and Changzhou, 182
Ali Music, 164
anonymity of blockchain, 3
anti-fraud behavior, 140
application-specific integrated circuit
  (ASIC), 17
ArcBlock, 22

architecture of blockchain, 10
  block capacity and expansion, 19
  consensus mechanisms, 19–20
  data authenticity guarantee, 20
  development, 10–12
  formal proofs, 20
  middleware, 18
  network, 18
  operating system, 18, 21–22
  platforms to support deployment
    of applications, 20
  problems and challenges, 12–17
  security and privacy, 20
  sharding, 19
  side chain technology, 18–19
  storage, 19, 32–33
artificial intelligence, 132–133
asset custody, 149–152
Autonomous Decentralized Peer-to-
  Peer Telemetry (ADEPT), 128

B

bank credit information system,
  139–140
beef cattle breeding, 82–85
Berners-Lee, Tim, 165

BFT-DPoS consensus algorithm, 21
Big Data
    agricultural and rural, 194
    application of blockchain in, 121–124
    in China, 46
    integration of blockchain with, 124–126
    problems with, 119–121
Big Data Investment Strategy, 44
Bitcoin, 3, 10, 15, 25, 29, 135
    mining, 16
    workload, 16
Bitshares/EOS, 31
"black swan" incident, 165
blockchain (*see also* architecture of blockchain)
    advantages, 56
    applications, features (*see also* cultural and creative industries, blockchain application in; digital copyright protection, blockchain application in; financial industry, blockchain application in; health and medical industry, blockchain application in; media industry, blockchain application in), 4–5
    business value, 5–6
    definition, 1–2
    development of, 2–4
    guidelines, 6
    openness of, 6
    supervision related to, 7
Blockchain +, 37
blockchain applications, requirements for
    access control, 17
    centralization of computing power, 17
    chain security, 15–16
    data authenticity, 16
    governance and supervision system, 17
    identity authentication, 17
    privacy, 15
    public key signature security, 16
    smart contract upgrade and monitoring, 17
    useful work, 16
Blockchain as a Service (BaaS) platform, 106
blockchain consensus mechanism, 31
blockchain events, 209–216
Blockchain + Hundred People Summit, 203
    business, 205–207
    core values, 204–205
    initiative, 203–204
blockchain-related development policies, 107–113
blockchain tokens (*see also* legal regulation of blockchain technology), 57–63
    payment medium, 57–58
    securitization certificate, 59–60
Break-in Contracts, 26
Break-out Contracts, 26
BurstCoin, 33
Buterin, Vitalik, 3
byzantine fault tolerance (BFT), 13, 21, 24, 26

C
CAP theory, 13
Casper consensus mechanism, 31
CDN (Content Delivery Network) functionality, 32
centralization of computing power, 17
Certificates of Authority (CA), 4
Chainalysis, 140

chain security, 15–16
ChangeHealthcare, 180
Changzhou Medical Association, 182
China Inspection and Certification
Group (CCIC), 107
China Inspection Group, 103
China's high-speed railways, 114
city management, 96–99
China's national conditions and
urbanization, 96–97
rules for parking management, 98
Code Obfuscation, 35
competitiveness, 79
consensus mechanisms, 19–20
core technology research, 113–114
cross-border e-commerce, 142–143
cross-chain interconnection, 18
cryptographic mechanisms, 2
CryptoKitties, 13, 164
cultural and creative industries,
161–162
cultural and entertainment
industry, 162–163
cultural IP creation, 163
development and
recommendations, 170–172
games industry, 164
music industry, 163–164
customs border inspection, 103–107

D
DAG directed acyclic graph system,
33–34
DApps, 18, 21
data authenticity, 16
DDoS (distributed denial of service),
15
disintermediation, 42
depository certificates, 71–73
development of blockchain
technology, 107–113
demonstrations, 114–115

industrial development and
application, 115–116
policy documents, 108–111
promotion of industrial chain and
ecosystem construction, 117
standards and normative systems,
116
digital bill, 141
digital China, 46
digital copyright protection,
167–170
digital economy, 45–51, 80
digital economy industrial park,
217–225
digital identity, 90–93
digital industrialization, 41–45
digitalization of industry, 30–41
digital medical technology, 174
digital tickets, 141–142
Ding Lei, 37
distributed hashing (DHT), 32
distributed ledger technology (DLT),
2, 80
DOT (Relay Chain Token), 25

E
ECDHM (Elliptic Curve Diffie–
Hellman–Merkle), 35, 35
education governance, 99–103
cost of learners, 102
integration and sharing of
educational resources,
100–101
protection of intellectual
achievements, 101–102
student credit file based on
blockchain, 101
E-Krona, 138
encrypted wallet, 181
ENIAC computer, 9
enterprise-level medical blockchain,
180

environmental protection, 131
EOP (Ecosystem Operating Platform
　or Ecological Operation Platform),
　42
EOS blockchain, 21–22
Ethereum, 3, 15, 19, 24, 27–31
　architecture, 13
Ethereum EVM, 25
Ethereum Virtual Machine (EVM)
　support, 22
European Commission, 167

F
Facebook, 167
feedback economy, 40
FEOP, 49–51
FileCoin, 32
financial industry, blockchain
　application in
　　asset custody, 149–152
　　bank credit information system,
　　　139–140
　　costs and efficiency, 135–136
　　credit lending, 145–148
　　cross-border e-commerce,
　　　142–143
　　decentralization, 136–137
　　digital bill, 141
　　digital currency, 137–138
　　digital notes, 140–142
　　digital tickets, 141–142
　　efficiency of financial
　　　transactions, 159–160
　　electronic voucher, 148
　　insurance business, 152–155
　　integration platform business
　　　plan, 148–149
　　realization of financial
　　　technology, 155–161
　　reduction of financial transaction
　　　costs, 157–159
　　securities trading, 143–145

　　security of financial transactions,
　　　160
　　transparency of transactions, 139
　　use of virtual "coins", 138
financing of token issuance, 7
Florence, 180
food and drug supervision, 87–90
　traceability approaches, 89–90
fragmentation mechanism, 30

G
Goldman Sachs, 160
Gossip about Gossip protocol, 34
governance and supervision system,
　17
Government digital reform, 179
government understanding and
　application of blockchain
　technology, 79–81
　　in city management, 96–99
　　in creating personal information
　　　file, 93
　　in customs border inspection,
　　　103–107
　　in digital identity, 90–93
　　in education governance,
　　　99–103
　　in food and drug supervision,
　　　87–90
　　in poverty alleviation, 81–87
　　for senior citizens' allowances,
　　　92–93
　　in tax management, 93–96
Guardian Life Insurance Company of
　America, 178

H
Hashgraph, 34
health and medical industry,
　blockchain application in, 173–182
　　blockchain technology trends,
　　　182

electronic medical records, 175, 181

encrypted wallet, 181

enterprise-level medical blockchain, 180

intelligent monitoring equipment, 180–181

medical Application Programming Interface (API), 178

medical blockchain application, 180

natural language processing (NLP) platform, 179

token trading, 178

Health Information Exchange (HIE) platform, 178

HealthWizz mobile platform, 181

Hedera (Ivy), 34

HSBC, 103, 105–107

HTLC (Hash Timelock Contract) funding, 23

Hyperledger, 4

I

identity authentication, 17

illegal public financing behaviors, 7

ILP, 27

industrial digitalization, 41–45

   data availability, 44

   ecological chain, 44

   fault tolerance, 45

   financial generalization, 44–45

   humanization of service provision, 43

   normalization of trial and error, 45

   simplification of service, 43

   socialization of (local) government functions, 43–44

industrial innovation panorama, 42

industry Internet, 41

Interledger, 28

Internet of Things (IoT), 5–6, 79, 81, 88, 126–127, 136, 193–194

   allocation of resources, 127–128

   application scenario, 130–132

   future prospects, 132

   privacy, 128

   security performance, 127

   status quo of development and application, 128–130

   technical principle, 130

IPFS (InterPlanetary File System), 32

IT development, 9–10

L

legal regulation of blockchain technology

   on application, 65–66

   in China, 56

   dimensions, 55

   ICO related legal issues, 60–62

   legal challenges, 56–57

   reconstruction of business model, 63–65

   status quo of, 55–56

   technology and, 53–54

   of tokens, 57–63

   in United Kingdom, 56

   virtual currency exchanges, 62–63

Lightning Network, 23

Linux Foundation, 3

M

Ma Huateng, 37

MaidSafe, 33

media industry, blockchain application in, 165–167

   content subscription, 166

   efficiency of news dissemination, 165

   new forms of online media, 166

news source certification and
news review, 165–166
medical blockchain application, 180
"Medical Link + Blockchain" pilot
project, 182
Merkle DAG, 32
Merkle proof, 26
MetaX, 167
micro-payment channel, 23
Moros, Nicolás Maduro, 138
multi-participating alliance
blockchain network, 98

N
Nakamoto, Satoshi, 3
National Institute of Standards and
Technology (NIST), 10
network project, blockchain, 22
Lightning, 23
Raiden, 24
Tendermint Cosmos, 24
NewBchain project, 132
NXT (PoS Consensus), 31

O
Occupationally Generated Content
(OGC), 38
off-chain computation, 19
"OneTouch Ping" insulin pump, 177
Ontology network, 22
OpenChain Access Layer, 22
openness of blockchain technology, 6
Oracle (source of truth) mechanism,
16

P
Parity Substrate, 27
Parity Technologies, 27
People's Daily, 37
Petro currency, 138
"pig-network" project, 50
Plasma, 28–29
PokitDok, 177–178

Polkadot, 25–27
POS (Proof of Stake) consensus
algorithm, 15
poverty alleviation, 81–87
characteristics of blockchain
technology, 85–87
solution, 83–87
P2P communication, 10
P2P Hypermedia protocol, 32
P2P protocol BitTorrent, 32
Practical Byzantine Fault Tolerance
(PBFT), 4
privacy, 15, 35
problems of blockchain platform
application support, 14
compatibility, 14
consensus mechanism
mathematical proof, 15
data synchronization
performance limit, 14
ease of use, 14
extensibility restrictions, 13
interoperability, 14
smart contract formal
verification, 14
storage restrictions, 14
transaction performance limit,
13
Professionally Generated Content
(PGC), 38
Professionally Produced Content
(PPC), 38
proof-of-existence, 75–76
BAOBAO blockchain, 73–74
of conventional data, 74
cost of, 69
dilemmas, 69–71
macro dilemma of, 68
nature of, 67
notarization and, 76–77
status-quo, 68–69
of trade secrets, 75
value of, 67

PSR (Pressure-State-Response) model, 40
public financing behavior, 7
public key signature security, 16
Pub/Sub Gateway Adapters (publish/ subscribe gateways), 22

Q
Quanzhou Petrochemical and Petroleum Company, 103

R
Raiden network, 24
R3 Corda, 33
real estate industry, blockchain application in
    advantages, 185–186
    asset management, 184
    ChromaWay, 188
    commercial properties' sales or leasing, payment methods, 186
    decision-making, 184–185
    efficiency of house due diligence, 184
    efficiency of real estate development, 189
    financing and payment processing, 185
    fraud elimination, 189
    "house chain" of Yiju (China) Co. Ltd., 188–189
    ownership of property, 190
    reliable real estate information, 183–184
    Rentberry decentralized leasing platform, 187–188
    smart contracts, 190–191
    "stepped shareholding" program, 190
    transparency in transactions, 190
    Xiong'an New District blockchain rental platform, 187

refinement process, 41
Reitwiessner, Christian, 30
replay attack, 15–16
Representational State Transfer (ReST) interface, 180
Ripple, 31
Rootstock Native Token RTC, 25
RSMC (Recoverable Sequence Maturity Contract), 23

S
Sanger, Larry, 167
securities trading, 143–145
sharding, 19, 29–30
Sia, 32
side chain technology, 18–19
    projects, 24–28
Sinochem Group, 103
Sinochem Quanzhou project, 104
smart contract, 3, 176, 190–191
smart contract upgrade and monitoring, 17
social economy, 46–47
Spotify, 164
State Channel, 30–31
state machine replication (SMR) consensus algorithm, 13
Stellar, 31
storage space, 19
Storj files and data fragments, 33
supervision of blockchain, 7
Swarm, 32
Sybil attack, 15

T
tax management, 93–96
    tax-related data sharing mechanism, 95–96
Tendermint Cosmos, 24
13th Five-Year National Informatization Plan, 1, 80, 108
token trading, 178

top-level design of blockchain
  development, 113
traceability of blockchain, 69–71,
  88–90, 95, 101–102, 122–125,
  129–130, 140, 144, 148, 151,
  160–161, 167, 173, 175, 177
transaction process, 5
Truebit project, 30
trust mechanism, 4

U
UGC (User Generated Content)
  commonplace, 37
UnionPay, 148–149
urbanization, 40
US DECENT platform, 166

V
Verady, 180
virtual currency, 57
    legal regulation of (*see also* legal
      regulation of blockchain
      technology)
virtual goods, 58–59
Virtual Voting consensus algorithm, 34

W
Wanda Group, 148–149
WebAssembly (WASM) virtual
  machine, 22
Web3 Foundation, 25
Wikipedia, 167
WiKIT, 39, 48
WiKi (wiki), 39
Woods, Gavin, 25
WSS (Working-Sensing-Smart)
  model, 40

X
Xiamen Customs, 103, 106
Xiaomi Company, 167
Xi Jinping, 46

Z
Zero Coin (ZCash), 35
zero knowledge proof (zk-SNARKs),
  35
Zhou Hongyi, 37
Zuckerberg, Mark, 167